Working the Clock

How to Win the Race for Productivity and Profits
with Workforce Management Technology

Acknowledgments

I'd like to thank Bruce Goldman for making the introduction that made this book possible. He was the first to make the connection between Oaklea Press and the ability and need to get the message out about workforce management technology.

Since being an author is far from my day job, I'd also like to express my appreciation to Stephen Hawley Martin, my editor, who worked skillfully to make the content of this book clear and easy to read. He made certain the project didn't get in the way of that day job, so that my customers would continue to be well served during the time that it was written. Steve also contributed some important material to the book drawn from his work with other business leaders.

I would also like to thank the software and hardware vendors and their customers for sharing their stories, including their successes and their difficulties. Some have chosen to remain anonymous so that the whole story could be told. I appreciate their willingness to share their journeys with you. The vendors also provided access to product specialists and inside experts who are working to meet the market's growing demand for ever more powerful workforce management tools. All of us in this business get charged up talking about this new technology and what we know it can do and have seen it accomplish. I hope our enthusiasm is contagious so that you will catch it too.

Michael (Mike) R. King deserves special recognition for the business acumen he has imparted to me during the years we've known each other — over lunches, via late night e-mails, and during the times we worked side-by-side. His contributions to the section of this book on business case development and ROI were invaluable. This book would not be in your hands today had I not come to know Mike and become his understudy.

And finally, I want to thank my family for their unending support and for making me take a break, go to bed, or just turn everything off every now and then. Those of you who are your own worst boss will know what I mean. Family, friends, coworkers -- they all have contributed by shaping how I view today's workplace. Whether it's a useful suggestion, a new or different perspective, or just the ability to see humor in certain situations — I hope I've done justice to the influence they have had.

Working the Clock

How to Win the Race for Productivity and Profits with Workforce Management Technology

by

Lisa Disselkamp

RICHMOND, VIRGINIA

ISBN 10: 1-892538-13-X
ISBN 13: 978-1-892538-13-0

If your bookseller does not have this book in stock, it can be ordered directly from the publisher. Contact us for information about discounts on quantity purchases.

The Oaklea Press
6912 Three Chopt Road, Suite B
Richmond, Virginia 23226

Voice: 1-800-295-4066
Facsimile: 1-804-281-5686
Email: Info@OakleaPress.com

This book can be purchased online at
http://www.LeanTransformation.com

Foreword

When was the last time you read something that made you dramatically change the way you manage your business? This book has that potential. If you're a CEO or a COO, there's a good chance you're going to be enlightened and fascinated by what this book contains. Even if your business already has an automated time and attendance payroll system, you may not be aware of the many ways it can be of benefit. The fact is, it can give you access to information that will enable you to do more than just run your operation more efficiently. It can help you serve your customers better and smarter, and that can lead to more sales and a bigger share of the market you serve.

It's been said that an organization's most important asset goes home at the end of every work day. If that's true, then your second-biggest asset could very well be the technology you use to track their activities. Your time and attendance technology should be saving your operation significant money in a number of ways that will be discussed. In addition, it can and should be an important tool to use in reaching your organization's strategic, operational and financial goals.

You're probably aware of the four levels of knowing. The lowest level is, "You don't know what you don't know." The second is, "You don't know what you know." This is followed by, "You know what you don't know," and at the top, "You know what you know."

The four levels of knowing:

4 You **know** what you **know**
3 You **know** what you **don't know**
2 You **don't know** what you **know**
1 You **don't know** what you **don't know**

When it comes to time and attendance technology today, many chief executives simply don't know what they don't know. But this book will tell you, and it will explain how to reach the point where you know what you know and use it to improve the bottom line. You see, workforce measurement and record-keeping technology has come a long way in the past few years. Never before has there been such a powerful management and deployment tool that can be placed literally at your fingertips. So sit back, relax, and soak up what this revolutionary new way to manage workers, labor costs, and work flow is all about.

Of course, not everyone who reads this book will be a CEO or COO. Perhaps you're a CFO, CIO, or the Vice President of Human Resources. You may be the Payroll Manager. Or perhaps someone recommended this book to you because you're intimately involved in an operational area that manages people and labor budgets. Whatever the case may be, I've got exciting news for you. If information technology, payroll, time and attendance, or labor activity planning and data collection fall into your area of responsibility, you may have come upon the career-enhancing elixir of a lifetime.

If you're a C level executive, allow me to suggest you take this opportunity to rethink some key functional areas in your organization and consider making some dramatic changes. You'll be able to take advantage of insights and practical applications your peers may not yet have considered.

If you haven't reached the boardroom yet, you can still use this book to your advantage. It's human nature to want to be more important to the organization. Who wouldn't want to have more responsibility, to garner a higher level of respect, to be paid more, to be included in high-level meetings, to manage an area acknowledged for its strategic importance and impact on the organization? You can use what you learn in this book to pursue all that. Your organization can greatly benefit from the knowledge that's in it. Put this together with what you know about your company, and everyone will benefit.

Let me ask and answer a big question: What's essential in every organization? Operations. That's where the rubber meets the road — the meat and potatoes. Improving operations — making them more efficient and less costly — is how things can get done better, faster, and more profitably. It's how your company can beat the competition, get investors investing and become the envy of every player in your field. And for some organizations, improving operations is what absolutely must be done in order to survive. As you read this book, it should become clear you're holding the key to greatly improved and considerably more cost-efficient operations.

Am I claiming too much? Well, I'm not going to absolutely promise you'll soon be arriving at meetings in a big black limousine, but I will say this. Soon you'll be able to show the powers that be how to make big improvements your organization's operations. Not just little improvements. Big ones. You may be sitting on data that can be of incredible strategic value, and it's possible that up until now no one in your organization knew about it, thought about, or if they did, imagined a way to access it. But there is a way, and you can be its champion and its keeper, which can't possibly hurt your career.

So hold onto your seat, grab a pencil to take notes, and step into a non-stop elevator to the executive floor and a more profitable future.

Stephen Hawley Martin
Publisher, The Oaklea Press

How Best to Use This Book

This book contains a great deal of information and ideas about workforce management technology (WMT). If this is not something you're already familiar with, you will benefit most by reading it from start to finish. But if you already know about the technology and understand what it can do, you may wish to skip ahead to the section or sections that will provide you with information and insights on the planning and installation of WMT systems.

The book is divided into four parts and contains additional material at the back. Part One sets the stage by explaining how time and attendance technology has evolved in recent years and how the author became involved with the technology and participated in its evolution.

Part Two draws on case histories and references existing WMT systems to elaborate, give examples, and to stimulate thinking concerning the use of the technology.

Part Three is intended to provide insights and to flag issues for consideration prior to making a decision to acquire this new technology.

Part Four identifies issues to consider when moving forward into the design and planning stages of a WMT system to answer specific needs. It also suggests a way to build a business case for the technology for presentation to upper management, and it explains a technique called "mission-based configuration," which is a system set up to do more than simply pay people. It means approaching each pay rule, each user workspace, each system feature as an action-oriented tool that can be configured and applied to help accomplish corporate goals.

After Part Four, in the section, "Especially for Payroll Managers," the author makes a case for the Payroll Department to be the repository and implementation arm of Workforce Management Technology. And finally, a section called, "Especially for Owners and C-Level Executives," contains a case for enhancing the attactiveness of a company for sale through WMT.

Consulting the Table of Contents pages that follow should help you determine the best starting point for you based on what you wish to derive from this book. There is also a topical index beginning on page 285 which you may find helpful.

Contents

Part One
How Business Technology Has Changed

How My Walking Around Strategy Paid Off
Suddenly, Accurate Estimating Was Possible
Real Time Labor Data Gives Visibility
The System Can Expand without Adding People
Can Jobs Be Cut by Automating Payroll?
A New Time and Attendance Opportunity Presents Itself
Eliminating Payroll Errors & Beyond — Exposing the Iceberg

Part Two
What Workforce Management Technology Can Do

Business Technology Has Come a Long Way, Baby
The Way We Used to Work
Bringing Time and Attendance into the Twenty-First Century
Employee Score Cards
Using Labor Data to Increase Retail Sales
The Case of the Chicago Public Schools
Engineering & Planning Use Time & Attendance Data
Define the Issues and Link Them to Labor Data
How One Manufacturing Company Used Labor Data Technology to
  Become a Leader in Its Field
Incentive Plan Cost Analysis
WMT Enables Modeling to Predict Effectiveness
Professional Service Organizations — The Case for Efficiency,
  Compliance & Revenue

Part Three
Workforce Management Technology Systems
and Installation Considerations

Part Four
Getting from Concept to Project

Part One
How Business Technology Has Changed

Chapter One: How I Got Started in This Business

I got my start in time and attendance technology when I landed a job at an airline — pun intended — in the Payroll Department shortly after I finished college. But it wasn't a job I'd been preparing for. With a degree in Japanese and in International Management, my goal was to work in international trade. That's right, I wanted to be an import/export specialist helping companies expand their businesses in the Far East.

Remember the "Japanese Miracle"? The concept emerged back in the 1980s when I was still in school. It may seem like ancient history now, but Japan was the place where business was experiencing tremendous quality improvement and market growth. All a person had to do was open the business pages of a daily newspaper to see headlines about an alarming and rapidly growing trade imbalance. My calling in life seemed clear. I didn't want to be an interpreter or translator, but I did want to be fluent in a second language. So, out of patriotic fervor and a sense that few others would be able to offer this skill set, I majored in Japanese and simultaneously pursued a business degree with the idea that I'd help American companies sell their wares to the Japanese. Surely there was an opportunity to show small and medium sized companies how to modify products and marketing approaches to appeal to Asian consumers. In this way, I believed I would be doing my part to help the trade imbalance disappear. I wrote a thesis that was in effect a marketing plan for The Richmond Baking Company, in Richmond, Indiana. It laid out a strategy to sell cookies and graham crackers to people raised on rice cakes and fish flavored crackers.

In order to be successful, I knew I'd have to convert these companies to an understanding they had to adapt their business to the Asian market, and not the other way around. The whole idea was for a company to modify the way it had always done business in order to be successful, competitive, and appealing in a totally foreign market. Now, when I look back, I realize that before consulting was something I'd even heard of, consulting was what I wanted to do. I wanted to help businesses by taking a hard, careful look at their products and practices and, when it made sense, to help them redesign those practices to better serve their customers, shareholders, and ultimately their employees. That's what I do now, but the Asian market doesn't figure into it — except to the extent that some of my client companies are competing with Asian businesses. What I now do is all about keeping American companies strong, about managing their employees smarter and compensating them in ways that will control labor costs, attract the best employees, motivate workers to meet the company's demand for their labor, and drive accountability and customer satisfaction. I'm constantly looking for new ways to meet a company's strategic, financial, and operational goals. What I do is help companies find ways to deploy and finance their most important resource — human capital — in ways that will bring the maximum return.

Perhaps it's not surprising that Payroll was the launching pad to my present career. After all, how many seasoned and well-established business executives do you suppose were going to listen to a fresh-faced twenty-two year old, obviously very non-Asian young woman from the Midwest tell them how to sell to the Japanese?

Not many.

I was also fighting complacency among American business leadership at that time. The imminent threat and the implications of the global economy hadn't yet sunk in. The Asian market seemed incredibly distant and strange. Most American businesses were accustomed to their international customers adapting to our ways of doing business. Although Japan was doing very well, we weren't doing that badly in America, and competitive forces hadn't yet compelled managers to think or act differently.

It didn't take long for me to realize there weren't many opportunities to engage companies in how to modify their products to appeal to and penetrate Asian markets. After pounding my head against a few brick walls, I decided to follow another passion — airplanes — and took a job with one of the largest charter airlines in the U.S.

I wasn't actually flying, of course, but it was invigorating just to be working in the industry. I suppose my enthusiasm for airplanes motivated me to learn as much as I could about the company and how an airline works. My "in" was a pretty lowly job in Payroll and it was there that I realized what a big disconnect existed between Payroll and Operations. The two areas never talked with the result that each knew very little about what the other did. They both provided only what the other side "needed to know" and busied themselves with their own responsibilities.

I've become a believer in what some call "shadowing," or temporary staff rotations. Organizations come out ahead when workers understand what the various business units within the company do and how they relate. Not only does such an activity provide an appreciation for the work being done outside an employee's immediate area, but once the uses and reasons for deliverables and deadlines or how one's own area is perceived are known, workers are more likely to apply that understanding of what they do to the business as a whole. They begin to think beyond the four walls and become aware of the inherent dependencies between departments. This builds a spirit of collaboration and appreciation.

When corporate personnel go out into the field and spend a day in a nursing home, for example, they not only appreciate how difficult the operational side of the business can be, but they also understand why that special report the facility requested is so important. Or when marketing types visit store locations they realize why — despite the fact that it looks really cool — that display rack is driving the floor sales associates crazy because it doesn't hold enough merchandise, so they continually have to restock the bins.

I was the sort of person who would take the long way to the copy center — back before there was a copy machine in every department — so that I could stop by the Chief Pilot or Chief Flight Attendant's offices and chat with any crew members who might be in the area. Or I might walk through the flight scheduling area and peek in on any situations that were in progress. I learned about crew protocol, Captain's checks, and a Captain's decision-making authority during flight in an emergency situation. I learned about the safety training that the flight attendants had to master and how much they knew about each airplane's equipment and emergency procedures. Did you know, for example, that crew members are routinely being "checked" by another senior crew member to insure they are going through all the proper safety procedures during flight? I learned about deadheading — flying a plane with no passengers — and how airlines cautiously ferry a plane when it is partially disabled and operating on only one engine. I discovered that this airline paid the airport a fee for every minute the plane is on the ground or tarmac. I even ventured out into the maintenance hangar at every opportunity, to get a glimpse of the aircraft, and also to find out what the A&P (airframe and power plant) mechanics had to do when a jet came in for routine maintenance. Did you know that at regular intervals an aircraft is almost completely disassembled that it's checked, has its engines, seats and tires replaced, and then reassembled to insure the plane is structurally sound, mechanically fit and safe to fly? These checks are required after a certain number of takeoffs and landings. As with most businesses, there was a lot of activity going on behind the scenes to get the product off the ground.

In retrospect I realize the important thing about my wanderings was that I didn't limit my curiosity to what other people were doing. I related it as much as I could to what I was responsible for — and that was "just Payroll." But to me it was all connected and I saw opportunities to bridge the gaps and enable the different areas to benefit one another.

It occurred to me a great deal was being overlooked that could be done to manage a company's workers and labor expenses in ways that could improve sales, boost quality and efficiency, increase employee satisfaction, and above all, have a positive impact on the bottom line. At the same time, it would significantly improve the processes and outputs of the payroll area. It was hard for me to believe the potential benefits being overlooked. All it would take was a little effort and the right technology.

Then one day, an opportunity began to unfold. The Payroll Department had a "disaster" that perhaps only a Payroll person can imagine or appreciate. A check for $50,000 made out to a single individual got pretty far along — well out Payroll's door — before it was caught. A misplaced decimal was a short lived lottery ticket for one employee when $500.00 became $50,000.00. It was an error that should not have gone unnoticed. Within a short time, the supervisor position of this dozen or so person Payroll Department became open. The thought struck me I might land the position, but common sense told me I didn't have much chance. After all, I was the youngest and least experienced person in the department. A number of others had been in place a dozen years or more. But I was young and fearless, and wanted to show my confidence and ambition. So I applied for the job.

A new manager position was created and someone was brought in to fill it, the department was restructured, and know what? To my surprise, I got the job of supervisor — reporting to the new manager. I had the good fortune of working for a truly wonderful lady who recognized and understood how to use my talents. Her name is Kathy Barras, and she is perhaps the best boss I have ever had. Not only was she extremely competent and easy to work with, she knew how to position and leverage an individual's skills and interests. You might say she had a talent for understanding where people would best fit and she knew how to employ their special aptitudes for the benefit of the department and the company. Personnel with technical skills were elevated, but not into supervisory roles. Others with great people skills and the respect of their peers, like my cohort Teresa Booth, were put in leadership positions.

As a relative greenie in the corporate world, I considered both Kathy and Teresa my mentors. Teresa had an incredible ability to read people. She and I complemented each other well and Kathy made certain our assignments fit our strengths. My talents had less to do with the nitty-gritty processing of payroll and more to do with analysis and improving processes. As time went by and I mastered my routine areas of responsibility, I took on special projects along with my supervisory duties.

It didn't take a very hard look to see our department had outgrown its processes. For example, there was a serious lack of auditing procedures. The $50,000 check had brought that to light. We also did much of our work on paper, and believe me a lot of paper was generated. We had approximately 200 cockpit crews composed of captains, first officers and flight engineers, and about 800 flight attendants. (The exact number varied depending on the time of year.) All of them submitted manual time sheets monthly. Obviously our department's tactical approach to getting its job done needed improvement.

How My Walking Around Strategy Paid Off

By getting out and networking with people in other areas and attempting to learn as much as I could about the business, I found out a database loaded with information existed on the other side of the building. It struck me that this was a gold mine that could make the manual time sheets we had to deal with obsolete. The FAA required the airline to include all kinds of information on the flight log of each aircraft every time a plane took off. The company maintained a computerized flight scheduling system that provided all scheduled flight activity. After every flight, a log sheet was submitted that included the names and positions of the crew members, their duties on the flight as well as the actual flight time recorded in what is called "block in" and "block out" time. A flight doesn't officially start until the blocks are removed from around the airplane's tires. Likewise, for payroll purposes, accounting for the crew's time didn't start until the flight was rolling.

This was nothing less than incredible. The information we required these employees to report on paper — that we collected on time sheets — was already being gathered. And the big deal was that it was being entered into a computer system. All that needed to be done to get the data for payroll was to tap into a flight operation system already in place. This would eliminate an enormous amount of paperwork and the potential problems that went along with it.

Imagine, for example, how prone to error and delays a paper system is. Time sheets are processed by passing them along from one person to the next as different information is reviewed, calculations are made, and data is collected. People in manufacturing, particularly those familiar with Six Sigma, know how difficult it is to deliver quality when a product goes through several steps in a process. What Six Sigma black belts call the "rolled throughput yield" is the final outcome. "Yield" refers to the percentage of good parts produced by an operation. For example, if there are four operations each with a 99 percent yield, the rolled throughput yield is $(0.99) \times (0.99) \times (0.99) \times (0.99) = 96$ percent. Imagine having four wrong checks distributed for every hundred employees. It can happen in a manual set up, but if the data is processed electronically the potential for human error is eliminated. Computers simply don't make processing errors the way people do.

Other benefits to this automated process were apparent as well. Crew members' activity was no longer reported twice — once on the log sheet and again for each employee on a time report. So this redundancy was eliminated. Omissions decreased because the information used for payroll was data that had been collected at the actual time it happened, not at the end of the month. Paper reports no longer had to be routed around for verification and supervisory evaluation and then gathered and mailed to the corporate office. The use of a single source of data meant payroll would be entirely in sync with operations data.

These were benefits anyone could quickly and easily grasp. What perhaps was more remarkable were ways the company could benefit beyond those that were so obvious.

Suddenly, Accurate Estimating Was Possible

I quickly realized more was to be gained from this than just the benefits to employees and payroll. As is the case with practically every organization, the airline had to package, price and sell its product. This meant it had to estimate costs and market forces and build a pricing model. Many overhead factors exist for an airline, and pricing factors are constantly changing. Fuel costs are a big one. Seasonal demand and of competitors' pricing are others. And of course, it takes people to fly the plane and to serve the passengers. Quoting a competitive price was one of these things that had to be done. You see, the company was a charter airline that did ad hoc flying. For example, a pro football team might win the division title and have a game next week in Green Bay. Teams contracted with the company for travel needs. The front office would make a last minute call and want to know the cost to fly the team to a particular city.

The need to project actual costs accurately was extremely important since doing so could determine whether the flight was profitable. The company had little trouble calculating the fuel cost and the landing fees. But no method existed to accurately estimate the cost of labor when a flight was added to the schedule because the amount could vary considerably. Once a crew member was in overtime, which was triggered by passing a certain number of flight hours in a month, he or she would be paid up to sixty dollars an hour on top of base pay. Overtime at a crew member's rate is no small amount. The company used averages and historical data, but no forecasting tool was in place that delivered reliable labor cost information.

The pricing process was fascinating to me. I imagined myself in the cost accounting area putting that pricing model together and being exactly on-target — how gratifying that would be. But I wondered, how the heck could I do it? I was in the Payroll Department and I couldn't even predict what the total crew payroll amount would be at the end of the month.

Then it came to me. We had labor data in our computer that was real-time. Tapping into it was all that was needed.

So I went to management and said, "Not only can we eliminate the manual processing of payroll — the need to collect time sheets, add them up, combine and total them, then compile the data into reports — not only will all that work and the manual effort be history — everything we need to predict the labor cost of a flight in advance will be in the computer."

Not surprisingly, they wanted to know what in the world I was talking about.

I explained they wouldn't have to wait until the end of a payroll cycle to get information about who had worked how many hours because the data in the computer was always up to date. Assuming the computer was programmed to do so, it would show if overtime would be triggered by adding a flight to any crew member's flight schedule. No longer would it be necessary to wet a finger and stick it in the air. We'd be able to calculate exactly what the cost of labor would be whenever a flight was added.

Real Time Labor Data Gives Visibility

The old saying goes, "You can't manage what you can't see." This applies to just about any industry. For example, depending on who is selected, adding an extra shift to a wing in a hospital or to an assembly line to get a rush order out might trigger overtime. With an automated time and attendance system in place, however, the computer would be able to show that assigning Justin Thyme to the extra shift would bump him into overtime. But by quickly determining who else on the team has the right qualifications, availability, and the fewest worked hours, adding Ima Werker to the extra shift would incur less cost because she has worked fewer hours and her base rate is lower. All that's required is for the computer to be programmed to calculate the cost of assigning a particular worker based on the hours the worker has already logged during the pay period along with the ability to determine who on the payroll has the right qualifications and skills to take her place without triggering overtime.

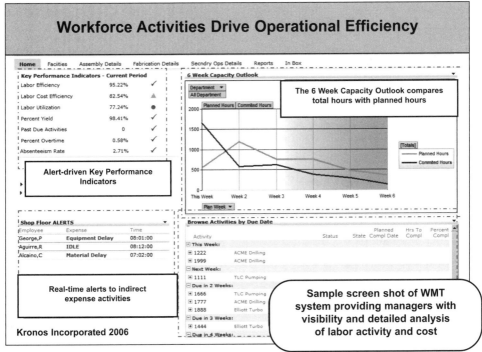

Workforce analytical modules play a big part in this. For example, Kronos recently acquired a company formerly known as Clarity Matters. The firm had developed a powerful analytical tool with over 150 key performance indicators and the ability to home in on problem areas by analyzing time and attendance data. At one hospital, for example, the product evaluated two years of time and attendance data. Based on an analysis that included more than 350 departments in the organization they discovered that if they could better manage just the top 25 outlier departments, bringing them in line with the median, 80% of the total overtime cost could be saved, an amount totaling approximately $2.5M. This analytical tool made the process of finding the biggest problems less of a "hunt and peck" process. It isolated the problem areas and quantified the impact of the worst offenders. Visibility took this organization from blind-man's buff to x-ray vision.

The System Can Expand without Adding People

At the airline, working with a management information systems (MIS) developer, we put in place a flight crew payroll system that generated payroll costs on the Crew member Activity Notification sheets (or C.A.N. Reports as we called them). A side benefit was that as the company grew, adding more aircraft and the crews to support them, we wouldn't have to add people in hub offices or the Payroll Department to handle the added volume. In the past, we'd had to, because manual systems entail a fairly fixed ratio of Payroll workers to employees.

Generally, workers are hired and managed so that they are tasked to capacity. Obviously, there's a limit to the additional work that can be put on existing workers. For a computer, however, the difference between processing 1,000 C.A.N. reports and 2,000 is not much. This provided the airline what's called "scalability."

I've worked with companies that have 200 employees and with companies that have tens of thousands of employees — both using the same basic technology. Using calculators and adding machines, it takes considerably more manpower to process 100,000 records than it does 200, but

26

when a computer is doing the work, it doesn't take many more people. It just takes more servers and bandwidth — more computer power.

This is a nice advantage to have for a company in a growth or acquisition mode. Not only will it assure economies of scale for the merged company. The merged company won't need two Payroll Departments — the challenge of adding new people from the acquired company to the payroll system will have been greatly simplified. As an organization grows in personnel or complexity, employing automation will actually keep the fixed costs somewhat stable.

Can Jobs Be Cut by Automating Payroll?

In some cases jobs can be eliminated or the growth of Payroll staff curtailed. This happened at the airline as a result of automating payroll functions. But in many cases the bulk of work to do with manual timecards is performed outside of Payroll by people who are administrators or supervisors of a department. They perform this function in addition to their regular primary jobs, usually monitoring, updating, and identifying problems on a daily, weekly or biweekly basis. Perhaps they have been spending a half a day each pay period attending to this. When a system is automated, the time devoted to this task will be reduced. The mundane tasks of validating the data, looking for missing information, checking entries and manually tabulating time are eliminated.

Sophisticated time and attendance systems verify an employee's identity and location. They can even restrict when an employee is able to report into the system. Problems are flagged and the system filters out the clean data so that only the questionable records must be personally reviewed. So the biggest impact in terms of hours saved is usually out in the field. Supervisors in a retail store, for example, can now spend more time on the floor, interacting with customers, keeping an eye on sales reps and cashiers, and making a positive impact on sales. Supervisors or production cell leaders in a manufacturing plant can spend more time training new workers, solving problems, clearing bottlenecks, and pitching in to help meet production quotas.

A New Time and Attendance Opportunity Presents Itself

After a job as full-time mom for a few years, I went to work for one of the nation's largest providers of care for the mentally and physically handicapped, with about 29,000 employees in 32 states at that time. This company also contracted with the government to provide job corps services for training youths in inner cities.

At the time, the company had a totally paper time and attendance system, and a centralized Payroll Department at its headquarters to process the incoming information. Management knew an upgrade to this operation was needed and believed savings and better labor cost control could be realized by implementing an automated time and attendance system.

Eliminating Payroll Errors & Beyond — Exposing the Iceberg

Imagine how much opportunity exists for error in a manual system with 29,000 employees. Each paper record has to pass through the employee, his or her supervisor, an area coordinator and the Payroll person. That's four opportunities for an error to be made. Mistakes in arithmetic and omissions may be commonplace. The possibility of fraud and abuse is also real. In any system, checks and balances must be in place. For example, one person should key in, and another should check what's been keyed. After all, adjustments and corrections can be costly. Depending on the policies of the company and the state in which they operate, a manual or "hand" check may have to be written when a mistake is made. Some companies will charge back the cost of this to the facility that generated the error.

At this organization, the estimated cost of a hand check was $50, and that's how much could be charged back to the local business unit. This company had 500 or 600 such checks on average per month. That's nearly $30,000 down the drain.

Beyond this, management was even more concerned that they had very little control over labor expenditures. A centralized, automated system was viewed as a way to get a handle on this. This company was very successful and had grown largely by acquisition. It had nearly 1,500 locations in different parts of the country. Most of the revenue was directly related to labor activity. Wisely, the time and attendance project was preceded by an effort to standardize compensation practices and systems in HR and Payroll areas at corporate headquarters. I say wisely because management knew that effort alone wasn't enough to achieve their goals. The greatest benefits came from instituting policies and activities that drove expenses and revenue potential into a workspace that could be managed and leveraged.

Automated workforce management systems can eliminate a host of problems and lead to all kinds of benefits. During this time my appreciation grew for how far "off the shelf" technology had evolved in this area. Instead of homegrown solutions such as were developed at the airline years earlier, companies could now purchase incredible systems which had been developed to meet business needs. As you read the next chapter, you will begin to see just how much can be done with this technology.

Part Two
What Workforce Management
Technology Can Do

Chapter Two: How Labor Data Technology Is Being Used to Run Companies Better

Automated time and attendance can be the vehicle for collecting extremely valuable data and information about worker activities and the costs associated with these activities. This can in turn become the wellspring for a new way to manage worker activity — what we'll call "workforce management technology" or WMT for short. WMT can become the very centerpiece of managing workers because the data can be used to evaluate all kinds of business issues and is the repository of information about what goes on in a business every day and the activities and the productivity of the individuals who make it happen.

The system deposits information into its memory banks, creating an

Develop a Platform for Workplace Analytics

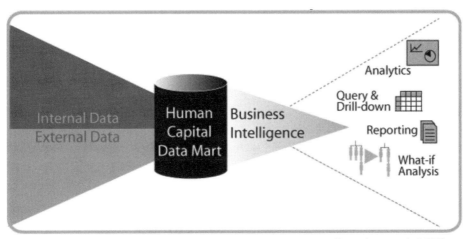

Konos Incorporated, 2006

ongoing history of the business and its workers. Best of all, when the data captures a pattern of success it can be shared throughout the organization, thus "institutionalizing" the success. On the other hand, if analysis of the data reveals patterns that are problematic, the technology can be used to provide solutions. If employee turnover is highest among people who work long shifts, for example, the system can limit the scheduling of excessive-duty periods. If a certain phase of a production is consistently creating delays and resulting in overtime, this may call for reevaluating the staffing assignments. The system can be used to develop solutions or to model alternatives.

WMT provides a natural platform for integrating all sorts of business intelligence. The more WMT information that's gathered, the more the WMT knows about the business, and the more meaningful the data will become. Data from external and internal systems can be plugged in. Scheduling software provides the background logic, and the human resources database supplies employee demographics and job information. The ERP (enterprise resource planning) system provides tracking labels and production volumes. Labor analytic tools can draw on WMT data and analyze the outputs. Training — or learning management systems (LMS) — can be integrated with job data, employee skill sets, schedules and pay-roll. Access control systems use WMT systems to control entry into the facility and track the flow of people on site. Billing systems use the data to eliminate redundancy and insure consistency between paid hours and billable hours. The WMT system becomes a Human Capital Data Mart of knowledge for further use. The business can draw upon the repository for

Collect the Details

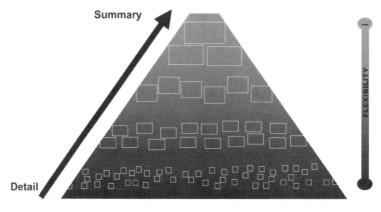

Kronos Incorporated, 2006

34

analytical, query, drill down and roll-up of details, reporting and modeling — what-if analysis.

Moreover, WMT is extremely efficient. Data needs to be entered just once, and then it can be shared among the various systems, making each one more intelligent. Instant access is possible because information is distributed immediately. Additionally, everyone will be analyzing the same data; everyone will have the same version of knowledge so that business units can better communicate and all will know the decisions will be based on the same information. When disparate units attempt to converse without integrated systems and a central repository of common human capital data, the organization can become like the Tower of Babel, each entity speaking its own language with its own facts and figures. WMT removes this barrier to communication and gets everyone speaking the same business language.

Business Technology Has Come a Long Way, Baby

When was the last time a secretary took a memo in shorthand?

Okay, maybe there's someone out there still working that way, probably pushing ninety. But people who have been around longer than I tell me it's been thirty years at least. Communications and technology in the workplace have come a long way.

How did payroll get done back then? How did companies collect information on workers' time and tabulate it?

Manually, and on paper, right?

How is it done in your company, today?

Perhaps your company is now collecting the information electronically, but even so, chances are that *what is done* with all the information being collected hasn't changed much. It could well represent a gold mine of data that management could use in ways you will soon learn about, to make things run more smoothly and efficiently.

Paper timecards may have been replaced, and your company may now be using electronic timeclocks. This may be a "mechanical improvement," but the only real difference is the way data is being moved from point A to point B. Such small incremental developments in collection methodology have delivered only limited benefits compared to what is actually possible.

The extinction of secretaries who took dictation, answered phones and took messages between typing letters, filing, and getting coffee came about as technology evolved. Desktop computers with word processing and list management programs began to proliferate. Telephone systems with voice mail made the companies that printed pink telephone message slips look for a new line of business. The *coup de grâce* came when nearly every office worker had a computer linked to the Internet, on his or her desk. Integrated, multimedia, real-time communication was now available to all. A whole new way of communicating emerged and this sent secretaries the way of the dinosaur. It was a dramatic change that occurred in just a few short years.

And you know what? One just as dramatic is now in the making.

The Way We Used to Work

My editor tells a story about when he went to work for an advertising agency right out of college. Like others, his firm developed and produced ads for its clients, some of which ran on TV, others in magazines or newspapers, some on radio, and of course there was the occasional outdoor billboard. Each job, whether it was a TV or radio spot or a print ad or billboard, had a job docket that traveled from one person who worked on it to the next. Everything to do with a job (which might have included briefing documents, background material, the copy and the layout once these were developed) traveled with this job docket. Also inside was a time sheet in triplicate, complete with carbon paper.

Remember carbon paper? Perhaps you recall the admonition, "Press hard, you're making three copies."

Or maybe not.

It was up to each person who worked on a job in my editor's ad agency to record his or her time on that card, along with what was done and the date. This meant people had to record time twice. Once for the job and again on a time sheet that was turned in to accounting and was used to calculate a person's pay. That's because the timecard in the job docket remained there until the job was completed and closed. Eventually, layout time would be billed at one rate, copy time at another and production time at yet another — even though the same person might be responsible for all three and be getting paid one hourly rate.

This is a good example of how Payroll is often compartmentalized and viewed as being unrelated to actual work. It's also an example of duplication of effort since employees had to do the same thing twice. Now it's possible to call up what in effect are time sheets on a web-based system that allow employees to post their time against specific jobs and tasks. The same posting also records their time for payroll purposes. The system will calculate client billing, and employees' paychecks. It also provides real-time data, so that if someone in management wants to know how much time has been posted to a particular job, he or she can find out up to the minute with a few clicks of a mouse.

In that ad agency of yesteryear, there were probably several hundred of these job dockets floating around at any given time. They represented what in manufacturing would be called work-in-progress (WIP). As would also be the case in a factory, this WIP was worth many thousands, if not hundreds of thousands of dollars. The accounting system at this firm considered time which had been posted to a job to be earned income even though it hadn't yet been billed. The work had been done, so it had been earned. It would be billed and become money in the bank unless some part of it had to be written off. Of course, no one really knew how much WIP there was at any given time. The best anyone could do was guess.

This being the case, what do you suppose happened at the end of each year? The controller of the company needed a tally of this work in progress in order to put it on the balance sheet as an asset. So a mad and frantic dash would take place to round up all the job dockets and total up all the timecards.

My editor hasn't been in advertising for a number of years, but he says that for all he knows this yearly ritual is still taking place during the last two weeks of December. Maybe so, but let's hope not. Just imagine how

TIMECLOCK EVOLUTION

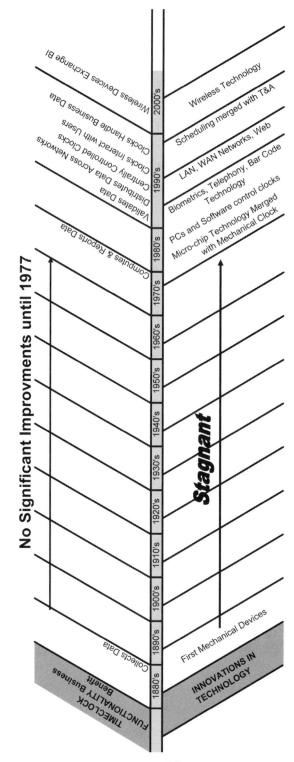

Timeclock technology remained relatively stagnant for almost a century until 1997 when Mark S. Ain of Kronos Incorporated first merged microchip technology with mechanical timeclocks. This created the first intelligent device that could capture, record and add employee time.

much easier it would be to have all that data entered into a central database. Not only would there be less chance of loss or error, but all the totaling and all the billing could be automated and immediately available. In addition, the controller of the firm would be able to know how much work in progress existed at any given moment simply by consulting the computer on his desk.

Bringing Time and Attendance into the Twenty-First Century

What would you think of a company that still had secretaries taking down memos in shorthand and typing them up on an IBM Selectric?

Okay, what would you think of a company that still processed payroll and looked at its data the way it did thirty or forty years ago?

You might think a lot of people in such a company would be doing work that could easily be eliminated, given the technology that exists today — work that could be spent in more productive ways. You might also think the people who run that company are probably missing out on a great deal of valuable information they could put to work if only they brought the way the company processes time and attendance and manages labor activity into the twenty-first century. This has happened in other departments, even in advertising agencies. Art directors no longer use t-squares and drawing tables. They use computers. Copywriters no longer use manual Underwoods. And it's a pretty good bet the general ledger isn't handwritten in ink and totaled by an adding machine. Human Resources probably uses up-to-date software and computer power to store and access the records it needs. And computers have done more than just make typing or compiling and storing records easier. They have assumed other functions as well — functions that used to be done by hand or with a slide rule or an adding machine. For example, engineers don't simply draw on a computer, they input variables and extrapolate results, make projections about viability and performance. CAD (computer aided design) software replaced the draftsman and the manual process of making mechanical drawings, but engineering technology went further putting the computerized drawing into intelligent design applications where stresses, temperature and materials are analyzed, giving engineers visibility as to where a plan could be prone to failure or exceed expectations.

Finance Departments and investors use data not simply as data points plotted on a line, but as analytical tools that demonstrate trends and deliver buy or sell signals. Procurement and Logistics Departments use systems that evaluate production data and supply needs and enable companies to operate "just-in-time," increasing efficiency and reducing costs.

Why should Payroll be different? Instead of just getting checks written, why shouldn't a time and attendance system deliver valuable information management can use to run things better. Why shouldn't it provide actionable data?

The fact of the matter is, it can. An example follows.

Employee Scorecards

Sports teams and fans have long understood the value of performance data. Look at baseball cards. Players are rated, traded and idolized for their "stats." Who goes up to bat is decidedly scientific — based on batting averages, runs batted in (RBI), and on base percentage. The player's performance determines how and when he is used in the game.

Imagine if employers had score cards for employees.

Integrating performance data (such as stats on workers or teams or

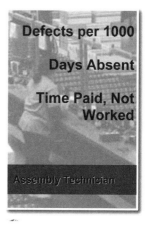

Kronos Incorporated, 2006

business units) with workforce systems can provide that kind of informa-tion. It can tell the employer who does what and when they do it best — at the individual, group of organizational levels. Workforce analytics is taking the labor data, measuring it, analyzing it and using it to improve performance. It's the coupling of the data from the various areas that reveal correlations and show where the company is batting a thousand and where some pinch hitters are needed.

It may reveal that more training is needed or where too many cooks in the kitchen actually slow down production. What's important is that it will enable companies to distinguish between what managers think or say their people do and what they actually do. Data provides the story, a his-tory. Analytics reveal causes and relationships and provide forecasts. Baseball managers don't just look at RBI numbers. Pro golfers don't just study their past scores. They understand what makes them great players and they constantly work to keep their eyes on the ball and improve their swing.

Using Labor Data to Increase Retail Sales

An outdoor equipment retailer in the northwestern United States, with dozens of stores located across the county, sells recreational and extreme sports equipment. Perhaps you've been in one of their stores. Each looks like a lodge, and the salespeople are all twenty-something with buff bodies and good tans. They sell hang gliding, skiing, cycling, camp-ing, hiking, backpacking, and mountain climbing gear, along with other extreme outdoor recreational equipment.

The company's management team recognized a connection between individual store sales and staffing. So the team decided to go to an auto-mated time and attendance system. In other words, WMT would be used to increase sales. Part of the strategy was to make the operation and imple-mentation of WMT by store managers a mandatory core competency.

The management team of this outfit "knew what they knew." They knew their numbers and understood their customer traffic patterns and sales trends. They also had a good feel for the "soft side" of the sales process. Their marketing approach included employing sales people who enjoyed and participated in the outdoor sporting activities for which the equipment being sold was designed. So they hired guys and gals who like to rock climb and rappel and hang-glide and put them in the department that sold these goods. They knew their customers were enthusiastic about such purchases and reacted positively to the workers who shared their interests. A certain "match" existed between sales staff, products and customers. When everything was aligned, the perfect "sales chemistry" was created. The goal was to create this chemistry and to staff at a level that would return the maximum ROI (return on investment). They also knew that customers eventually get tired of waiting for someone to help them and will go somewhere else if they don't get service within a reasonable length of time; this made the right number of sales personnel for the amount of traffic on a given day a must.

Along with knowledge about what made the cash registers ring was an appreciation of how difficult it was to create this perfect chemistry without assistance. The team also realized that not every store manager was a natural "chemist." Some were better than others at conjuring up this staffing magic. So they studied what the best managers did and figured out why and how they were successful.

In this way, the management team came up with its own "best practices" based on what had worked in the past. Coupling statistical data on customer traffic along with sales and best practices, they knew their employees' "score card stats" and were able to build a model for staffing. They knew what types of workers to schedule during specific seasons and during special sales events. You might say they viewed the work day as a sports team would game day. The team could predict with a fair degree of accuracy what store traffic would be at different times of year and on different days of the week. They knew what could be expected during a sales event such as a ski equipment sale, or a mountain climbing bonanza. They developed a game plan, knew their players, and set out to break records. All they needed was the mechanism to make it happen.

The retailer selected a workforce management technology vendor that understood the relationship between time and attendance and business objectives — such as maximizing sales — and offered a software product that fit the bill. For this retailer, Workbrain, Inc. became their partner. Management was purchasing a new tool. They were not simply installing a new timekeeping and scheduling system. Knowing what the expected outcomes were, the system had to be rolled out with a means for ensuring results.

There's a saying in engineering — "you cannot expect what you are not willing to inspect." The new owners of the time and attendance system must have come across this expression because they decided early on in the development of their plan to institute new job expectations for managers along with the new system. Not only would they train the managers on how to use the system, they planned to change how managers were evaluated at their annual performance reviews. Using set goals and best practices, a measurement for competency was determined. Management provided the targets — increasing store sales — along with the methods for reaching the targets — best practices configured into the time and attendance system — and the timetable for evaluating their aim — "come to papa time" at the annual review.

What this employer instituted was measurable accountability with tangible processes and tracking tools. Much more was involved than establishing a sales target. Ways were developed to evaluate how the managers worked within the system by considering actual inputs, decisions, deployments, mitigating factors and results. The managers knew their planning and reactions to the system indicators would be tracked and compared to the effect they had on store income. A hands-on tool was given to them to use every day in the pursuit of company targets. They knew it provided their leaders with visibility into how they were doing. The result was, this business tool became a part of the daily routine — a front-end business driver. It became a tuning instrument to channel each store manger's use of labor through a system with built-in standards, allowing the company to institutionalize best practices and to produce the desired sales results.

Not only did the company achieve success and reach its sales goals, the technology also resulted in smarter, more cost-effective use of labor resources. If they scheduled the "kayaking king" to work even though he was paid a higher wage than the local novice, they expected better results. Better results meant more money, and enough more money meant more value for the labor dollars expended — in other words, a better return on investment.

This approach makes sense intuitively, but until now the benefits,if any, were difficult to quantify. For example, ski enthusiasts who are passionate about the equipment they use are going to sell more skis and equipment than someone who has never been on the slopes. A key is to have the optimum number of such sales people available to take customers by the hand during a major sales event or just your average day.

Let's say a family is going skiing this year during spring break. The man of the house has found a pair of skis he likes, and he's talking with a sales rep about the skis and about the trip.

The salesman says, "Wow! You're going skiing for a week at Steamboat Springs? Fabulous! Snows practically every day there 'cause it's right next to the Continental Divide — best powder in the Rockies — 'champagne' powder they call it because it's so light and fluffy. I'll tell you what, you're going to need some powder skis in addition to those Salomons. Take a look at these. See, they're a lot wider. Otherwise, on a big powder day, you're going to sink up to your knees—"

The management of this chain had its store managers match the right people in the right numbers to anticipated store traffic at the right time. They also wanted to get the supervisors and managers out of the back office — away from the tasks of scheduling and checking timecards — and out on the floor where they, too, could sell.

And you know what? Come game time — when the doors open at stores across the country — the strategy works.

The Case of the Chicago Public Schools

One big user of time and attendance technology is the Chicago Public School System. Chicago is the third largest school district in the county, and it's the biggest employer in Chicago, with 58,000 employees, 620 locations, 435,000 students, and an annual payroll budget of about $2.3 billion. The Chicago schools have been using automated time and attendance for about fifteen years as of this writing. I spoke with Mike Edwards, Deputy Chief Fiscal Officer, about their system from Kronos, Inc. He says the technology has been helpful in a number of instances, but one in particular is its handling of the different ways Chicago teachers get paid. Edwards estimates about 8,000 different types of buckets or positions they can work in exist. Which one a worker fills depends on whether he or she is an hourly worker or salaried, what jobs she performs, union rules, and so on. This was not easy to administer in a manual set up, but a computerized system keeps it all straight without missing a beat.

But there's more. Before Chicago's system was instituted, each employee at each of the 600-plus schools had to fill out paper time sheets. At that time, the system had about 42,000 employees. Clerks would collect these and transcribe them to summary sheets. All this paper had to be transported to a central location and be key punched by data entry personnel. In a paper system of this magnitude, mistakes were bound to occur. Edwards estimates there were about 48,000 adjustments annually because of errors and omissions. Not surprisingly, people got upset when they were not paid correctly. In a highly unionized situation such as this one, workers and teachers would complain to their unions, and the unions would file complaints. Edwards says you cannot imagine the disruption.

The school system's labor agreements allowed employees who experienced a payroll error to leave the classroom — during school — and go to the downtown office on working time an dispute their pay. For that "missing in action" teacher a substitute had to be called in — and paid — while the teacher, was out of the building. Now *that's* an expensive payroll adjustment!

Another factor that led to complaints under the old system was that people sometime felt they were treated differently at different schools. One clerk might allow a five-minute grace period for tardy workers. Another might give ten minutes. Or it might depend on how the clerk felt about a particular employee. One she liked might get a pass. Another might be held accountable to the letter of the rule book. Of course, teachers and school workers frequently moved from one school to another and would notice these inconsistencies. The result was hundreds of grievances filed each year by the union. Every complaint required a hearing and testimony to be given as to what had occurred. The school system employed four full-time individuals in labor relations devoted to handling these complaints, and top management spent a large amount of time and effort on this sort of thing.

But a computerized time and attendance system does not make human errors and it does not play favorites. It administers the rules fairly and consistently as they are written and programmed into it. Edwards says that last year (2005) under the automated system, a total of only 37 grievances were filed. The labor relations agents handling these cases have dwindled to only one staff member. The burden and distraction of these cases has virtually been eliminated. Imagine the time and money this has saved.

Mike told me that when the system was just being implemented, the employees were dead set against it. The union filed a legal grievance and the case went to arbitration where the union lost their case. The Chicago *Sun* paper wrote a scathing editorial, titled "Untimely Clocks," about the folly he was getting the school system into with this new technology. The unions and employees were upset. He wasn't popular by any means. But Mike had big plans.

Mike convinced the unions and employees that things were going to get better. People would be paid fairly and consistently and the error rate would improve. In fact the errors went from 48,000 to around 10,000. Not bad for an organization this large and operating with employees moving about and having varying schedules.

Mike looked beyond Payroll for more opportunities for improvement. The education world is commonly funded through grant money. These funds are made available to individual schools for specific programs and administered largely at the local (school) level. Teachers are compensated out of these but it requires tracking, reporting and reconciling the hours spent on the program against the pool of grant money. In Chicago, it was very common for school administrators to struggle to keep track of teacher activities and they often exceeded their grant budgets. Spending money you don't have is a big problem.

But Mike understood the power behind the workforce management system he'd purchased from Kronos. He implemented the system in a way that local school officials were able to track and schedule their teachers and programs so that they spent only their allotted amount of grant money. When the system registered that budget spending reached 75% a caution was issued, 85% a warning and at 95% all activity was cut off. In the first year the system saved $15 Million for the school system. On the flip side, the school system didn't want to leave grant money on the table. Analytics looked at spending over the grant period and checked on how program managers planned to spend all the money. Instead of finding out at the last minute that programs had a lot of money and then going on a spending spree — attending workshops and the like — the dollars could be spent more effectively as they were intended. Quality was being managed as well as the financial side.

Mike soon got an award from the Mayor of Chicago. The city was now touting his success. The Mayor remarked to him, "Mike, you've gone from being on the hit list to the hit parade". Mike made the connection between a business problem and a workforce technology solution.

Engineering & Planning Use Time & Attendance Data

One company client of mine builds water towers — those big things that look like giant mushrooms rising up around communities and industrial parks across America. The company uses WMT to track the status of its projects. As you can imagine, just one of these huge tanks takes weeks to fabricate. Managers from engineering, supervisors, and sales personnel now track the time spent on each project and the progress toward completion. Employees enter into the system the amount of time it takes to complete certain tasks — for example, coating a large assembly. On any given day, this enables the company to see how many hours have been put against a particular tank, and what steps in the build have been performed. It identifies who is working on a project right now and who is going to work on it tomorrow.

Let's say a customer wants to know the status of a particular water tower under construction, and he calls his service rep. The people at the company can tell him exactly where it stands up to the minute by calling up real-time information in the computer. Yep, it's on time and on budget. Hallelujah! And that's not just a "best guess" based on last month's reports.

You see, the company's president had a vision. He realized how outdated the company's systems were when he heard about the new technology. He imagined, and he planned what it could do at *his* company. This was not a huge corporation. At the time Kronos' Workforce Timekeeper application was installed, the HR Department was still doing things on paper for the 400+ employees on the payroll. But the obvious lack of investment in information technology to that point didn't deter him from seizing the opportunities he saw.

For this particular business, the technology can also be used to create incentives for workers to get things done faster and more efficiently. Let's take a welder. Say Steve is scheduled to weld one of the panels today. He clocks in when he starts on the welding work order by swiping a bar code representing the specific task he's about to perform. This task is part of the purchase order and project plan. The time and attendance system now tracks his time on that task. Then he swipes again when he finishes. If he completes the job before the standard time, he might get points toward a bonus. Operational objectives and time and labor data have now been linked.

What are the business objectives in this? (1) The work is more likely to be completed on time; (2) the project is completed at the lowest cost and shortest timeframe (3); Steve is motivated; (4) management can see labor activity and cost in real time and measure progress against budgets and milestones; and (5) Steve's performance is tracked.

How did the time and attendance system help reach these goals?

The manufacturing schedule became the employee's work schedule. The assembly process put the work order on Steve's task list. Of course, that process probably hasn't changed and has been ongoing for the company. What has changed was that instead of Steve just reporting that he is at work today — "Hi time and attendance system, Steve here. It's 8:00 a.m. and I'm at work" — Steve now tells the system, "I will be working on Work Order 4566 starting at 8:00 a.m." The Supervisor can even put the work order in Steve's work schedule in the WMT system along with the next work order he has to complete, and the next. When Steve goes to the timeclock, or swipes a barcode, the work order becomes "in progress." The computer system can now compare what was scheduled to occur against what is actually occurring or has already occurred.

Anyone who needs to monitor this project can see, in real time, what is being worked on, what is complete, how much time it took, and what is scheduled to be worked on next. And the person doesn't have to be in Farmville where the water tower is being built or out on the shop floor. He doesn't have to be in the same building. Or on the same continent. He doesn't have to call Steve's supervisor.

Is the work being done at the lowest cost? The WMT system can help manage that, too. The system contains Steve's pay information. Time multiplied by hourly rate equals the cost. The system may even have suggested assigning this work order to Steve because he is the welder with the lowest hourly rate. Once Steve is finished with the task, the system can compute the cost of that particular work order adding in all the welders, fabricators, painters, and so forth who logged time against that project.

Steve knows the system is tracking the time it takes him to complete the job, and that if he finishes quickly, he may qualify for a bonus. This bonus may add to the cost, but it also will move Steve along faster to the next work order and help keep the project on schedule. This may make sense since not meeting the schedule could cost the company more than a small bonus. Further, if Steve's manager reviews the schedule and notices that Steve is about to exceed 40 hours this week if he picks up the next work order, the manager has the opportunity to change Steve's schedule and to assign another worker to that task, keeping Steve's total hours in check and avoiding an overtime payment.

In this case, the WMT system helped meet three objectives — on time completion, cost control, and visibility — and it did so by putting front-line management in control.

Define the Issues and Link Them to Labor Data

Beyond the possibilities for imaginative incentive plans, time and task data like this can be invaluable. Company management needs to take a hard look at the issues being faced, see where the costs are, what's driving the business, and link that to labor activity and compensation. Studies have shown that not everyone in the typical company is working to move the ball forward. According to a Gallup survey shared at an industry conference, about 25% the workforce is actively engaged and working the way management would like and hope, and approximately 50% are what is termed "neutrally" engaged. They come to work. They warm their chairs. They muddle along and don't hurt the company. The remaining 25% of the workforce is activity working *against* the company they work for. You might label them "disgruntled." That's an enormous number, and a very scary one if true. These people might be stealing from their employers, involved in fraud or in some other counterproductive activity. Is your company doing anything to combat this malady?

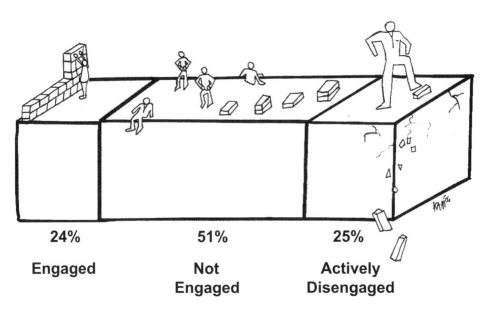

24%	51%	25%
Engaged	**Not Engaged**	**Actively Disengaged**

Source: Gallup Organization

Perhaps you can't believe you have employees who are actively working against you. But think about this: Another study, a survey done in 2005, indicates most American workers could fit a lot more work into each day. Conducted by America Online and Salary.com, it says the average worker wastes 2.09 hours a day chatting with coworkers, running errands, surfing the Internet or making personal phone calls. That lost time costs U.S. employers about $759 billion a year in unproductive labor expense.

Human Capital Management

Four Basic Tenets	
1	Every company's workforce structure, attributes and culture are unique
2	Three principles of Human Capital Measurement: • Think and operate systemically (connect the dots) • Get the right facts (you have them) • Focus on value (creation and destruction)
3	Go beyond perception (*what people "say"*) and focus on actual behavior (*what they "do"*)
4	It is possible to identify and understand the real human capital drivers of business performance

There are four basic tenets of establishing an effective human capital management strategy. We all know our company is special — no two organizations are exactly the same, and the response made to the differences is critical. Use your understanding of your company to design what will work best for your organization. Secondly, operate from a top down approach when developing a plan. Identify what you want to achieve, what you have — in terms of people — to get it done, and what has the greatest potential value. Designing from high level objectives down to the detail of specific tasks will insure there is a connection between how employees are tasked, who is tasked, and the outcomes of their efforts.

51

Make certain you are operating from the top level of the "Four levels of Knowing" as mentioned on page 5. Find out who is engaged. Next, focus on activities, skills and preferences not job titles. And lastly, get in touch with the things that make your business successful — such as the retailer we discussed earlier and the next example.

So what's new about collecting data?

I hate to admit it but some very smart people have actually been rather skeptical when I tell them about this technology. "Those systems don't offer anything new. You can't tell me the technology doesn't already exist." The use of labor activity data to drive business productivity and profits makes so much sense they simply cannot believe that companies aren't already using it. In fact, many companies have tried and many continue to put effort into this area. Walk any manufacturing floor and you'll see they are evaluating production levels, parts complete, all sorts of business data. However, one industry analyst told me that 75-80% of that data is out of date within two weeks to a month or more. The systems and processes to collect and analyze the data aren't yielding much value to the organization when the data is that stale. The tools for collection are cumbersome, the data originates from disparate systems and participants in the process don't have much motivation to keep things 100% complete and up to date.

Go into any organization and ask workers to walk around with a clipboard and collect data. After a period of time, the participants begin to lag in their duties and the entire process declines in value. What's new with workforce management technology entering into the mix is that workers are able to report data and *see the results in real time*. Why does that matter? Let's go back to our discussion about worker behavior and attitudes. If a worker has been around awhile, they've seen more than one young whippersnapper come along asking for information. They know they are going to outlive the latest fad in productivity studies. It may be that nothing anyone has ever done with the information has ever made their life any better.

Most people, at some point — usually early on in a job — want to be successful. Older systems asked workers to collect and report information, but the effort did little to quantify the challenges they were facing on the shop floor to help reduce cycle times, to expose problems and high producers, and make reaching their goals easier. When employees know the information is being tracked and measured, that non-value added activities are being identified (i.e. the daily challenges and obstacles they encounter are illuminated), they are more willing to participate. More importantly, the technology can give them a visualization of exactly what is happening — the cumulative effect or outputs — in real time. What's new is that the technology gives them a way to see how they are moving the needle. Workers can see that "it's Wednesday and I'm behind on reaching my target, so I'd better report the problems I'm having and see what can be done to help".

In a real world example with a manufacturer, workforce analytics identified a "hidden factory" within its production process. A wiring harness was being shipped with wires crossed and line workers were fixing this problem. This non-value-added time was reducing their productivity. When the activity was reported the problem was identified in real time and a value engineer was called to the floor to evaluate the low outputs. The problem was quickly resolved. Another discovery at the same plant was that when work orders were released to the floor without 100% parts complete, the job took twice as long. The analytics tool played a major role in uncovering this non-intuitive problem and allowing the manufacturer to resolve this impediment to productivity. The result was that they exceeded their cycle time goal for that product, reducing it by more than half.

What's new is that the technology empowers the employees to reach their goals, to be successful at an individual level. They can monitor their performance and know their supervisor is monitoring it as well in real time. Instant feedback, instant recognition, spotlights on obstacles and challenges — add those individual benefits up and the company benefits as well. Unlike the lean and quality initiatives that satisfy the needs and interests of workers higher up on the management ladder, these systems impact the front line workers. The advantages for *them* compel them to support the system, to continue to give the system the information everyone needs, and to react to the data — changing behavior to reach their goals. That's different.

How One Manufacturing Company Used Labor Data Technology to Become a Leader in Its Field

One company, Nucor Steel, has found a way to turn this situation around. What Nucor has done is tie a big percentage of employees' and managers' compensation directly to steel output and quality. Nucor's management is aware that for employees, compensation is where the rubber meets the road, and that management gets what it pays for and measures.

An experienced steelworker at anohter steel company can easily earn $16 to $21 an hour. At Nucor the guarantee is closer to $10. But get this — a bonus system tied to the number of batches of defect-free steel produced by the shifts an employee works can triple a worker's take-home pay.

Nucor gave out more than $220 million in profit sharing and bonuses to the rank and file in 2005. What did that mean to the average Nucor steelworker? He or she took home nearly $79,000. A $2,000 one-time bonus to mark the company's record earnings in 2005 and almost $18,000, on average, in profit sharing can be added to that $79,000 paycheck.

But that's only part of the story. At Nucor, not only is good work rewarded, but bad work is penalized. Bonuses are calculated on every order and paid out every week. If workers make a bad batch of steel, and if they catch it before it has moved on, they lose the bonus they otherwise would have made on that shipment. But if it gets to the customer, they lose three times the amount.

Steel plant workers at Nucor aren't the only ones with a big percentage of their pay at risk. The take-home of managers depends heavily on results as well. Department managers typically get a base pay that's 75% to 90% of the market average. But in a great year, that same manager might get a bonus of 75% or even 90% of his base pay, depending on the return on assets of the whole plant.

This adds up to managers and workers who think and act like owners of a business rather than workers who are there to put in their time so they can pick up a paycheck. When workers act like owners, good things happen for the business and its shareholders. The proof is in the results. Nucor had sales of $12.7 billion in 2005, up from $4.6 billion in 2000. In 2005, net income was $1.3 billion, up from $311 million in 2000. The company's return to shareholders was 387% over the 2000 through 2005 period. This puts rust-belt-industry Nucor ahead of New Economy icons such as Amazon.com, Starbucks, and eBay in terms of ROI over that period.

Hard to argue with performance like that, isn't it? And it happened because the technology was in place to keep accurate records of who worked when and where and to relate that to each and every batch of steel produced. Points toward bonuses could then be automated, calculated, and bonuses disbursed when paychecks were cut. There is no lag between good performance and reward, and this keeps workers positively engaged.

Incentive Plan Cost Analysis

One thing is true in just about any business. As with Nucor, you get what you measure and pay for. When people's jobs and livelihoods depend on something getting done, it is more likely to be done. This means it's important to keep score in order to know precisely how the business is doing in each key area and to hand out rewards to employees when they meet the goals they've been given. That's why management in industries other than steel might also consider tying a percentage of workers' compensation to achieving company goals.

WMT Enables Modeling to Predict Effectiveness

A good incentive plan can have a big impact on a company's bottom line. The right WMT system can be helpful in developing a plan because modeling can be used to determine what the financial impact might be. Suppose someone comes up with an incentive plan to get people to work weekends. Before instituting it, management would be wise to see how much it's going to cost. This won't be difficult with an automated system.

Take last year's weekend time and attendance data, for example, overlay the proposed incentive program on top of it, and presto, the cost of the new incentive program can be compared to the current compensation plan. The technology is, for the first time, introducing simulations into human capital management.

This is particularly helpful when the plan involves qualifiers such as minimum number of hours, overall attendance or limits on stacking the new plan on top of other premium programs. These qualified plans are useful when the incentive is designed to provide a consistent labor supply. They are weighted to discourage employees who might consider working something less than 100% of what is required. They become "vested" and risk losing all of their "bonus" if they fail to work as they promised. Overlaying a new commitment plan against employee work patterns is a more realistic estimate of the cost than any educated guess or "calculation." The question can then be asked, assuming the plan produces the hoped-for behavior modification, if employees do begin to work weekend shifts consistently, can the company afford the additional expense? Or does the additional expense offset the avoided costs of what happened when workers could not be persuaded to work the weekend?

The converse can also be determined. Say there is already a weekend differential but management senses there is ample supply of workers willing to work the weekend. By removing, or reducing it, and running the numbers, it's possible to see what the potential savings would be.

It's not always necessary to use historical data. These systems are designed to help management determine how they should operate in real-time or in the future. It's the integration of the business knowledge — creating correlations between operational demand and labor supply — that provides the manager with a forecast and a barometer of his labor situation. In heathcare, for example, a certain number of each category of worker — based on skills and roles — must to be present during a hospital shift, depending on the number of patients on a particular floor or in a unit and the patients' acuity level (i.e., how sick the patients are and how much care they require). Set ratios can be programmed into the software so that "what if" scenarios can be run. If the cost of the incentive program seems too high, the conditions can be tweaked. Instead of a 24 hour minimum before the incentive is earned, bump it up to 30 hours and see what happens. How many employees would still meet the minimum and be eligible for the bonus? How much would be saved? This ability to tweak and adjust is one of the things that make this feature so useful.

Software vendors offer scheduling solutions for use by manufacturers that help them optimize output based on the variables of workload and staff. They use optimization routines with sophisticated algorithms to run and compare scenarios in order to calculate the best possible schedule in terms of the work to be done and the employees needed to perform it. An employer can define the parameters and the priorities so that the system takes desired limits and goals into account. This brings scheduling to an entirely new level — to demand-driven labor forecasting.

A manufacturing operation that builds complex and highly variable products, for example, can realize impressive gains by using such a system. It can dramatically increase efficient use of labor and production space by scheduling products in a sequence that keeps wait time between assembly operations to a minimum. A book by international consultant Jorge Larco called *Lean Manufacturing in Build-to-Order Environments,* due to be published by Oaklea Press in 2007, deals extensively with this.

There are other ways sophisticated scheduling tools such as this can be helpful. In a nursing home, for example, healthcare payers have standards that tell what's acceptable in terms of billing — according to the level of care deemed needed. If ten residents are on a hall, they will reimburse for a certain number of providers in each job category, depending on the level of acuity. The amount of care these patients are to receive has been predetermined by that agency. To staff at a lower level would be to underdeliver — to provide less care than required — thereby exposing the provider to noncompliance and quality issues. To overstaff the hall is to overdeliver and incur non-reimbursable labor expenses.

To schedule properly some workforce management systems provide configurable staffing templates that integrate the patient information with predefined staffing requirements and worker data. Based on a projected census and current staffing, the system will show the slots that need to be filled as those census numbers change.

The same modeling system can be used in a factory. Once the number and types of widgets to be turned out by each production cell during a shift are entered, the system can calculate how many of each product configuration needs to be produced during a given period of time, which is called the "takt" rate, as well as the skills and number of workers needed to accomplish this. In other words, it will project the types and the number of positions to be filled so that each workstation can be manned properly. The same system can also work in retail, hospitality, or education, using a projection of what customer traffic or student enrollment is likely to be.

The key is to feed the system the proper data — which the organization already knows — and deploy the system and its information to managers. It helps to make using the tool a specific job responsibility. The onus is then put on these managers to demonstrate they are using the system to manage staffing and to control costs and generate maximum revenue.

Professional Service Organizations — The Case for Efficiency, Compliance & Revenue

Some organizations don't happen to have hourly laborers. But even so, they don't have to miss out on benefits that stem from the advances in automation. Unanet Technologies specializes in providing solutions for project-oriented organizations. The market for products that satisfy the challenges in the government sector, internal service organizations, consulting and advanced technology firms, is growing. Frances B. Craig, president of Unanet, explains that these organizations face three primary challenges — paper based accounting processes, legal requirements and managing to insure top operational performance.

It's easy to understand how automation would improve the inefficiencies, inaccuracies and timeliness of processes that have historically been done manually. Once an organization grows beyond 25 or more employees, business leaders dealing with paper or even electronic spreadsheet-based processes can become overwhelmed with managing the "paper" instead of the core business. Errors in processing in these business models can mean not only overpaying employees, but also under-collecting earned revenue from customers.

The regulations imposed on this industry are also a major concern. Frances lists but a few of the alphabet soup of laws that can have an impact, including:

- DCAA (Defense Contract Audit Agency) DCAAP 7641.90
- Per Diem Rates dictated by the Department of Defense (DOD), General Services Administration (GSA) and State Department (DOS).
- SOX (Sarbanes Oxley) — internal controls
- OMB Circular No. A.11 Planning, Budgeting, Acquisition, and Management of Capital Assets & ANSI Standard 748 — Mandating Earned Value Management Reporting

For anyone who may not be familiar with, or is considering government work, the DCAA governs the rules for any government contractor charging for labor. Some of the key rules include:

- Proper accounting of direct costs by contract.
- Time must be recorded on a daily basis and changes in time must be appended with comments.
- "Total Time Accounting" (a.k.a. adjusted rate, time dilution). All hours worked must be recorded.
- Signatures and approvals are required from employees and supervisors
- DCAA dictates how policies must be written concerning timecard responsibilities.
- Penalties for incorrectly charging labor.

Srict guidelines, reporting requirements and the likelihood of being audited necessitate having an intelligent system to enforce policy, consistency and insure proper reporting. Without automation, imagine the manpower that would be required and the attendant cost an organization would incur just to stay in compliance.

Finally, like any other business, these organizations have to stay on top of performance. Resource scheduling is crucial in the project world. What may be unique is that workers may be assigned to multiple projects concurrently, and the mix of how they spend their time can vary widely. Complicating project work is that resources can be overbooked or under booked if labor isn't managed effectively. This can lead to project delays or underutilized resources. Unanet's solution not only manages this, but it also provides forecasting tools to predict and evaluate revenue and project completion targets.

One feature needed in professional service labor tracking is the ability to keep tabs on hours worked relative to project completion. For agencies servicing government entities, requirements exist for *how* hours are to be tracked. The Unanet technology allows users to append comments and "Estimated Time to Completion" to the labor hours, adding another level to the usefulness of the data. Project expenses must also be tracked along with project hours. Unlike internal project expenses generally absorbed by overhead accounts or built in rate margins, these may be billed directly to the customer and have to be tracked alongside the work. Having one place to store all of this data is immensely helpful. The systems also integrate to project tracking formats such as Gantt charting so that data transfers seamlessly between different schedule mechanisms.

Project profitability for service organizations can be managed using dashboards and tools that can track profitability by project, person and task. It's important to know where companies are working under cost and truly making money. Summary reports offer high-level overviews and drill down so that managers at every level can understand at whatever level of detail required how the work is getting done. Revenue management is also key in project-oriented companies. And finally, systems like Unanet's provide "Earned Value Management" tools to analyze this component of the work.

Workforce management technology is growing in the professional services industry. Companies in this segment concerned with efficiency, compliance and long term profitability cannot afford to overlook the importance of automating their processes and integrating the areas of Payroll, Accounting, and Project Management.

Benefits of a software tool such as Unanet include:

- Rapid Invoicing and Payables — typically improves from 20 to 2 days
- Profitable Projects — Overruns are avoided early on
- Better Decision Making — Real-time reports provide data for making decisions when it matters, not after it is too late
- Improved Compliance — Rules enforced so that compliance nears 100%
- Enforcement of Corporate Policies — Corporate rules are enforced across the organization
- Reduced Costs (eliminates paper, fax, storage) — typically 90% improvement in costs — companies have saved $100 to $150 per employee in each year for time reporting and $30 per expense report
- Reduced Errors — typically 90% of the errors are eliminated; companies have been able to bill hundreds of thousands of dollars formerly unbillable or unrecorded.
- Employee Satisfaction — many companies report that their accounting staffs no longer have to work weekends to record a projects's time and expenses.

Chapter Three: Using Labor Data to Achieve Financial Goals & Maximize Profits

When business objectives, human capital strategies and technology are integrated into a single workspace for managers, achieving financial goals not only becomes possible, it becomes more likely. For example, an intelligent, automated system can help reduce overtime hours. This is probably one of the most clear-cut ways WMT can provide a positive return on investment, and it is one of the easiest to implement. In fact, overtime reduction produces one of the fastest "time to value" results out of WMT.

Overtime is a premium paid on hours worked in excess of a set periodic limit of total hours worked. The Fair Labor Standards Act (FLSA) stipulates a weekly overtime threshold of forty hours in a seven day work week. The pay week can start on any day of the week but it must remain consistent. An employer cannot decide that the pay week starts on Sunday this week and Monday next week — particularly if this is done in an effort to avoid paying overtime. Employees who work more than forty hours in a week must be paid time and a half (1.5 x their base rate) for the time worked that exceeds 40 hours. The actual rate of pay should be calculated on the average hourly wage earned during the work week in question. This is commonly referred to as the "blended overtime rate." Many employers fail to accurately calculate the overtime rate. Before making a selection, it's important to make certain a time and attendance and payroll program can accommodate the mechanism used to derive this blended rate for the overtime payment, and whether that mechanism is internal or external to the system. Otherwise, someone will be forced to come up with creative ways to calculate this rate.

In addition to the FLSA regulations — which are considered the minimum statutes for overtime pay — many states add their own rules regarding overtime payments. Some states, such as California, have instituted daily and consecutive day overtime guidelines. Unions often stipulate special overtime rules for their members requiring overtime payments on certain days of the week, such as Sunday, or double time beyond a certain number of hours worked in a shift.

The good news is that these overtime limits are well known and easily defined. Better yet, WMT systems can forecast when an employee is likely to work beyond the point when overtime will begin to accrue and create a warning signal to alert the appropriate supervisor or manager. The system does this by constantly compiling data, minute by minute, hour by hour, day by day. Unlike old technology that used clocks or paper timecards, it doesn't wait until the end of the week or the pay period to tally a report. As a result, the point at which an employee will exceed an overtime limit can easily be determined, and the system can detect this and produce an alert, thus allowing management to take action to prevent overtime from occurring.

Rolled Up Information

A WMT system can roll up information in practically any way management may find helpful or revealing. It can take the data from a group of employees and combine it into a department. Departments can be combined into divisions, divisions into districts, and so on. This is important so that actual expenses can be compared with budgets at every level. Employees who work in multiple roles or departments or facilities can be accounted for in the cost center where they actually work. Regular, holiday, weekend, overtime, even nonproductive time can be segmented and then rolled up across job, department and facility lines as an expense type instead of as an aggregate by business unit. Such roll-ups give the organization a total picture of the cost of compensation programs. What's different about WMT roll-ups compared to payroll registers is that the data can be totaled for any time frame (not just payroll cycles) and related to actual business events and activities performed. Nonproductive time can be parsed or classified into travel time, training time, administrative, and so forth. These categories — which may be considered overhead — can be rolled up across the organization and evaluated as well. Totals for nonproductive time relative to output may reveal things about staffing levels that were otherwise undetectable.

**Data Shows Where and How Value-Added Time Is Spent —
Toyota's Story**

Comparing actual value-added time spent by workers who in theory do the same jobs can cause employers to completely rethink how they do business. A study conducted by the National Center for Manufacturing Science (NCMS), for example, determined that Toyota's product development engineers were, on average, four times more productive than their American and European counterparts. Western engineers spend about 20% of their time actually creating something of value for consumers; Toyota's spend 80%.

According to Michael N. Kennedy, who wrote a book about the Toyota development system, *Product Development for the Lean Enterprise,* the reason is that Western systems follow a somewhat bureaucratic, linear approach that focuses engineers on individual tasks and due dates for each new model under development. Toyota does not focus its efforts on the development of specific vehicles or on completing deadline-oriented tasks such as detailed drawings or schematics. Rather, Toyota's engineers focus on developing the many subsystems that come together to form automobiles and trucks. The result is that Toyota engineers are less concerned with non value-added minutiae. They concentrate instead on developing auto and truck components in the belief the resulting superior subsystems can be mixed and matched to create a whole host of new product possibilities. Because of Toyota's obvious success, many Western companies that depend on new products to keep them competitive are now striving to emulate the Toyota product development system.

If there are internal sources of excellence that ought to be emulated within your organization, roll-ups and comparisons may spotlight these performers. With data that can be parsed in any segment, timeframe and related to key performance indicators for the business and delivered in real time, the proliferation of this excellence doesn't have to wait until the annual report.

Evaluating Incentive Programs

Roll ups are just one way this new technology helps executives "see" what's really going on. All kinds of things can now be tracked. For example, how about programs like student loan repayment plans, employer assisted home loans, help with buying a personal computer, attendance and referral bonuses, and other incentives? How effective are these programs? Do they lead to employee retention? Do they lead to more profit? Now it's possible to find out.

The ability to track *total* compensation packages vis a vis the competition is often overlooked. Think of all the ways employees might be compensated. Overtime, incentives to work on holidays, weekend incentives, travel pay, new hire bonuses, overnight pay, and call-in pay are just a few examples. An employee whose base salary is $50,000 per year can make $80,000 if he's figured out the system and works it. Suppose he gets overtime after 40 hours, plus an incentive to work weekends. If he's reached 40 hours by Friday, why wouldn't he sign up for the weekend, too? And if a potential employer across the street offers a better return, guess what? If won't be long before the employee knows all about it, and it could be enough to draw him away. Have a look at the difference between base earnings and total pay for your employees. That "icing" on top of the base pay is often entirely unmanaged. No one evaluates the total cost, the impact and the return on investment.

Speaking of what worked and what didn't, what about sign-on bonuses? As of this writing, RNs can easily get a $5000 incentive to take an open position. This usually comes with the stipulation the nurse will work for the organization for at least a year. But are commitments such as these being enforced? In a manual system, perhaps not. Are these bonuses impacting recruitment, retention and overall quality? WMT enables the business to take the cost, the actual labor contributions, the business results (quality, revenue, retention rates, and so forth) and analyze the program — as is done in other parts of the business.

Off Shore Operations Best Practice Monitoring

On a commercial airline flight last year, I sat next to a fellow who manages manufacturing plants around the globe, including China. He and I chatted for some time about his experience with Chinese management. As a student of Asian business practices, I was naturally curious. One of the truly frustrating things he related was how resistant the Chinese are to change. Initially, the management and workers would consume the information about this company's standard operating procedures and replicate these practices quite nicely during the initial operations. At this point in the relationship, U.S. oversight of the Chinese operations was intense. He would be on site for extended periods, monitoring progress and achieving relatively good production output. His company in the U.S. was a lean manufacturer with streamlined operations and state-of-the art equipment that kept labor needs to a minimum. U.S. management was proud of its accomplishments in these areas and felt the lean approach had served the company well.

In all lean environments, demand-driven scheduling is a key component. During the initial operations, the Chinese plants staffed like the U.S. operations. My seat mate said that as soon as that phase had ended, however, and the intense on premises American management presence ended, the Chinese plant managers altered their staffing significantly. In China, where the population has reached 1.3 billion, employment is an issue. There's an abundance of labor, and full employment is the goal. So the Chinese abandoned the U.S. owners' staffing models and tripled the staff, significantly increasing the labor to production ratio. Suddenly, the advantage of low-cost Chinese labor was offset by the number of employees now working in the plant. Cultural expectations had overridden the business's standards, and my seat mate was tearing his hair out. Little could be done to manage the situation remotely from U.S. headquarters.

I let this man know that with a WMT system in place, he would have had the ability to observe and control these issues from afar, even from his office in the States. What was going on may have been half way around the world, but the system could have been his window into what was happening in real time. The costs associated with the Chinese managers' actions would have been readily accessible over the web. Instead of finding out about this "alternate" labor model weeks into production, his company would have found out about it in real time, well before the situation got out of hand. It's something important to consider when a company is operating across a cultural and geographic divide that inhibits having a representative from headquarters on premises. This is a perfect illustration of the value of this new way to enforce policies and practices regardless of physical or attitudinal barriers.

Asking for Forgiveness, Not Permission

The first concern of a front line supervisor is usually to get the work done. Higher level managers want the work done, too, of course, but they are also probably more concerned about doing so within the confines of a budget. Sometimes this disparity — the disconnect between the guy getting the job done and the big guy worrying about money — results in budgets that look nothing like the actual dollars showing up on the payroll reports.

What's the cause of this divergence between what has been allocated and what eventually is spent? Workforce management technology can deliver two things that can help close the gap between budgeted and actual expenditures — visibility and accountability.

In order to know what's going on, a manager has to "see" it. He must be cognizant of what's happening. That's what's meant by visibility. After all, how can anyone manage what is invisible? No one would go to the store and shop for items that have no price tags, pay for them at checkout and simply live with whatever amount arrived on the monthly credit card bill. No one would hire a contractor to remodel a home without reviewing the design and the bid. No one in his right mind would leave for six months and return later to simply pay whatever it cost to get the job done. Anyone who's ever dealt with a contractor knows there is always *something* unexpected that arises that demands *more*.

To manage, we have to know what's going on, such as how much things cost as the shopping cart fills up and items are checked off the list. We want to decide if fixing that old furnace is worth it, or if we should buy a new one. Managing money means knowing how it is about to be spent and giving approvals along the way. If costs get too high, it may mean changing plans and making other choices.

It should be the same with employees and payroll. Managers need to know what is going on and how much is owed for the work that's being done. What happens all too often in the workplace, however, is that supervisors and schedulers — who are intently focused on getting the job done — are managing the work with little scrutiny by management when it comes to the costs they are racking up. Today, they'll be judged by whether the activity was completed. It won't be until tomorrow that anyone looks at the cost, and then it's "a done deal" justified by the fact that the work *did* get done.

What WMT provides is visibility and accountability into the accumulation of labor costs. It gives managers an opportunity to review and approve or not approve the way labor dollars are being spent. It may be that supervisors and schedulers will welcome a system that provides a justification for and stamp of approval on the scheduling decisions they make. Say farewell to forgiveness, priorities shall prevail!

Using WMT to Manage Budgets — *Today!*

What tools have managers above the front line supervisory level had in the past to manage their budgets? Typically, they received after-the-fact payroll reports. This group is not likely to be inclined to sit down and sift through a stack of timecards and payroll reports. They may have had a budgetary monitoring process and some stand alone scheduling software. These tools were probably not integrated, however, and the targets were primarily at the department level. Until now, organizations as a whole have generally lacked a consistent approach or standardized productivity measurements.

Some companies use HR related applications or reporting budgetary programs such as Cognos and Hyperion or Lawson and Ultimate Software packages. But these solutions are geared to midlevel management in businesses where labor usage and costs fluctuate little. What's more, they offer no dynamic evaluation of skill mix and activity in the labor to budget picture.

Kronos' Visionware product — an analytical module that works closely with this provider's timekeeping and scheduling components — allows both front line and higher levels of management to blend data from operations, HR, time and attendance, and finance to evaluate the different types of labor being employed across the organization. This tool also helps shorten the evaluation cycle, and for companies where billable hours must be submitted within time limits, this heightened accuracy increases revenue potential. A study by Nucleus Research revealed a facility that recovered hundreds of thousands of dollars by putting Visionware to work .

Businesses that experience frequent or unforeseen peaks in labor demand and rely on supplemental labor, such as contract or agency workers, are well positioned to benefit in the budget process. Significant cost savings and return on investment can be realized. In studies conducted by Nucleus, Visionware customers were able to "improve labor productivity and control costs by increasing accountability for labor usage and driving adherence to productivity standards."[1]

In the public sector, organizations are beginning to manage budgets in the same way business has traditionally approached the process. Chicago Public Schools, for example, created a new position of CFO in an attempt to improve in this regard. The new CFO quickly noticed the district was continually over budget on many projects, probably due to a lack of timely information. School administrators may have wanted to stay on budget, but they had no idea at any given time where they stood because reports often were not available until weeks or even months after the fact in many cases.

To operate the system as a well-run business, and to make administrators accountable, the CFO and his staff began using the analytics tools available in the Kronos system the Chicago Public Schools already had in place. Budgets were tracked by grant or project and reports were distributed to the owners daily. The CFO's office then took the bold move of shutting down projects that went over budget. This demonstrated to everyone that budgets had to be managed and that the old way of operating would not be tolerated. As you might imagine, not many projects had to be shut down before everyone got the message.

Why weren't Excel® spreadsheets used to manage these budgets? It's best if the tools to manage budgets are resident in the work life of the users and the users are familiar with the applications employed. These users already were using a time and attendance system on a daily basis, so it made sense to deliver the budget information in the same environment. Employees were compelled to go into the time and attendance daily so they would be paid correctly. This made it easy to take care of other business in the same workspace. And from an administrative perspective, integrating this type of budgetary information with time and attendance made reconciliation between the two systems automatic, which made sense since any audit of grant money spent for hours worked would require a match between Payroll's numbers and the grant report.

Approvals Force Accountability

Requiring supervisors, managers, even employees to register approvals throughout the pay cycle, instead of only at after the period ends, gives them the responsibility to evaluate, adjust and confirm the activity and payments before they go over the budget or exceed limits.

Depending on the product, approvals can be set up as being required or they can be optional. Users can enter them daily, weekly, or periodically. Multiple users can be allowed to approve the same employee timecard when appropriate. Approvals can be tagged with comments, adding more description and value to the data. WMT systems can put payments into pending status until the record is stamped approved for payment.

Be aware, however, that it is not legal to disapprove and thus deny payment for actual hours worked as in the case of "unapproved overtime." Employees who actually work hours in excess of the overtime limits — 40 hours weekly — must be paid for their time according to wage and hour guidelines. Employers cannot refuse to pay overtime because the employee did not get approval for the hours worked. But they can track an employee's time and label overtime payments as "unapproved" as a disciplinary matter. It's best to consult your state's department of labor, a consultant or your legal counsel for classifications of possible overtime exemptions for workers by industry, trade and position. There are exceptions. What is useful is that tracking unapproved OT distinguishes this cost from approved (i.e. operationally required) OT and draws attention to unnecessary costs that ought to be controlled. In other words, management will know who is answerable for these costs and can take action as necessary.

Recording of Approvals — A Trail of "Whodunit"

Eliminating the paper trail requires that we have a place to record approvals, so it makes sense that this should be a feature of the technology. This isn't just about replacing the supervisor's signature at the bottom of the time sheet at the end of the pay period. That happens when the supervisor communicates his timecards are ready for Payroll, whatever the process. Electronic approvals can be a form of "checking in" on activity throughout the pay cycle. They can be used to verify that "I have observed this record of activity and have made adjustments where needed." It can be a method of hand-off. Each layer of management can input approvals so that the final approving authority is certain all managers have completed a review of the data before it's finalized for payment.

What if a policy is in place that says a manager's approval must be obtained before certain types of extra pay or thresholds are awarded? Before a check is cut, the system can flag this for the manager to approve. The activity then gains visibility as the records are examined at each level. The supervisor will feel a greater sense of accountability as the data migrates up the chain of command and he or she realizes that the discretionary use of labor is being monitored by a number of stakeholders.

You may not fully anticipate the impact such monitoring can have. The exceptions and filters that database logic and queries generate become "red flags" to managers, who can usually identify the problems and outliers easily. Would you continue to shop at a store with no price tags if your spouse got an e-mail alert that you were exceeding your credit limit as you loaded your cart? Rest assured, the disparity between budget and actual labor costs will shrink when supervisors feel the spotlight's glare on their use of labor. No longer will it be possible to ask forgiveness after the fact.

Ghost Employees Become Visible

A ghost employee is one who is on the books but does not exist. This can and does happen in organizations — regardless of size. It may be that a fictitious employee has been "hired" and someone is fraudulently collecting his pay. It can also come into play when an employee is terminated and an internal person hijacks the record of termination before it is recorded, diverting the exemployee's pay to his or her own personal account. New regulations, such as Sarbanes-Oxley, are designed in part to make certain that companies institute checks and balances to reduce the potential for such fraud, among other things.

To meet these requirements, a company ought to be able to demonstrate that the person who sets up new hires in the payroll system is not also someone who can approve timecards and distribute checks. The more hands involved, the better. Even so, some companies do have locations where everything to do with payroll is performed by one individual because there may not be enough people at the required level. The problem is, what's to keep that individual from creating a person, filling out timecards for her, getting a check every week made out to that nonexistent person and depositing it into a fake account? There's little in manual systems to enforce the necessary checks and balances. Technology offers a more secure way by involving more people in the process, validating a person's identity and existence, and monitoring his or her productivity. It's hard to create a productive ghost.

There's also a scam called "shadow employment" where the person really did exist at one point, but has since quit or been terminated.

Through simple collusion, the individual may still be getting paid. Let's say Darla Goins quit, for example, but her Supervisor, Anita Raze, didn't let anyone in Payroll know. Anita gets Darla's checks and splits the money with her. It's difficult if not impossible to pull this off in an automated system, particularly when timekeeping is tied in to the scheduling of employees based on work to be performed.

Another method of fleshing out ghost employment is that a system workspace can be set up to automatically list terminated employees as well as those on leave of absence who are still getting paid. timecards with photo IDs can also help, but the goal of totally eliminating the possibility of ghost and shadow employees may be sufficient justification to use biometrics such as finger, palm or retina scans or to install a voice validation system, any of which will make this sort of fraud much more difficult to pull off.

Preventing Overdrafts of Time-off

Banks are good at preventing customers from withdrawing more money from their accounts than they have on deposit. Unfortunately, companies don't always control time-off benefits as carefully. But putting an automated system in place can prevent people from taking PTO (paid time off) they haven't earned. The system can also enforce that minimums be taken. Exempt employees, for example, usually are required to take PTO in full eight-hour increments representing a "day." Hourly workers will often have to take time off in quarter-, half-, or full-hour increments. Otherwise, what's to keep someone from leaving ten or fifteen minutes early and charging it to PTO? That kind of erratic disruption to staffing is not what PTO was intended to provide. This way, the company disburses the benefit in an orderly, manageable manner that diminishes the impact on operations and administration.

No More Double Coupon Days at Work

Have you been to the grocery store and noticed the frugal shoppers —

women with the coupon pouch as fat as a bookie's wallet? They study advertisements in the Sunday paper. They time their trips to the store to optimize savings by shopping just when the sales start, or the freshness date markdowns hit, or the double coupon deals go into effect. They are there to get double, triple deals.

Many employees approach work the same way. They read up on the compensation policies. Their union contract is their compensation Bible. They talk to other workers about how much they get paid. They scope out the schedule. They know that when Jupiter aligns with Mars they can work that shift and qualify for overtime plus shift premium holiday pay. They'll earn double, or even triple time for a single shift. An associate related a newspaper article, for example, that told about a nurse who was earning six figures despite a base salary in the neighborhood of $50,000. She was making more than some senior-level managers.

Why does this occur? First we need to look at these compensation programs and how they came about. Most were offered to satisfy a demand in the labor market for incentive compensation for certain classes of workers, or during especially difficult-to-staff periods such as holidays and weekends. Unfortunately, these well-intended programs are rarely considered as a package. In the minds, they are created and managed in what might be called silos. The programs become entitlements of employees, meaning that once one is in place, it's difficult for an employer to retire it. Then, when another influence on labor creates another new pay policy, an additional program is written and implemented as though it were just one more item in a buffet line. Instead of replacing the red Jell-O with a healthy spinach salad, employers simply add the salad to the menu.

Even though they are usually not, pay programs ought to be designed in concert with one another. If a particular situation qualifies an employee for a financial incentive, the program should define exactly what is required in order to qualify and how that program pays if the employee also qualifies for one or more   programs at the same time. If, for example, employees can earn a shift premium for working second shift and a weekend premium for working the weekend, what happens when the employee works the second shift on the weekend? Does the employee qualify for both? What happens if the employee is also working overtime during the second weekend shift? That shift might also fall on a holiday making the employee eligible for the second premium + the weekend premium + overtime + holiday pay.

Count the number of programs in any company's compensation policy book. That may possibly be how many programs that can be "stacked" on top of one another to pile money on one fat and happily overcompensated employee.

Is this really what it would take to get an employee to work that shift?

Workforce management technology systems can institute a hierarchy structure to compensation programs, capping the amount an employee can earn for working any shift. The employee above may have been earning $2.00/hr extra for shift two, $3.50 more for weekend, 1.5 x their base rate for overtime and double time for holiday. At a base rate of $10.00 per hour that's now a rate of $30.50 per hour or more when blended OT is also taken into account. Automating this process could allow management to enforce a cap on this combined rate limiting the rate to a certain multiple of the base, say two times the base rate.

Or there's another option. The hierarchy could institute a matrix structure where employees who qualify for multiple programs are paid the premiums in a certain order until a set limit is reached. The matrix can be used to enforce a policy that stipulates how payment is to be handled when two or more programs coincide. In this scenario, perhaps OT is always paid so the holiday double-time would be in effect. That limit having been reached, nothing more would be paid. Or, if the employee is in OT and also weekend second shift, the weekend pay might take precedence because it is the higher rate of the two shift premiums. Suffice it to say technology offers a way to build equitable compensation to meet business needs without obligating the company to pay excessive compounding of premiums.

A system can also be set up to help avoid double-paying overtime. In some states, California being one, daily overtime is mandatory. In that state, overtime also must be paid to someone who works more than 40 hours in a week. If someone works more than eight hours in a day, that person is entitled to overtime on the extra hours worked that day. If someone works more than 12 hours in a day, the person starts earning double time. If a person works seven consecutive days, even though they may only work one hour on each day, the seventh day is automatically paid at the overtime rate. After eight hours on the seventh day, double time kicks in. Confused? When manually administered, these payments can easily be overdone. Imagine being able to set up a system that understands the intricacies of these regulations, avoids noncompliance and better yet eliminates double payments.

It's easy to see why programs in existence for many years are often vaguely written and lack limits and qualifiers. They would have required considerable manual intervention to compute. But time and attendance systems can automate those processes and allow the programs to mature in complexity. Compensation programs and stacking guidelines should be written clearly in every compensation document, union contract and employee handbook. The write-up should support and concur with the configuration of the program in the time and attendance system. It makes sense to assemble a binder with a printed copy of each compensation policy and place it where it is accessible to employees, supervisors and Payroll personnel. It should be kept up to date at all times. If an employee questions her pay, the binder will become the backup to support how a payment amount was calculated. In segments of the heathcare industry this is required.

Keeping Track of Compensation Programs

Those who handle payroll in today's large, enterprise organizations that do business in many different states have a confusing array of overtime rules and compensation programs to deal with. For example, not only does California mandate more than weekly overtime, so do Colorado and Kentucky, among others. Later, we will touch on the different holidays that vary by region and locality. One company I know of has dozens of overtime rules to keep track of, and even more premium rules. Prior to installing a sophisticated time and attendance system, these programs had to be administered locally. Without centralized administration, the corporation had even less control and visibility into these programs than would be advisable. In some companies there could be so much "leakage" (excessive compensation), I wonder how anyone who recognized the situation internally could sleep at night.

There Are No Payroll Police

Kentucky has an interesting wrinkle in its overtime regulations. Overtime must be paid on the seventh consecutive day, but not until 40 hours are reached. So, if someone has worked 35 hours the first six days of the pay week and only works two more hours on the seventh day, for a total of 37, no overtime is due. On the other hand, let's say six hours per day were worked during the first six days and eight hours on the seventh day, for a total of 44 hours. One might assume only four hours of overtime is due, but that would be wrong. The entire eight hours is to be paid at the overtime rate according to Kentucky regulations.[2]

Compliance could be the simplest solution to controlling labor costs. Some programs are written very clearly and spell out the exact conditions under which payment can be earned. For example, there are programs we refer to as "bonus programs," wherein employees work a specified number of hours to earn a special bonus payment. In manual systems, compliance with the strict requirements becomes a relative matter, dispensed at the discretion of managers. Automated systems don't know what a "good excuse" is, and they don't play favorites. The rule is hard-coded and exceptions need not apply. The system can play the bad guy because managers are loath to be Payroll police.

Complexities Abound in Payroll

In some cases, a person working on a particular day of the week has to be paid at the overtime rate. Sunday work, for example, may have to be paid at double time or time and a half. Another twist on overtime is known as "8 and 80." In this case, a person becomes eligible for OT under multiple conditions. For workers, there is not just one way to qualify, there are two. If the employee works more than 80 hours in two weeks he gets overtime, or if he works more than eight hours in a single day, he starts earning OT. In big, complex organizations, especially those doing business in multiple states, many different categories of labor compensation can exist. One company I know of has fifty or more different overtime rules. Keeping up with this can be complicated and difficult in a manual setup. But no matter how complex the rules and regulations may be — they might be different in different locations, or change because of the time of day or the shift worked — they will be taken care of once programmed into an automated system.

Judging the Value of Pork

Employers rearely evaluate compensation and benefit programs for effectiveness. Without picking political sides, I'll bet that almost everyone would agree that Congress hands out bushels of money — often for very good reasons and at other times not — but it certainly seems that we hardly ever get an accounting of the effectiveness of that spending. Sometimes the money is only supposed to be spent for certain things or go to certain people, but invariably it ends up in non-qualifying hands.

It's like that with companies, too. I was talking with an HR director whose company had a sign-on bonus program. The company is in a tight labor market, and it was a great incentive package for workers to hire on with that company. The intent of the program was to attract and retain the best workers. New hires received the bonus immediately in exchange for a promise that they'd work for a certain length of time — six months to two years is typical of these programs.

I asked the HR director two questions: 1.) Is it working? 2.) How do you recoup the money when employees leave before their time is up?

What do you suppose were the answers?

"I don't know," and "We don't track whether they work as long as required, so we don't have a collection [repayment] process."

Apparently, one department processes the payments. No department was responsible for the collection. There was no tracking of employees in the program — no evaluation of whether the program attracted "good" employees or how long they stayed.

Let me ask — would the marketing department get away with such a thing? If a car dealer offered $1000 cash back and didn't sell any more cars than normal, would management continue that campaign? If a retailer offered a rebate for purchases of $100 or more but the cashier paid it out to everyone who came in the store, would that person have a job tomorrow?

We'll assume the company — which was very large, keeping the human resources and Payroll Departments very busy — simply could not manage the new hire sign-on bonus any better than it did because it had to work with a manual system. Maybe the cost of manually handling the extra workload compared to the bonus payments that might have been returned did not justify the extra manhours that would have been required. Perhaps. With an automated time and attendance system, however, this program could easily have been monitored for both effectiveness and compliance. Participants receiving the bonus payment could be flagged in the system. Their employment commitment could be tracked so that if they left the company prior to fulfilling their time in service, the supervisor and Payroll Department could be notified to collect the bonus amount from the final paycheck. If an individual had insufficient payroll dollars coming to her to reimburse the employer, then further action could be taken to recover the money. Not only is the recovery of those funds important, the employer ought to be concerned about the message conveyed when such programs are not policed. Employees talk to each other. Workers study compensation programs and become experts on them — not just what is written, but what is enforced. They are smart, and when it comes to money, they don't miss much.

Annual Budgeting — the Story of 3M

There are other ways WMT can help companies save. On average, companies spend 36% of their revenues on human capital expenses but only 16% say they have anything more than a moderate understanding of the return on their human capital expenditures. [3]

For example, wouldn't it make a lot of sense to budget for Payroll based on the amount of work anticipated? Budgets haven't been put together this way in the past, perhaps, because useful data wasn't available. Now it can be. Sales trends and company goals need to be taken into account, of course, but with the right WMT system it's not difficult to know how much work can be turned out — how many widgets can be produced, how many patients can be served — based on historical data.

Bill Monahan, a top 3M executive, was put in charge of a new company that came into being as the result of the spinoff of six business units from that company. All at once, Bill was in charge of those six units. In listening for the first time to reports from leaders of the spun-off businesses, he says he probably believed 50 to 75% of what he heard. Even though he took much of what was said with a grain of salt, he did not examine the details of the plans they presented as aggressively as he now realizes he should have, according to his book, *Billion Dollar Turnaround*. In retrospect, he believes he should have started by believing nothing and requiring each business unit leader to prove every aspect of his portion of the plan. This is called zero-base budgeting. In other words, they should have been instructed to work budgets up from zero revenue rather than adjusting from the other direction, which he says often included unrealistic growth projections. Executives who have come out of GE say that company does a good job at this. Bill says he learned his lesson the hard way, and this delayed the turnaround he orchestrated by at least a year. As Bill moved forward, he used companies like GE as benchmarks, but not doing so sooner cost him time, energy, and a lot of indigestion. With the proper labor data, the first look Bill took at those new business units would have been transparent. Also, having workforce management technology in place would have made it easier for each business unit leader to build a budget from the ground up.

How many companies simply stick a wet finger in the air to determine how much to budget for payroll for the coming year? In firms that are guilty of this, management typically takes a broad look at the business. They determine what it cost to run the business for the year that is ending, take note of the inflation rate or annual revenue growth, and budget an increase of 2%, 3%, 10%, or whatever the case may be for the upcoming year. You might say payroll budgeting is done in much the same way that profit sharing is determined. The amount is then divvied out to department heads. Department heads in turn take a subjective look at staff and try to figure how much it will take to keep each person happy. The entire salary budget is often allocated among the staff as an annual or hourly base rate increase. Often, no margin is set aside for staffing changes, overtime or incentives. The budget is merely a bonus payment spread out over time.

This is hardly the way to plan labor expenditures.

I continue to be amazed at how labor is often treated compared to other business resources and assets. If the purchasing department decided on New Year's Day that it was going to pay each vendor a set amount on a weekly basis for the rest of the year, the company would be putting itself on "autopilot" — unable to react to any turbulence or headwind, unable to avoid catastrophe or to seize opportunities for improvement. The company would have lost any power those funds could have wielded as unexpected needs arose or services failed to meet expectations. The budgetary process for labor needs to be more intelligent and more closely related to productivity.

Choose Wisely, Young Grasshopper

If you've been around a while, you may remember the television show Kung Fu with David Carradine. For some reason certain scenes from that show have stuck with me. I remember Carradine's instructor casting a long glance at him and knowingly prodding him to "choose wisely, young grasshopper." As I recall, it was when the Kung Fu novice was trapped in a cave and had to figure out how to escape. His only option? Move a scalding caldron with his bare arms so he could get out. This resulted in a brand on his forearms. It seemed so ominous. I just ached for him to make the right decision because if he didn't, well, I didn't want to imagine the result.

It can seem that way in business, too. I see businesses struggling with problems and unable to come up with new solutions, unable to see the future. The choices can be painful. The budget process is somewhat like that. Where should dollars be put to best serve the company going forward? Who should the company invest in, and how much should we expect to pay? That goes for labor budgets, project budgets, capital, and marketing budgets. Any time money is spent, a choice is made.

It's best to analyze every budget plan thoroughly and to pay attention to the details. As part of the process, it's important to study the alternatives, including the possibility of keeping things the same. This is where WMT modeling can really come in handy by identifying the amount and cost of labor required to produce a certain amount of goods or to generate a particular level of revenue. It will allow you to quantify and qualify the rationale for budget expenditures.

Proposals based on data and analysis and presented in a familiar format are easy to produce and hard to refute. Making workforce management technology data part of the process will remove personality issues, give the data credibility and level the playing field. It's a flashlight, a magnifying glass and a scale all rolled into one and applied to the decision process.

My advice is to position the budgeting process as an investment activity and go about it as diligently as if the objective was to fund your own retirement. This goes for labor costs and salary budgets as well as operating expenses and capital expenditures. Resources are almost always limited and some ventures are potentially risky. It's important to determine whether something is a "nice to have," such as a store greeter or an ergonomic engineer, or whether it will bring a return on the investment. If so, what will the return be? How does that compare to other ways that money might be used?

Bill Monahan says that before approving an expenditure to pursue a new venture, three questions need to be asked an answered:

1. Is it real? In other words, is there really a market (a need) for whatever has been proposed?

2. Can we win? In other words, is this something the organization can pull off given its competition, resources, and expertise?

3. Is it worth it? The answer to this is the projected return on investment. Wise investment choices are those that offer the greatest returns.

Workforce management technology allows the organization to evaluate the value of labor dollars spent. Tracking workers and activity against key performance indicators and in ways that give incentives to productivity and engagement eliminates the disconnect between workers, output, and cost.

American industry has advanced in its understanding of commodities and purchasing. It has adopted and developed lean manufacturing and sophisticated supply chain management techniques. Highly competitive companies such as GE force vendors to bid for contracts and supply ever less costly components and materials. Some companies, particularly airlines and manufacturers, are struggling and are doing what they can to negotiate away expensive benefit programs. It seems apparent, however, that efficiency programs have not gone far enough in the area of human capital. Knowing the true value of human output enables management to put labor dollars to work in areas where they will generate the greatest return. Regarding labor as a manageable commodity opens up new possibilities for acquiring this resource at more cost-competitive rates.

Introducing Supply and Demand to Labor Management

I love television commercials that make me look at life differently. Often, they are designed to make us, the consumer, feel as though we're in control, to take the proverbial driver's seat in the dog-eat-dog world we live in but are often victim to.

Take the advertisements for online mortgage brokers. A husband and wife sit at a table contemplating a document before them. An anxious banker sits across the table awaiting their reply. They hand the paper back to him, show him the door and say, "Next" to the waiting throng of eager bankers standing in line outside their door. What if mortgage lenders competed for your business? Wouldn't you be empowered? Wouldn't it be to your advantage?

In the world of WMT, something approaching that scene is beginning to occur. Vendors have seized the supply and demand concept and put it to work for companies and employees. Human Resources has traditionally been focused on making HR *processes* more efficient. WMT systems are making the *workforce* more *effective*.

What software vendors have produced is an intelligent tool to supply the appropriate type and amount of labor based on the business needs. Shift bidding or more aptly put *competitive* shift bidding is at the doorstep.

In scheduling systems that allow employees to bid for shifts, a workload template is created indicating how many workers in each job category are needed, at what times, and at what locations. Employees can log onto the system, review the open slots on the schedule and submit bids for particular shifts. This is different from basic self-scheduling where employees either sign themselves up or request shifts without regard to pay. Shift bidding is able to add a money component. For highly desirable shifts, a company may be able to acquire its labor for the lowest cost by allowing the employees to submit their best "price."

Controls on Self Scheduling

Such bidding systems can allow those with more seniority to request a shift before people with less seniority can do so. Union rules might even require that a certain class of employee gets first dibs. So the system can automatically let these employees in to make their requests for a set period of time before opening up for others to make requests. In this way, the technology eliminates the distraction that employee grievances and gripes cause when protocol isn't followed.

Alternatively, a system can be programmed to take into account employee preferences. Employees enter the days and times they'd most like to work. Once their preferences are established, the scheduling program takes these preferences into account. Why is that important? Two reasons: Reduced absenteeism and improved job satisfaction. That equals lower costs and more engaged employees.

Of course, rules can be applied to all of this. For example, state or union regulations may require that only people with specific qualifications work a job or shift. A scheduling workspace can be programmed to insure a worker with the right skill set is scheduled for a shift. The company sets up the criteria specific to its needs and the regulations to which it must adhere. In healthcare, for example, these needs are based on the

patient population and acuity. The employer may need respiratory thera-pists or G-tube certified staff on the ward with the addition of new patients. Only a sophisticated, rule driven system can facilitate ensuring such compliance in a self-scheduling process. The risks of delivering the wrong type of workers to the work site are almost nil.

Compliance with staffing requirements often makes employers subject to audits by outside regulatory agencies. In some industries guidelines dictate rest periods between shifts or maximum number of hours worked that can be worked in a set period of time. If the employer has gotten an exemption from overtime or minimum wages government agencies will periodically monitor compliance. Records are pored over to determine whether a facility has been staffing and paying personnel according to the rules and regulations. This makes it very important to have a system to help the company comply with the rules while still allowing supply and demand to work to the company's advantage.

Payroll Corrections and Cost Accounting

WMT can help manage financial affairs in other ways as well. Management may not realize the impact, for example, on cost accounting when payroll corrections are not factored into the reporting. Eliminating or reducing manual check adjustments is the first step to insure payments (labor expense) can accurately be related to productivity. The next is attributing the payments to the proper time frame and labor events so that payroll records reflect the total accumulated cost of those activities. Systems that report costs based on payment dates alone are not an accurate tool to use in understanding true business costs. Payroll calendars do not relate well to business cycles, and manual check payments are rarely married up to business activity time frames.

To get a handle on this, let's say a department suffers from poor reporting, a high incidence of payroll adjustments and no ability to record those adjustments properly. Last week, most of those in the department worked overtime to complete an important project on deadline. Due to long hours the tired workers put in, and Payroll's willingness to fix employee mistakes, several employees forgot to report all of their additional time by the regular deadline. When paychecks were distributed, these employees instantly realized their mistakes and presented Payroll with corrected time sheets. The added hours substantially increase overtime hours and costs to the department. Let's say Payroll processes hand checks the following week — which also happened to fall in the next month.

When the department manager receives his monthly payroll report, he will probably not realize that much of the cost for that crunch week will in fact be on next month's report. With what he has been given, relating his production numbers to labor expenses and the cost of pushing to get the order completed is not possible. If a historical edit capability were a part of that company's WMT system, however, the monthly report would accurately reflect the additional costs incurred during the peak level of activity. Historical edit functionality allows Payroll to attribute the manual checks — and their inherent labor expenses — to the appropriate timeframe and activity.

Delayed reporting can also be an avoidance technique or a true attempt to defraud the company. An employee's request for payment after time has passed may mean his manager who must approve the additional expense will be less resistant because he can't remember what actually went on that week, so long ago. Historical data and recalculation functionality gives the manager the ability to rewrite the history himself and determine, just as he would have at the time, whether an additional request was justified or has already been paid.

Such rewrite features give visibility into what happened, what should have happened, how it was fixed and what the correction does to the budget numbers. Historical edits update the accrued expenses relative to the activity they represent. Overlaying payroll amounts that include corrections from prior periods and omissions from the current cycle (to be paid out later) to a production-based budget doesn't lend itself to much accountability. Applying historical updates into this tally helps keep managers on target.

An Assembly Process Benefits

Some companies run sideline businesses or build certain products that lose money, and they don't know it. Overall, the company might be making money, but a few products or business units may be very profitable and make up for the losers. An automated time and attendance system can help determine the winners and the losers.

One company I know of, for example, manufactures a product for which a single subassembly, one that may or may not be required depending on a customer's purchase request, takes seven hours to complete. By tracking the labor time on units with and without the subassembly and calculating the actual cost to build them, management was able to determine that customers who require this subassembly were being undercharged.

The same product has another optional subassembly that requires 25 hours of labor. Sometimes customers want both of these subassemblies. At other times, only one or the other is required. Accurate labor data enabled the manufacturer to take a realistic look at what the various combinations actually cost to build. Pricing was adjusted up on some units and down on others so that each variation remained competitively priced, but at levels that made all of them profitable. Without WMT to track and provide activity based costing the employer had no way to calculate labor costs by product.

In this case, the data also helped the company get smart about how work was scheduled through the plant. Imagine the wasted manpower and poor plant utilization if an entire line was held up for 25 hours because a unit needed a particular subassembly. Alternative routes were created that sent products requiring extra steps along different paths. At times units would rejoin the main line, and then veer off again while an infrequently called for subassembly was installed. This might be compared to scheduling local trains that stop at every station and express trains that run nonstop from one large city to another. At times the local train will need to get off the main line onto a side track so the express can speed by and not have to slow down and wait. Looking at labor from this perspective gave them unexpected insight into improving their processes and costing. That increased the company's profit margin.

How to Eliminate Paying the Maytag Repair Man

Yet another example comes from healthcare. I suppose we talk so much about this industry because it is under tremendous pressure where labor is concerned and may be the canary in the coal mine for other industries. The supply of qualified labor in the healthcare field is increasingly tight. Overall costs are spiraling out of control and providers are forced to do more with less. Competition and reimbursement rates are capping the income of providers. Labor is one of the biggest expenses and executives are working to understand it and spend labor dollars wisely.

We all know the Maytag man — the lonely maintenance guy who sits with his feet perched on the desk waiting for the phone to ring, hoping for something to break down and need his attention. Well, he does exist. Health care facilities — nursing homes and small hospitals in particular house a lot of equipment. They have HVAC systems, electrical, phone and plumbing systems, institutional-sized kitchens and special equipment for disabled residents. They also have a maintenance man or two. These guys are often much like the Maytag man, on duty to fix what gets broken and perform routine maintenance. They are handy guys to have around when things go wrong. But they are expensive, too, and not necessarily busy all the time — in other words, when the time they actually spent fixing or maintaining something is added up, it may be found they are actually quite unproductive. And nonproductive labor is an expensive luxury.

I met Doug Heisler, Vice President of Parsons, some time ago. He told me about a business model that eliminates this excess payroll item and still meets the operational needs of the facility. These companies identify the maintenance needs of a site and put together a routine maintenance plan for the equipment. The facilities don't really need someone on site 40 hours a week. We all know the furnace only goes out on nights and weekends anyway. So what these providers do is to allow the customer to outsource the maintenance role, rotating their contract personnel among several facilities as needed, providing support and actually extending the life of the equipment through their proactive maintenance program, while reducing the overall cost for both the maintenance function and the equipment itself.

It seems to me, however, that instead of Doug having to point out this reality to healthcare administrators, these managers should be recognizing the situation and calling him. Why doesn't it happen? Because of visibility. Maintenance worker activity isn't tracked, and emergency work orders and system breakdowns aren't linked to the overall labor cost to fix them. Overall facility maintenance isn't measured or reported against labor utilization. No one knows the cost of the friendly Maytag man relative to the true need for his services. Managers don't even stop to ask. And since the disparity between the need for the labor and the labor supplied isn't reported, no one sees a problem. Time and attendance technology, used as an intelligent business tool, would bring this story to light. Wouldn't you wonder what else is going unseen?

You Don't Have to Be Big to Benefit

I'm often asked how big a company needs to be to use workforce management technology. I answer that there's no minimum size, but it does make sense to evaluate how reasonable it is to expect benefits sufficient to justify the investment. There are companies with only a few dozen employees who are using time and attendance systems. The key is finding a vendor with the right product and pricing structure to fit an organization's needs and budget. Small organizations typically have concerns about system administration, and they don't want to have to buy more complexity than they need. Of course, they are subject to the same needs for accuracy, compliance and savings as big operations, but there may be areas where overly sophisticated technology simply isn't necessary.

Legiant is one vendor that offers time and attendance software to companies in the small to mid-sized market. Legiant's customer, DPT Laboratories, for example, selected the Legiant product for its ability to deliver greater accuracy to the company's processes, its easy-to-use training materials, and for its growth potential (since DPT plans to expand in the future). DPT anticipated the improvements to their processes that were realized. But management was pleasantly surprised when savings added up to $30,000 annually for this 500 employee company. Three years after implementation, savings are still apparent in overtime and the processing effort, and accuracy has been achieved that could not otherwise have been realized. In a case like this, the question should not be, "How much will the system cost?" but rather, "How much will it cost if we don't purchase a system?"

Chapter Four: Using WMT to Enhance Operations, Quality & Compliance

A friend of mine, who works for a large heathcare operation, was recently given the newly created title Vice President of Patient Satisfaction. His organization has the goal of becoming the heathcare provider of choice in its region. A WMT system can provide data to help in achieving this goal. Set up the right way, it will allow the organization to track individual employees' contact with patients and relate this to patient satisfaction levels — provided satisfaction levels were measured through questionnaires or post discharge interviews.

How might this work? Let's say Mr. Amal Well was on such and such a floor in such and such a room on specific days. A patient questionnaire designed to measure his level of satisfaction might be given to him when he leaves the hospital. It would be a matter of using the time and attendance system data to track "customers" and then relate Mr. Well's survey feedback to the employees who provided care during his stay. It might even track the specific dates and times of activities about which Mr. Well had particular concerns. The patient survey data and the employee activity data could be linked and compiled to assess whether satisfaction was related to specific employees or to events, and whether certain employees or activities generated higher patient ratings than others.

It could also overlay other aspects that may have impacted Mr. Well's level of satisfaction and the employees charged with his care. Were they unable to respond due to being short-staffed? Had the employees been working double shifts? Did other patients during the same timeframe, dealing with the same staff members, register the same responses? Are trends evident in how employees are scheduled, or are put together in teams, that relate to the level of patient satisfaction? Do higher paid employees deliver more satisfactory care? And so on.

It's likely some caregivers would prove to be more proficient than others at turning out happy patients. It might be that certain employees work better under particular supervisors or on certain shifts, and that this results in better patient satisfaction outcomes. The hospital might discover that ratings drop toward the end of a double shift worked by an employee or when an employee is called in from a day off. Linking time and attendance data to operational data, such as patient surveys, would add one more dimension to the organization's understanding of what patients experience and the way employees are scheduled to work and be compensated. If there is a correlation between them, employee performance can be viewed as a key indicator of success in generating patient satisfaction.

What to Do with Data

Employees are the face of the organization, the deliverers of products and service. It makes sense to strive to identify the exceptional performers, as well as the poor performers. It would make sense to find out what each group is doing or not doing that others aren't. Specifically, what makes them different? Do nurse scheduling practices impact client satisfaction?

What might supervisors do with this information on client satisfaction and can it be related to the staff? Training is one obvious possibility. Modifying procedures is another. Applicants with certain traits might be targeted for future hires. It would also be possible to set up an incentive program based on satisfaction levels of clients. In Chapter Two I described an incentive plan at Nucor Steel that has proven itself to be extremely effective. It tracks individual employees and the quality of each and every batch of steel they had a hand in making. The point is, with cause and effect identified, steps can be taken to improve performance. You need not take "client" too literally either. The client might be the next department down the line internally in the chain of processes that the work goes through.

Keeping Track of Who's on Site / Remote Monitoring

Perhaps some remote sites in a company are not staffed with management personnel during late-night shifts. The technology discussed in the case history in Chapter Two can be put to work in these situations. Since the new technology is real-time, it's possible to know who is on premises at any given moment. If someone has punched the clock, called in from a phone or logged into a PC at a work location, that person is there. This means a quick check on the computer, a text message, a cell phone page or an e-mail can notify management if someone failed to show up at each facility or workstation, who that person should have been, and who might replace him.

This feature is particularly important in certain segments of some industries. Home construction contractors, 24 hour convenience stores and gas stations are examples. Employees travel on their own to these work locations, get there, and begin the day. Often, they are the only worker on site. In a manual system, the employee reports work activity on a paper time sheet or an old timeclock punch card that's rounded up and submitted at the end of the week or pay period. On a day-to-day or hourly basis, management has little or no ability to monitor whether an employee is actually on premises. How can anyone at headquarters be sure a store is even open? In the case of heathcare providers, employees sometimes travel to residential locations to deliver care. Often, the services provided are critical to a patient's well-being. Certain activities may literally be matters of life and death. Failure to provide such services could put both the patient and the healthcare provider at risk. It's critical that companies with such issues do the job they've been contracted to do, and a WMT system can help insure this.

For retail businesses and contractors, not being open or having workers on a job site can mean lost revenue or delays. Managers *must* know when they have a kink in the human-resource supply chain, so they can address it immediately. Like a production line shutting down, it simply can't be ignored. This is why visibility into what is going on in remote locations represents such a big improvement.

Enforcing Policy Compliance

Automation can also insure incentive plans, wage and hour guidelines and overtime are administered properly. Let's say a policy is instituted that if an employee works an extra shift, he or she will get as an incentive two dollars more per hour. But a requirement is that the employee must work at least four hours beyond the regular shift. In a manual system, this might be tricky to administer, and there will be the ever-present temptation to bend the rules. An automated system will eliminate this temptation and administer the guidelines without missing a beat. More important, the most sophisticated systems can be programmed to prevent managers from scheduling employees into overtime situations by setting up overtime "violations" and warnings. This would be almost impossible to do in a manual system.

Some companies have policies that require points to be given for poor attendance. Attendance issues that create staffing problems for companies include absences, late and even early arrivals, long shifts, short shifts and unscheduled shifts. Leaves of absence for jury duty, military duty, personal or medical reasons or sabbaticals also interrupt the supply of labor.

Companies that recognize these attendance issues and want to do something about them create attendance programs to monitor the activity and manage the employees. At each occurrence the employee racks up a point. In some programs, the various types of attendance problems carry different weights. These points accumulate, and after a specified number is reached, an individual may be "written up." This citation may need to be considered immediately or taken into consideration at the annual employee evaluation time.

Conversely, there are "perfect attendance" programs designed to motivate employees to come to work on a regular basis. Obviously, just getting one's basic hourly rate isn't enough of a motivator.

Time and attendance systems come right off the shelf with mechanisms that track and count these types of work exceptions. This is, of course, a supervisor issue. But what supervisor wants to spend time keeping track of absences? How much time does the tracking take away from more productive work? What is that time worth? When does absenteeism reach a point when it becomes grounds for dismissal? With guidelines in place, an automated system can keep track and give an answer.

It's important to mention that things are changing in this arena as well. The Family Medical Leave Act (FMLA) is wreaking havoc on employers.

In June, 2005, the U.S. Senate held a roundtable discussion of FMLA as a competitive threat to US manufacturing. Case study examples of the abuse of FMLA leave and the impact on businesses were cited with disturbing implications. Intermittent leave — including tardy, early departure and Monday and Friday absences — has grown five times as fast as use of the program for continued leaves. For example, on Super Bowl Sunday one employer experienced a 50% spike in FMLA absences during game time. Occurrences of tardy and early dismissal at this employer averaged 110 per month, equal to six employees calling in late or leaving early *every day of the month.*

Industry representatives at the Senate hearing complained that FMLA regulations negate any contractual agreements between employers, employees and unions leaving the employer with little or no recourse to contest FMLA absences or to apply attendance policies to employees with habitual attendance problems. FMLA use has exploded in manufacturing and is circumventing employers' efforts to curtail poor attendance through policy. Unions have even held on site classes to "train" employees in the use of FMLA. One employer estimated FMLA absences cost them $8.1 million annually. All an employer can do in the present regulatory environment under FMLA is to react effectively to the disruption and work to mitigate the costs. If your company is caught in this situation and does not have a powerful tool to respond to employee absences you may pay a very heavy price.

Companies Can Improve Performance and Save

When lean manufacturing strategies are employed companies typically experience significant performance improvements such as reducing lead time by 50-90%, increasing throughput by 40 to 80%, and increasing overall productivity a whopping 75-125%.

Six Sigma is another methodology employed to deliver quality and performance improvements. This scientific approach's credo is Define, Measure, Analyze, Improve and Control. To oversimplify it a bit, Six Sigma focuses on using data to identify problems such as defects, errors, and bottlenecks. The process is then repeated, and refinements are made. This continues indefinitely so that improvements are continuously made.

Applying this to workforce management makes a lot of sense. The key is to focus on continuous improvement and to use data as a tool. After all, the goals of reducing cost and waste, eliminating risk and improving output and resource utilization are very similar. Both rely on good data — and providing that data is well worth the effort as the results show. Isn't that what every business should be concerned with when they look at labor?

Absence Management: Out of Sight and Out of Pocket

Absenteeism as a business problem is a little like the common cold. We all expect to suffer from it, and we usually try to ignore the symptoms and continue to chug along despite how it drags us down. It's contagious and annoying. We spend a lot of money treating the symptoms because doctors have yet to find a cure. We know exactly how long we spent on crutches or in the hospital but we have no idea how much time we spent blowing our noses last year. A cold can lead to much more serious ailments but we generally believe we just have to live with it and eventually we'll be all right.

Business leaders suffer from a similar affliction called absenteeism. Every manager knows his employees will be absent some of the time but rarely complains about or takes time to evaluate how it impacts him. Absenteeism can spread, infecting employees with its sense of entitlement, racking up the costs as its symptoms must be dealt with. No single manager in the company owns the direct and indirect costs of absenteeism as a line item in the budget. Most companies have only limited ability to track the time and expense this malady creates. Leaving it unexamined and untreated, most companies simply don't understand the cumulative affect it has on the business — the costs, the reduced productivity, the risks and the negative effects on morale and turnover. As some business leaders begin to recognize the price of absenteeism and start to manage attendance better to become more competitive employers of choice, executives who ignore absenteeism will pay dearly in lost profits, productivity and employee morale.

Absenteeism comes in three "strains":

1. *Planned* (scheduled) absences: Vacation, PTO, Leaves (military, jury duty, personal, and so forth)
2. *Unplanned* and unscheduled absences: Sick, Disability, FMLA, Worker's Comp, leaves such as unpaid, bereavement, and so forth.
3. *Partial shift* absences: Late arrival, early departure, long breaks, personal appointments and so forth.

Unplanned absences are perhaps the most costly of all. One in ten hourly employees in the U.S. is absent on average, or 10% of the workforce. This represents a chronic problem with an estimated price tag of $3,600 per hourly employee per year. The higher the rate of absenteeism, the greater the costs. According to Circadian Technologies. Inc., a leading international research firm, overtime is 28% higher in companies where absenteeism is high. Idle time is 3.6% higher in these companies and turnover rates are greater in companies that suffer from poor attendance.

Productivity suffers because of absenteeism. Unexpected call-offs, late arrivals and illnesses all disrupt the planned activities and waste the time of managers and supervisors who have to process them and adjust staffing. The quality and speed of the work may also be diminished because less qualified employees may have to take over. Employees who have to take up the slack can also become overworked and overburdened.

Absenteeism of any type not only increases costs and impedes productivity, employees who work excessive overtime to cover for absent workers, or who work in jobs for which they are not properly skilled, are more likely to have accidents and succumb to poor health. The indirect costs that result include those from additional worker's compensation claims and greater healthcare costs and represent very expensive side effects.

Financial managers need to be concerned about accurately tracking attendance because without adequate estimates of the company's accrued benefit liabilities they may not be able to meet the minimum accounting requirements of regulations such as Sarbanes-Oxley. This can not only be costly, the implications for these managers should give them a scare on a personal level — think Enron executives. Out of sight, out of mind takes on a new meaning. It may mean money coming out of the personal pockets of these executives when they are forced to defend inadequate accounting processes and practices.

That's the diagnosis. The good news is that the prognosis can be good. WMT offers a remedy that's very easy to swallow. The keys to effectively manage absenteeism include:

- Communication and alignment — visibility, infomation, timing, alignment, and control
- Standardization of policies, terms, processes and objectives
- Tools
- Training

Organizations need a way to track absenteeism and to identify the patterns and root causes. Such a system needs to enforce tracking consistently across the organization and total the findings to show the overall magnitude of the problem. Once this is understood, managers should share the information about patterns, offenders and seasonal issues with supervisors. They ought then to set absenteeism goals in line with the company's strategic objectives. A standard plan of action needs to be created that includes common terms, policies and practices that are clearly defined and easily followed. These standards should next be configured into the system which will become the new workspace for absence management throughout the company. Training is the final key to success. This will be necessary not only because a new system is being introduced, but because roles, responsibilities and expectations will be different than in the past, and employees will need coaching and follow-up for these to take effect. Remember, we're talking about a serious "illness" and periodic checkups are needed to measure progress and eventually keep the "patient" well.

Planning that engages everyone in the effort to manage attendance can be a benefit unto itself because it will raise consciousness about the issue — as will the use of new technology and data that measure and forecast absenteeism. Software applications can empower employees to manage

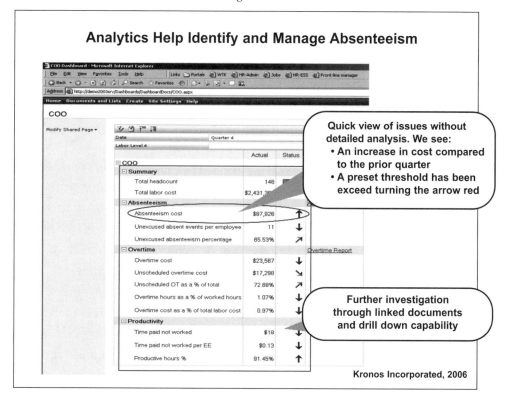

Kronos Incorporated, 2006

their own time off and influence the schedules to which they are assigned. Automating scheduling will enforce leave and compensation policies resulting in more equitable treatment and improved employee satisfaction. Circadian researchers have found that absenteeism is lowest where specialized software is used to manage schedules and attendance. Its effects are even more dramatic where employees are allowed to manage their work and home life balance. The difference could mean savings of up to $3 million per year for a company with 5,000 employees.

The effects of FMLA represent a growing problem for companies, but applying technology to this category of time off can significantly reduce its financial and operational impact. Employees aren't simply using this program for long term absences such as medical leave, the birth of a child or caring for an ill family member. Increasingly, they are becoming aware of the leniency this program offers and use it as a "wild card" for intermittent, last minute call-offs and partial shift absences. Automated systems enable companies to accurately track this manipulation of the system and to compile total time off. Lacking such a tool, companies are hard pressed to prevent overuse of the program. It's a generous program on the employee side, failing to track it adequately will obligate the company to excessive "generosity" and expense.

Tracking of Certificate Requirements

In certain industries employees must maintain specialized certifications that require recurring training. Employees whose certification expires may no longer be eligible to work until they become "current." Absence management systems track these certification requirements and alert managers to upcoming due dates and violations. The ability to forecast training absences and sunsetting skills enables companies to plan around these staffing issues. Some systems tightly integrate training with scheduling and time and attendance giving managers the full picture of availability and qualifications for a pool of workers.

Best practices for absence management include tracking and identifying patterns and root causes of absenteeism. Using this information, smart organizations learn to manage, forecast and plan for absenteeism. They use the system to enforce compliance and tracking and this reduces their risks as well as the negative impact of excessive absenteeism on cost and productivity. The technology allows them to react in real time to staffing issues and to take corrective action to change behavior.

Each type of absenteeism involves a different reaction time:

Planned Absences — Advance notification of vacation requests and planned leaves allows for schedule adjustments and staffing solutions to be provided at a lower cost; less disruption to services; better ability to staff with appropriate skill match (less impact on productivity); *Circadian: An average employee takes three days of unreported PTO per year.*

Unplanned Absences — Real-time response is required. Data is required from operations to assess needs, resources and costs. Unplanned absences can disrupt operations immediately, cause delays, increase costs, decrease morale and leave an employer understaffed in the number of employees and the skills required. *Circadian: Two-thirds of unplanned* absences are non-illness related, i.e., for personal reasons, entitlement-related, family issues and so forth.

Partial Shift Absences — Absences are often are unseen in real time. Immediate response required. Needs must be assessed, as well as resources and costs. Others on premises become burdened and productivity is hampered. Over payment often occurs due to workers being paid for non-worked time or because time off was not charged toward accrued benefit time. *Circadian: 0.72% is average payroll inflation cost due to partial absences.*

Benefits of WMT applied to absence management:
- Reduced costs — *Circadian: A company of 5,000 hourly employees has the potential to reduce costs by $7.9 million or more per year, or 3.2% of payroll on average, using WMT/Absence Management*
- Improved compliance, consistency and reduced risk
- Faster reaction time
- Better scheduling decisions
- Improved productivity and resource utilization
- Improved quality and service
- Increased employee morale and retention

Including Exempt Employees in WMT

Exempt employees are another group where time reporting and analysis of labor activity may be lacking. Normally set up for a straight 40 hours per week or 80 hours of pay per biweekly pay period, these employees often are required to report only exceptions. If one takes a sick day, the onus is on the employee to report that he didn't work, and a day of sick time will be deducted from the employee's available balance. If a salaried employee fails to report this, he will still be paid the full biweekly amount. Often, exempt employees don't submit time sheets for approval so the day off can easily be overlooked. The payroll coordinator has no idea whether the salaried employee worked or took time off, so the automatic 80 hours passes through the system as normal. The practice of exempt "autopay" has also put companies on "autopilot" when it comes to managing exempt labor.

What's the motivation for the employee to report that he was sick? If no one notices, he'll be able to use that eight hours another day. Using an automated labor management system requiring exempt employees to report into the system at least once a day validates they were at work that day. Plus, having some form of verification, such as biometrics, will validate that the employee was physically on site.

There is a widespread misconception, I believe, or perhaps an overly cautious approach about how to handle the reporting of exempt worker time. Exempt status is a well-defined classification of worker types. All sorts of criteria are used to establish whether people's job responsibilities — not just their titles — qualify them as exempt from overtime. Wrapped up in this characterization, or litmus test, is tracking time worked. Employers are under the impression they cannot track an exempt worker's hours without being obligated to pay overtime. But this is not so. It is an exaggeration of the guidelines. Employers have every right to keep a history of a worker's time. I'm not a labor attorney but I've spoken with some who assure me that when handled properly, exempt employees may be required to use an automated time and attendance reporting system without endangering their exempt status. It's not the existence of this information that counts, it's what employers do with it relative to compensation. So don't be afraid to include exempts in the process of implementing workforce management technology and thereby get the full benefit of having this data in the system.

Adhering to Worker Age Regulations

Employing minors under a certain age involves restrictions because in some states limitations exist on the number of hours they can work, as well as which shifts they can work, particularly during the school year. For this reason, minors can be flagged in the system so that their hours are limited, and other regulations are abided by — such as not being able to work past 10 p.m. on school nights. Eager teenagers may want to work the late shift and weary supervisors may welcome a helping hand at closing time, but the system can prevent these violations of wage and hour regulations. Automated scheduling can make this sort of thing easy, enforce compliance and put labor to work at the optimum place and time.

Travel Time and Mileage

Then there's the issue of travel time and mileage. Some companies pay employees at a different rate when they drive on company time between job sites. They may also reimburse for mileage. But how do they know the mileage charge is reasonable? With a manual system they probably don't attempt to verify everything. But with an automated setup, metrics such as the distance between work site A — reported in the system when an employee clocks in for work — and work site B, his second stop, where he also clocks in, can be integrated with the WMT data.

Making Sure the Right Unit Is Charged

Which business unit is charged for travel time and mileage can be handled automatically as well. Should it be the location the employee was traveling from (Site A), or the one he was traveling to (Site B) ? The employee can punch a clock, use a phone or PDA when he leaves location A, then clock into the new location when he arrives, marking the start and stop time of the trip. The system will allocate this to the unit management has determined should be charged.

What if the employee earns a different rate of pay at each facility? Won't he want the higher rate to apply? Putting this payment process within WMT will make the payments consistent. There may also be opportunities to reduce this expense. Is this nonproductive time required to be paid at the employee's normal base rate or could a lower rate, say minimum wage, apply? What if the employee takes his lunch break during the travel period — is that compensated time? Could travel be charged entirely to an overhead account and not the work locations? What if the answers are different based on the job or work location? The complexities might be practically endless but still are manageable and controllable within WMT systems.

Demonstrating Equal and Fair Treatment of Workers — Reducing Risk

Having detailed time and attendance data at one's fingertips can help in other ways. Suppose an employee claims his employer didn't pay or treat him fairly. For example, most states require employers to give employees breaks after working a set number of hours. Some states allow an employee to waive his right to a break and work through the break period. A policy might be set up so that a supervisor is required to give his approval in such an instance, and the supervisor in turn might have the employee sign a release. This can be entered in the system, which will be important when troublemaker Charlie gets canned for habitually being late. He may realize his habitual tardiness has been documented but still want a pound of flesh.

"They wouldn't let me take lunch," he might say to his lawyer, "I should be paid for all those lunches they made me work."

When an employee makes such a claim, it's up to the employer to prove that either the employee was actually given the breaks or that he waived his right to them, and was paid for the time he worked. Without documentation, the employer would be up the proverbial creek. With it, a disgruntled employee will simply have to move along and put the squeeze on someone else.

A labor attorney once told me a story about one of her clients. One supervisor in a company decided to institute a policy that if an employee under him didn't give two weeks notice before quitting, that employee would not be paid for accumulated paid time off (PTO). According to the attorney, this practice is illegal in the state where this company is located and one employee complained to the state about her client's company. This precipitated an investigation.

The lawyer went on to say that the state authorities didn't look at just that one employee record. Of course not. The company's entire system was audited. The authorities assumed that if one employee was mistreated, the company potentially mistreated them all. It happened that this company's problem was systemic, and its exposure to penalties and additional financial obligations turned out to be much more serious than what was indicated by just that single employee's complaint.

Let's think about the company where Charlie claimed he didn't get his required break. If management had employed the WMT system we've been discussing, this might not have happened, and if it did, after documentation upholding the company's position was presented, it's less likely that the authorities would have moved forward to take a look at all the records. In the first place, employees could have been required to clock in and out for all break periods. In the second, supervisors would have been entering in an employee's waiving of his break rights. The system would have forced each employee to be handled in the same way as every other employee in the company. The authorities would quickly see this and have less cause to investigate further. Automation would have prevented a wayward supervisor from making up his own rules for his department.

The reduction of risk — exposure to liabilities for noncompliance, employee grievances, external audits, fines, etc. — is often understated and undervalued. The financial benefit of reducing expenses related to these issues should not be overlooked. Workforce Management technology will elevate your organization to a higher plane, thereby mitigating risk.

"I owe my soul to the company store"

Company stores exist in many businesses. Hopefully they've come a long way since the time when coal miners and mill town workers relied on them for daily needs. For today's worker in a heathcare institution, the gift shop in a hospital is an example. In retail, an example might be discounted in-store purchases. Employees often are allowed to make purchases using their payroll ID number and badge like a debit card. In many cases they receive a discount, and the purchase amount is deducted gradually in small increments from upcoming pay.

Systems are available that will integrate the sale at the cash register with the time and attendance system. This can head off potential problems many employers have experienced when employees run up large balances. Suppose, for example, a part-time employee makes purchases totaling $300, and this amount would take several pay periods to be repaid out of that individual's small earnings. The system can check the current credit balance this employee has and impose a limit on how much more the particular individual can charge. Or it can set other parameters.

What about the employee who quits his job and goes on a shopping spree at the gift shop on his way out the door? He still has a badge. The cashier knows him. She has no reason to question him. First, the system might check to see how much the employee currently owes and compare this to upcoming pay to determine whether the charge should be allowed. If Greta has just just resigned or been let go, the system will not allow the transaction, and the cashier will be alerted that Greta is no longer an employee.

Keeping Track of Unproductive or "Down" Time

What about unproductive time? If a person is doing something that's not his primary responsibility, such as cleaning up, that's still considered compensable time. Even so, a company might want to segment this time since it didn't contribute directly to production or sales or providing service and account for it differently since it wasn't spent directly adding value to an end product.

WMT systems are designed to allow employers to keep track of any type of activity. For example, if workers have to dress in clean-room outfits before they actually get to a work area, they might be required to punch in when they arrive at the dressing room and punch in again when they arrive at their workstations. In this way, the time getting dressed and moving from the dressing room to the production area will be captured in a separate category. The best setup for data capture in this work environment would be two devices — one near the entrance or dressing area and one closer to the production area.

Speaking of unproductive time, many union contracts guarantee employees a minimum number of hours even thought they may be sent home after five minutes, which reminds me of the one about the hammer and the broken furnace. A repairman was called during the weekend. He arrived, assessed the problem, took out his hammer, hit the furnace, and it started working. He charged $51 — a dollar for his time and $50 for knowing where to hit the furnace. In real life, an off duty repairman might be called in during the night shift and spend five minutes fixing something that was holding up production. The company may have a guaranteed minimum of two hours pay if someone is called in to work this way. So the repairman must be paid two hours for five minutes work, an hour and 55 minutes of which is non-worked time. According to wage and hour guidelines, this time does not count towards "hours worked" and doesn't have to be counted toward overtime. The company is also not obligated to count those hours towards the accumulation of paid time off (PTO) or other benefits. But in a manual system, if Mr. Fixit has already worked 40 hours, and two more are put on his time sheet, he's likely to be paid at an overtime rate because the people keeping track aren't aware of, or may overlook, this detail.

Similar programs are known as "On Call" and "Call In." On Call staff are routinely scheduled for "On Call" duty. The employee is to remain on standby, easily reachable by management who may need to call in additional staff at a moment's notice. The employee may be paid a flat rate for this duty period. The time is not considered "worked time." If the employee is contacted and required to report to work, however, the time the employee works is "Call In" time. To compensate the employee for this interruption to her off-duty hours, the company may guarantee that she will be paid a minimum number of hours — regardless of the actual time worked and possibly at a special rate of pay. Again, if the employee works only a short span of time and the rest of the "guarantee" is paid as a "bonus," the hours can be treated differently from true "worked time," and the cost of those bonus hours reduced. In a manual system, particularly in large organizations, this complexity in pay practices is difficult to administer consistently and accurately. It also requires a good deal of training and data manipulation. WMT takes care of all of that.

We see a lot of cleanup in this area when WMT systems are installed. Call-in is a favorite device for "working the clock" by employees. Many executives have little idea how employees set themselves up for repeated Call-ins, racking up bonus hours like frequent flyer miles. We encourage rewriting these policies and setting up the system to shut down these "frequent flyers" and cap the well on call-in bonus time. Moreover, tracking Call-in pay will reveal the real problem, which usually has to do with attendance and understaffing issues such as poorly executed labor deployment. Why not use the data base available through WMT to reduce the dependency on Call-In and On-Call or whatever mechanism is in place to supply workers at a moment's notice?

Eliminating Flex Time Abuse

Flex time is what comes about when employees are allowed to work a flexible schedule by adjusting their work hours accommodate special, personal needs. Or it may be offered simply to provide greater flexibility to employees who want time off during normal business hours. Some examples of flex time are programs that allow employees to work longer shifts and take a day or a portion of a shift off without penalty. For example, employees work "eight nines" which means they work eight nine hour shifts accumulating eight hours of flex time. They then use the flex time as a paid day off. Flex time might also be used to compensate employees who worked an especially long shift in order to handle an emergency or who were required to travel and experienced long work days because of the time required to get to a distant work location. Let's say a person works ten hours one day. The person may only work six the next in order to make up for this. In a paper system, the individual may simply write down eight hours for each day. But this misrepresentation of actual time worked cannot be accomplished in a system where data is time-stamped when entered and "actual" arrival and departure times are accurately represented.

In a manual system, it's easy for flex time to be ripe for abuse. One common misuse occurs when a supervisor hands it out as a discretionary bonus to a favored employee. It can also easily be overstated or overdrawn. Employers may unwittingly violate wage and hour regulations by allowing flex time to cross pay weeks or pay periods and not pay overtime appropriately. These are serious infractions in the eyes of regulators. In addition, flex time that is not recorded accurately can skew labor cost reporting by attributing productive time to timeframes when no hours were actually worked.

But there is a solution. An intelligent system can bank flex time and insure it is used in accordance with company policy. It can apportion productive time accurately and reflect compensated non-worked time appropriately. Incorporating flex time policy into an automated system insures that the time is used and paid in alignment with labor regulations. And it can do all this while providing visibility into how the benefit flex program is being used.

Tracking flex time allows employers to evaluate the flextime program against operational and staffing needs. Since it represents a variance from the normal work schedule, it makes sense to monitor it to make sure it doesn't impede productivity. Tracking flex time allows the employer to measure the true cost of the program by relating flex time hours to any additional labor expenses that arise because an employee has to be replaced during the missed shift. Often, the flex benefit means others have to work overtime, or, in extreme circumstances, that agency or contract labor have to be brought in. The resulting additional expenses incurred need to be taken into account when evaluating such a program.

On the other hand, flex time might encourage employees to defer using other benefit time. Benefits such as paid vacations and holidays mean employees receive pay for nonproductive time off. The flex time program presumably pays employees for productive time and may create an illusion of paid time off similar to a vacation or holiday. This might actually work to an employer's benefit if employees get caught with excess vacation time in a "use it or lose it" program. In such a situation, the employer's obligation to pay for vacation time is eliminated when the employee fails to take the time off within the allotted time frame. The employee may have received several days off — away from work — during the period, but the employer may actually have paid only for productive time. He's making a payment for something the employer received — hours worked. With benefits, he's not paying for services rendered. So from the company's perspective, it could be that a flextime program may be a viable alternative to a vacation benefit program.

Whether or not such a program is appropriate for your industry and category of workers depends on how competitive the labor market is, as well as regulatory factors. But it may be something your Compensation Manager should evaluate. Using workforce management technology to develop a critical analysis of the program can provide valuable data upon which to base a decision.

Using an Automated System to Spot Inefficiencies

One company found through its new automated system that fork lift drivers were causing a tie up around timeclocks. Kronos recently acquired a company called Clarity Matters and integrated it into their suite of products. Clarity Matters developed a labor analytics product that evaluates the activity reported through time and attendance for operational issues. The company was engaged by a major manufacturer to apply this tool to the manufacturer's labor data and determine if employees were "working the clock." What Clarity Matters uncovered was that the plant's drivers would pull their fork lifts as close to the timeclock as they could get them before punching out at the end of their shift. The next shift spent a good deal of unproductive time untangling the resulting fork-lift jam. This discovery was made through a root cause analysis of the labor data that tracked time between arrival and activity. Obviously people knew about this logjam but they didn't understand the cost and impact on productivity. WMT technology added value to information — it replaced what people knew with what they didn't know about a situation.

Foiling Those Who are Working the Clock

What's "working the clock"? It's a lot of things. Most companies don't pay minute to minute, so a cutoff usually exists for rounding the time of a punch. For example, if someone punches in at 8:08, this might be rounded to 8:15, while a punch of 8:07 might be rounded to 8:00. Employees know this and are savvy about its implications.

At what time will employees aim to arrive? Some might come at 8:07

every da, and play this game at every punch. They punch in, punch out and in for lunch and punch out at the end of the day right at eight minutes before or seven minutes after. This can add up to a half hour of non worked time every day. That's two and a half hours a week. In a year that's 130 hours, more than three weeks of paid-for time that wasn't worked. In a company that employees hundreds or maybe thousands, this can add up to big money.

Of course, it can be argued that this rounding mechanism works to the company's advantage as well. Employees' time can be rounded back in a way that shaves minutes off what is paid. In theory, it's six to one, a half dozen to another. This may be true, but only for the computer. People aren't computers and they quickly learn how to "work the clock" and do so with abandon.

Let's talk about the lunch break because it's a slightly different animal. A lunch period is a span of time. It's an interval between two punches. At lunch time, an employee could leave at 11:53, knowing this will be counted as 12 o'clock. He could come back at 12:37, knowing this will show as 12:30. According to time records, he took a half-hour lunch. In fact, he took 44 minutes — almost 50% more. Interval rounding enables employers to shut down this game and pay employees for their true time.

Interval Rounding

What's interval rounding? WMT systems can be set to round the interval or span of time rather than the punch time. Jane punched out for lunch at 11:53 and back in at 12:37. That's 44 minutes, which rounds to 45. The entire shift can be rounded as well. Please be aware, however, that if your company bills based on hours worked and you decide to try shift interval rounding, you need to make certain this method is consistent with your billing policies and contracts.

The system can also be set up to flag those workers who do not punch at all for lunch. If they couldn't take lunch because they had to work, they should be paid for it. But if they forgot to punch, or just didn't bother to punch and took lunch, they should not be paid for that time. WMT systems can easily be set up for automatic deductions.

One of my customers requested an on-screen workspace that would display the employees who did *not* punch for lunch. Upon hearing this request, I was taken aback.

"You mean, we've got to get the system to tell us something based on data that isn't in the system?"

After all, the tool would be used to report employees who were not punching. *Show me what doesn't exist* was what I'd heard my customer say. Plus, for this tool to be actionable, we had to ignore missing punches (the nonexistent data) if the employee worked only a few hours and should not have taken lunch. This was incredible. Sometimes my client wanted to know whether a meal had not been punched, and sometimes he didn't.

The good news was the technology could do it. We devised a way to configure the pay rules and build logic into the system that told the computer to *expect* a set of lunch punches and what they would look like and under what conditions. If the system registered this activity, then nothing happened. But when the expected activity didn't appear — the system sent up a "Missed Meal" flag, giving the names of employees who may have forgotten to punch for lunch. An individual's supervisor could then look into what happened. Mind you — we did not customize the system, we configured it. WMT systems are designed as tool kits.

Early and late punches — relative to when the employee is scheduled to arrive and depart — can easily be dealt with in an automated system. Here's another scenario. Suppose Earl E. Bird likes to get to the factory at 7:30, punch in and then go have a cup of coffee at the cafeteria until his shift starts at 8 o'clock. If Earl isn't supposed to clock in before eight o'clock, the data collection device can be programmed so that it won't allow Earl to clock in before 8 o'clock. Or the system can allow the punch but round to the scheduled start time — unless a Supervisor overrides this restriction because Earl E. Bird really was supposed to come in early.

Good old Mr. Bird. Doggone it. Back in the good old days, he used to get paid for drinking that cup of coffee.

And don't forget to document this new restriction for early birds in your compensation policies so employees clearly understand what they will be paid for.

Sometimes you feel like you pull the rabbit out of the hat — the technology is invigorating when you see what it can do.

Not So Surprising Surprises

A parallel is the running of old and new systems simultaneously for testing and comparison. When going from paper to PC, the manual system is kept going while the automated system comes up to speed. Something I've frequently noticed during this time is that payroll costs go down during and immediately following the parallel period. People are aware of the additional scrutiny — they know that the two systems are being compared. So you might call this the "Big Brother syndrome." As the parallel process is used to validate the data, a dip will occur in the amount of payroll dollars paid out. Somehow, reported time becomes very credible. Paper system "fudging" disappears. As the paper system goes away, the payroll figure may creep back up. The good news is it often will not reach its previous high level.

Why? Controls are put in place and what's going on is more visible. As time goes by, if it's possible to do so, some people will learn subtle ways to work the new system. That's why it's important to devise controls that discourage and limit the amount of manipulation which can be done that results in "working the clock."

Does this mean people are dishonest? Perhaps some are. But consider what you'd do in a typical situation. For example, think about what might happen when a person is late, and it isn't really that individual's fault.

"Doggone it, there was a huge backup on the expressway. A tractor trailer turned over. I shouldn't be docked for that."

With the old manual system, it was easy enough for that person's supervisor to fix the problem. All he had to do to help his friend out was to add the time back in by adjusting the punch time. But in an automated system, doing this will not be so easy, and if everything is set up correctly, such an adjustment won't go undetected.

Controlling Exits and Entrances

Automated systems also can provide what's called gatekeeper technology. While clocking in to the time and attendance system the employee simultaneously is granted entry into the facility. The matter of controlling who gains entry into a building, a hall, even a room can be easily managed and monitored. You might call this killing two birds with one stone. In this case the two birds translate into two separate technologies, redundant equipment, essentially providing the same functionality.

The increasing need for such technology says a lot about our modern society. It reminds us that we are often anonymous, unidentified, presumed untrustworthy occupants of the places we go. We live with the expectation that daily life is full of activities where we encounter "transients." We expect out of town coworkers to fly in for a meeting. We work "remotely" from our home offices doing our time on the "cyber-shift" where our business associates are known by their user names and web addresses instead of their faces. We actually see fewer and fewer people routinely except for our closest "cube-mates." We are temporary patients in large institutions with specialist doctors we do not know well so staff wear photo IDs. Unexpected "visitors" cannot enter our schools without signing in and sticking Visitor labels on their lapels. As random customers at convenience stores we are videotaped on the chance we may turn into shoplifters or robbers. All this lack of familiarity — along with a media culture that feeds our insecurities — has fostered the fear that people are not where they should be, doing what they ought to be doing. The bottom line is that identification is a big issue.

Fortunately, the technology exists to help us verify identity, to replace knowing all of those around us and working in close proximity with a confirmation that we're interacting with the right person, that the right person is working for us, and that people are where they say they are, doing what they should be doing. Integrating WMT to door locks prevents unauthorized entry by person or by time of day and tracks movements of people in the workplace. When I worked at the airline — nearly twenty years ago — the Federal Aviation Administration (FAA) required security controls and ID badges in the airline headquarters because of the sensitive nature of the business — the systems the building housed that controlled planes flying up in the air around the country. It seems the dangers are now even more commonplace. This aspect of WMT is referred to as gatekeeper technology or access control. It's worth considering for the modern workplace.

The Case of the Missing Tools

For one of my clients, the value of access control addressed a perplexing problem. Management suspected tools were "clocking out" — leaving the premises and walking off with workers at the end of the late night shift. People who wanted to take tools with them could go out a rear side door where lighting was poor and no security guard was posted. Few workers used the door because it was some distance from the parking lot. Barring the door wasn't an option because it had to be accessible for emergency and fire evacuation.

The solution to this turned out to be fairly simple. What was the absolute last thing workers did before they left? They had to clock out. Restricting third shift employees from using the clock by that back door during the third shift was the answer. This way, everyone would be forced to use the exit in a high traffic area where workers could be observed leaving the premises. Further, the system could report anyone who attempted to use the clock near the rear door during third shift.

Making a change to how clocks were used was certainly cheaper than adding a security guard, or the cost of stolen equipment.

Chapter Five: How Automated Systems Make Life Easier

I mentioned earlier that one of my pet peeves is manual checks created by the Payroll Department to correct an employee's pay. No one is perfect and mistakes and omissions are bound to occur. But the degree to which Payroll is expected to accommodate the inaccuracies and oversights of other employees makes no sense in my opinion. No other business area would accept so much bad data, particularly when it directly impacts a business area's workload and efficiency.

Can you imagine the sales department making a bid on a project and then being expected to retrieve the bid, make corrections, and resubmit because procurement forgot to tell sales that there was a price increase in raw goods? Can you imagine this happening every week? From the same internal procurement personnel? Would that staff member even be employed after a few weeks of this kind of sloppiness? During summer break from college one year, for example, I worked at a publishing distribution center. The line workers filled book orders from elementary schools, picking inventory from the shelves that lined the conveyor belt "alleys" according to detailed purchase orders. It wasn't acceptable for those who took the orders to come out to the floor and tell the stock pickers they would have to re-pick that order they had just finished because the order-taker had forgotten something. Employees were expected to do their job.

What it comes down to is that Payroll managers and corporate management often make the mistake of positioning Payroll as they would customer service with employees as the customers. But employees are not customers. Customers purchase goods and services and whether customers are satisfied with the company is critical to survival. "The customer is always right" is an appropriate credo for maintaining a good relationship. Customers are not obligated to buy a company's products or use its services. Customers can do business with whichever company they please. It makes sense that companies should work hard and bend over backwards to keep them happy.

Employees, on the other hand, might be considered more like vendors or business partners than customers, and it seems to me they should be treated as such. Employees engage with companies in formal relationships. Companies and employees depend on one another to provide accurate and timely information. A vendor who does not submit an accurate, timely invoice will not be paid correctly or on time. Companies do not go around asking for un-submitted vendor invoices, send friendly reminders, or create special checks for vendors who forget to submit a bill. Companies don't make special check runs for vendors that forgot to include the cost of materials on the invoice. They demand a corrected invoice, or an additional bill, and process it for payment in the next billing cycle. Part of a vendor's "job" is to submit his invoice.

Employees have a job to do, too, and part of it is to submit their time spent and work activity information. It's one of the most important things they do. Without that time sheet, they should not get paid. No one is more motivated to make certain he gets paid than the employee himself. Unfortunately, many companies baby their employees and provide "service" to the detriment of the employee, the Payroll Department and the company.

But times are changing. Paying people accurately the first time is so much easier, faster, and more reliable with the technology today. Instituting a system and supporting it with a policy that puts the responsibility on the employee is the key to improving payroll production. When employees look at themselves as small business owners and recognize that the "revenue" (their paycheck) for their services won't be disbursed until they submit an "invoice" (their timesheet), then they take ownership of that process and make certain it's done right. After all, they shouldn't want their "business partner" — employer — to waste money generating manual checks, updating historical payroll records with updated check data, distributing secondary payments, refunding employee bounced-check fees, and spending countless hours reconciling manual check registers, bank statements and tax deposits. The money this costs could be used to increase wages, offer better benefits, and generate more profit for both employee and employer.

It becomes even more important when payroll data is being used in real time to manage labor more effectively, as we've discussed earlier. Payroll data is undoubtedly highly accurate. However, corrections and manual checks impede timely delivery of this valuable information to the organization and will prevent the greatest business benefits from being achieved if it they are not curtailed.

The Importance of Configurable Software

The beauty of a configurable system built on a tool kit of parameters, settings, queries and workspaces is that it can be made more powerful. It becomes customized for your organization. Perhaps the vendor did not design every feature into the system, but their software engineers did design in the capacity to make them possible. The lesson is, if you don't see what you need in the canned product, look for a system robust and flexible enough to be configured to suit your needs.

What makes a system robust and flexible are the parameters, qualifiers, counter mechanisms and zone features. The system needs to support the types of logic that your policies stipulate. Payroll practices are often built on Boolean logic, which says, "If so and so, then such and such." In a sense, employees qualify for their compensation and the complexities of the qualification process can seem endless. A setup's features must be able to account for eligibility criteria in multiple layers, i.e., if X then Y but only if $A + B = C$ on Saturdays. It must be possible to define settings and expand them. So in selecting the right software, it's important to look for the ability to combine the parameters, review data in the future and in the past, total data, average it and compute the data before a result is given.

We've seen incredibly complex compensation programs configured to entirely automate the qualification and calculations of pay. The key is to know your practices. Know how and why you pay employees today and what you need to be able to do tomorrow. Then find a system that can best handle those requirements, sit back and enjoy the evolution.

Rewriting Payroll History

As is the case with politicians and modern movies, Payroll is frequent-ly "rewriting history" — trying to revise the record of what happened in the past. For Payroll, however, unlike political pundits and Hollywood producers, that history must be 100% accurate. Payroll history is checked and rechecked — by government revenue agencies and internal auditors. Payroll records are subject to checks and balances — reconciling bank statements and general ledger accounts. They must square vertically with subtotals and grand totals and horizontally within every individual with-holding account. This becomes increasingly challenging with each adjust-ment, correction and manual check that must be written.

Manual processes for payroll corrections and hand checks are fraught with difficulty and prone to error. Payments cannot simply be made based on newly submitted information. The past must be reviewed and the new information applied to the historical data in order to determine if the new information changes the old. A good record of the adjustment must be maintained so that when subsequent inquiries occur, the inquirer can locate and comprehend the history of those changes. Time sheets must be recalculated, notes made and new records appended to the original time submissions. The new payment must be tracked both in terms of its his-torical impact and for its inclusion in current payroll data.

Praise be, however, with the introduction of computer-based time and attendance systems, rewriting history is much easier than in the past. Date and activity-specific records exist that can be updated with new informa-tion, recalculated and merged with current payroll data for payment. Adjustment entries are electronically appended to historical records so that finding the corrections and preventing duplicate adjustments is avoided. Software products today include historical edit features that allow everyone in the process to keep track of records and payments. Payroll can append employee timecards with a record of an additional payment, whether it is paid with the next normal payroll cycle or done with a manual checkoff cycle. Reports can be run with labor management software that show labor costs for specific periods of time or activity as they were actually paid in real time or as accumulated over time with additional adjustments and corrections.

The Ease of Making Group Edits

Let's say a supervisor has a group of people attend an off site meeting. Since they weren't at the plant, they couldn't punch a timeclock. In a manual setup, this would have meant locating the timecard for each of those individuals and manually adding the time. Or a report would have been sent to Payroll and Payroll would have had to manually add the time to each individual employee's payroll record before processing.

Today we have the ability to grab all of those employees at once — whether they are all in the same department, all work the same shift across the plant, or even if they all are working on a common project but represent a diverse group of employees and different functional areas. After the "group" has been selected we can now input the activity and apply it to all the selected employees in a single stroke. This works well for bonus payments, too, and systems often provide a confirmation that each record was updated successfully. No more need to find each employee's paper timecard or electronic record individually and input the same thing over and over.

This is a tremendous time-saver.

Reason and Comment Tracking

Is it important to your organization to know the reasons why? What value does attaching a reason or description to labor activity and payments add? From an audit perspective knowing "why" can be crucial in determining if a user made a change in the system for an appropriate reason.

In many organizations attendance is a big issue. Many systems now available can do "reason" tracking. For example, each time a person is late or absent, the record may be appended with a reason why. Maybe he overslept, or got stuck in traffic, or the baby-sitter didn't show. When tracking trends in employee attendance, a spike in late arrivals due to road construction may be revealed. You might ask, "So what? What can an employer do who knows traffic is a problem on the second shift?" Having the second shift employees consistently arrive late is going to disrupt the first shift, the customers being served and production schedules underway during the transition. The employer may decide a temporary change in the schedule would alleviate this problem by allowing employees to travel during nonpeak traffic periods, thereby making it more likely they will arrive at work on time. Or the employer could simply remind employees that they will need to leave for work earlier in order to insure on-time arrival.

Attendance can immediately impact a business's bottom line. If no one performs an authorized, reimbursable, billable service, the revenue that would have been gained is lost. The retail industry is particularly sensitive to the attendance problem. A retail store may not be able to open until a manager is on duty or enough cashiers are in place. I once went to the movie theater and stood at the back of a very long line. As the crowd grew we noticed workers behind the concession stand inside but soon realized no one was manning the ticket windows. The line grew longer and longer as show time approached. Finally, the manager came out and let us all in for free. Ouch! A couple of hourly workers missing and scores of customers walked in without paying a cent. Would it have been useful later, when looking at weekly revenues and expenses, to have recorded that occurrence and plan better for it next time?

In manufacturing, someone missing from a line can throw production off kilter. This is particularly true in lean environments that operate according to predetermined takt times. The line may have to "flex down" to a significantly lower output level if not enough people are available to staff each workstation because those who are present will have to be redistributed in a way that keeps the line in balance.

Error Reporting and Employee Interaction

Another important thing automation can do is identify errors in transmission. For example, it can automatically answer such questions as, "Who is not going to be paid?" And "Who is going to be paid who shouldn't?"

In a manual system, when timecards are being keyed in and one slips under the desk, unless someone happens to spot it, no one may suspect something's wrong until the employee goes to her supervisor when she doesn't get a check. If a terminated person happens to receive a direct deposit into her account, how quickly do you suppose she will report the error? But filters can be established in an automated system that will raise a flag if an employee is missing from the register who shouldn't be, or if an employee who has been terminated is going to be paid. All that's necessary is for an automatic audit to be in place ensuring inactive employees are not being paid and that all active, working employees are.

Variances in payment amounts can be monitored as well. Managers can review significant increases or decreases in payroll by having the system compare today's figures to a base line or to prior periods. Remember the $50,000 check I mentioned in Chapter One? If anyone had been reviewing just the totals for that group of employees the increase from any prior period would have jumped right out. It's even easier for an automated system to catch this type of problem.

Dealing with Chronic Tardiness or Absences

Let's say a company has a few employees who have attendance problems. They might be habitually late or absent. Management would like to replace these people, but firing can be difficult these days. On top of this, a person with an attendance problem is also likely to be someone with an attitude problem — a person looking for a reason to make things difficult for the company. So what the boss needs is good, solid documentation that enables him to let that person go without fear of repercussions. The right automated system can deliver this. For example, it will allow the employer to review the past six months or year and identify every time that person was late or absent and the reason given.

If the employer wishes, he might make a note in the system that on such as such a date, a first warning was given, and on such and such a date a second warning was issued. That way, if wage and hour, an Equal

Employment Opportunity Commission (EEOC) representative, or a labor attorney were to get involved and say it looks as though an employee was dismissed unfairly, the documentation would be readily available to demonstrate the opposite. With a manual system, it could take many man hours and several bottles of Advil to go through filing cabinets and pull out timecards in order to support a case. Be aware as well, it's also possible to integrate WMT with HR systems that administer disciplinary tracking, making HR's job easier as well.

The ways employees will attempt to slip past controls are practically unlimited. People can be quite skilled at avoidance techniques. "Slippery" folks will try it all. Late arrival? — "I forgot to punch." Late arrival again? "I lost my badge and couldn't punch." Late arrival again? "The clock wasn't working." Like children, aren't they? Why do people try this sort of thing? Because it works! In a manual system supervisors can be like parents. They're busy, distracted, and forgetful. They don't have time to keep track of the excuses, and are usually relieved the employee has finally arrived so the work can begin. And like children who quickly catch on to the latest, such employees with avoidance techniques can be "contagious." Suddenly, other employees have forgotten their badges. But this little game can be cut short in a hurry with an automated system. Marking occurrences with reasons and comments will bring to light problems and the frequency with which they occur. And you know what? It won't be long before word of this gets around.

While we're on the subject of tracking, here's another story. During a WMT implementation at a large hospital, I overheard a nurse commenting about a new regulation requiring employers to track staff illnesses. I asked how she was planning to comply with this new rule. She looked at me with a twinge of incredulity and replied something to the effect she'd have to create some sort of new paper report.

Absences would automatically be a part of the new system, so I suggested to the project team that they flag employee absences with a comment describing the illness causing an absence. This seemed the most logical place to store this data. All that was needed to help fulfill the new reporting requirement was to include the type of illness associated with each in the comment list of the system the hospital had already purchased. With this feature in place, the supervisor could easily add the comment when adjusting the schedule to reflect the absence or when entering time-off so the employee would receive benefit pay. This solution proved to be quite handy. Management could not only record events by individual, any spread of the contagion across the organization could be mapped and a record compiled of when and where it started, how many employees were affected, and when it tapered off. If an epidemic occurred, the cost could be tracked. It would be possible to see if some areas were immune or contained the spread more effectively. Because tracking was a requirement, an outside entity looking at this data would have an easy time applying standards and ratings to this organization's figures. What better way to insure the hospital scored well than to be actively collecting data and managing any problems?

Tracking Reasons Why in Payroll

The Payroll area can also benefit from tracking the reasons why things go awry. We don't live in a perfect world and there are times when Payroll makes mistakes and checks are wrong. Employees are rarely willing to simply wait until the next pay period to receive their hard-earned money. What usually happens, of course, is that Payroll generates an adjustment to correct the payment using a manually-written check. This rework in the payroll process is costly. I've known companies that put out more hand checks than some companies put out regular checks. For one organization with tens of thousands of people, such checks can run into the hundreds every pay cycle. Remember the company that decided to charge the business unit that requested a hand check $50 in the hopes of encouraging more accurate payroll reporting?

Automation facilitates tracking, and tracking the reasons that the Payroll Department has to process a large number of hand checks last month might reveal a bottleneck in the flow of the paperwork or a supervisor who apparently isn't checking the data before it's approved. It would reveal who and what is causing the rework. Tracking the reasons could be a valuable tool in eliminating the problems. The information could quantify in dollars the true costs of these problems and lead to their getting taken care of. It could well be that the more tracking is done now, the less will have to be done in the future.

Is Every Day a Holiday?

Holidays are so pervasive and widespread there are web sites devoted entirely to all the holidays ever imagined and set aside as special days. One, http://www.earthcalendar.net, will tell you what today is. You see, somewhere in the world, today is bound to be a holiday. I happened to type this sentence on August 8. Did you know August 8 boasts two international holidays plus holidays in six different countries?

Queen's Name Day — Sweden
Father's Day — Taiwan
Independence Day — Bhutan
Day of the World's Indigenous People — International
Peace Day (End of the Iran/Iraq war) — Iraq
Peasants' Day — Tanzania
Universal & International Infinity Day — International
Saint Mary MacKillop Day — Australia

Let's face it. We like our holidays, our heroes, our celebrations — any excuse to have fun or just to take time off. In addition to holidays most of us have never heard of, there are six "standard" ones — New Year's Day, Memorial Day, Independence Day, Labor Day, Thanksgiving Day and Christmas Day. Additional government and bankers' holidays include Martin Luther King Day, Columbus Day and Veteran's Day, and of course, there are regional holidays such as Patriot's day in the northeast, and local holidays such as Mardi Gras in New Orleans and Oaks Day in Louisville — the day before the Kentucky Derby. In Virginia, state employees take off work to mark Martin Luther King's birthday and salute to Confederate army generals Stonewall Jackson and Robert E. Lee on the same day — making for an interesting combination of lives to celebrate. And there are religious holidays, such as Easter, Good Friday and Yom Kippur.

Holidays can be observed on different schedules. Some observe the day as midnight to midnight. Others observe the holiday from the start of first shift on the holiday to the end of the third shift on the day after the holiday. Some holidays begin on the "eve" of the holiday. This is often true of New Year's and Christmas. For example, the Christmas holiday might start at 3 p.m. on December 24 and run to 3 p.m. on Christmas Day. Some companies will tack on extra holiday hours to Christmas Eve making the Christmas holiday longer than 24 hours. There are floating holiday programs where an employee can take off her birthday or bank an unused holiday for future use. Some industries that operate 24 hours a day, 7 days a week may designate when the holidays will be observed — particularly those that fall on weekends. Within an organization, holidays may differ based on the functional area. Administration may observe standard Monday-Friday holidays and operational employees may see their holidays fall on weekends.

Are you beginning to feel overwhelmed or left out? Imagine how difficult it is for Payroll to administer this monstrosity in a company with a manual system that administers to employees in multiple states, numerous unions, while employees enjoy any variety of holiday benefits.

Some employers have holiday programs that are administered as a benefit in the same way as vacation and sick days. As with other non-worked paid time off, every employee may not qualify because he or she may not meet the eligibility requirement. For example, such a holiday program might stipulate that the employee "must be employed at least 90 days prior to the holiday" or "must work the scheduled shift before and after the holiday" so that no one can make a four-day weekend out of it.

Holiday pay can be granted in a set number of hours or based on an employee's regularly-scheduled shift time. More equitable programs base holiday pay on the average number of hours worked per shift for a certain number of days prior to the holiday. There are endless ways to specify who gets how much.

Holidays are also opportunities to pay employees an additional incentive for working on a day most would like to take off. Holiday-worked time usually must meet qualifying criteria. The payable time must fall within certain zones of time or may not be paid in combination with other premiums such as overtime or shift. And finally, benefit holidays as mentioned above — those non-worked paid days — may not be the same dates as holidays which are payable for working the designated holiday.

This discussion may open your eyes to new holiday possibilities. Or it may make you shudder. What is great about technology now available is that no matter how your organization administers holidays, enough flexibility exists to handle a variety of policies, even within a single institution. And generally the systems handle these programs entirely hands-off. When assessing your holiday programs, or given the opportunity to tweak what you have in place prior to automation, the important thing to keep in mind is that the more consistent your guidelines are the better. Avoid too many "if ____ then ____" criteria and determine what happens when other pay programs are also payable on the holiday.

In addition, consider that these time-off benefits impact labor availability and the company's ability to produce products and services. Integrating holidays into schedules and timekeeping and planning for holiday shortages and premium payments are essential when trying to optimize human capital.

Programming for Bonus Policy

Here's a tricky one that's a piece of cake for an automated system. The policy stated that if someone worked five of seven holidays a year, he or she would earn a $500 bonus. Manual tracking of a program such as this presents several difficulties. As the year draws to a close, employees invariably will want to know whether they have worked enough holidays to be eligible for the program since they want to decide whether to work the remaining holidays. Where do they get this information? They either have to keep their own records or ask their supervisors. How will supervisors know? They either have to keep a manual tracking system up to date or go through a year's worth of timecards for each employee who asks. In addition, when a supervisor puts a holiday schedule together, she will often have no idea whether scheduling specific employees will obligate the company to more bonus payments or fewer.

During one implementation I uncovered this program being administered jointly by HR and Payroll. I started to ask some probing questions and found management had issues with this policy as well. How was such an incentive program being budgeted for? Technically, there were no program limits to the gross amount that might have to be paid out. Every employee was eligible who worked the required days. In a 10,000 employee organization, a lot of money might be involved. Before automation, estimating the funding of the payroll bank account including the holiday bonus was practically impossible.

Look Out for Such Programs to Slip in Under the Radar

It's not uncommon for such practices to elude the radar of the discovery team that's preparing for time and attendance automation. A program may have been handled in a certain way for a long time. It may have existed outside the time and attendance system entirely or partially, with the result no one thought to include it in the requirements for the new system. Fortunately, in the example given above, our thorough examination of the company's pay programs during initial project discovery identified this as a great opportunity to replace an unwieldy manual process.

The solution we designed enabled the customer to instantly identify any and all eligible employees at any point during the year. Employees could quickly determine their eligibility, supervisors could quickly find out how many holidays each employee had worked year-to-date, and management could extrapolate the financial obligation from the list of employees and their rates of pay. The customer gained ease of management, accessibility, and a financial forecasting tool.

Calculating Paid Days Off

Some companies and organizations compensate their employees for time off on holidays based on the average shift length they have worked during the past, say, six months. In other words, someone doesn't automatically get eight hours pay for Labor Day if their average shift worked has been six hours. This is very difficult to keep track of in a manual system, but easy to do in one that's automated. Simply ask the computer to go back over the past six months for each employee and calculate the average length of shifts worked. If someone is only working six hour shifts, it would be unfair to those working eight hour shifts to give that person eight hours pay for a holiday.

This type of program rewards employees based on hours worked. It also provides a way to reduce the cost of the benefit if the current policy is to pay all employees the full benefit amount regardless of their contribution of time, thus keeping the benefit in line with the business.

The message of this chapter is that rules and regulations can become quite complicated, and tracking attendance and compensation over time may be difficult using old technology. But what can be programmed into computer software can be programmed into an automated WMT system. This can make life easier for those in Payroll, HR, Finance, and in supervisory positions. But that's really not the point of this book. These improvements also save significant sums of money and improve processes. But these benefits are only the beginning. A properly conceived and executed WMT system will lead to even larger, more significant advantages for the organization and help achieve its strategic mission.

Chapter Six: Boosting Employee Retention and *Esprit de Corps*

A serious problem confronts many companies today — the difficulty they have attracting workers and retaining them. Some must replace up to 70% of their workforce each and every year. There are industries in which the average turnover rate is 30%. Why is this a serious problem? Not too long ago when a study was made of the manufacturing companies in the S&P 500, for example, 80% of their assets were in capital equipment and tangible goods. The remaining 20% of assets were intangibles, related somewhat to labor. Today, that allocation has been turned upside down. Now 80% of an average company's assets are intangible, and most of that is wrapped up in the quality of the workers. (See exhibit, page 132..)

Today's paradigm is knowledge and information, and this requires businesses to look at the "machines of knowledge" (i.e. labor) differently. The entire process of acquiring, managing and maintaining this new "machine" is changing. Like an asset it must be selected, recruited, installed (brought on board and oriented), scheduled into the process (assigned a job and task) and maintained (trained, provided benefits and supervised). Like equipment, labor has a life cycle that involves team-building, gaining tribal knowledge, promotions and mentoring. Eventually it will be retired and replaced with younger assets. The problem is, there's a limited supply of this resource and quality can be hard to come by. The investments companies make in labor are significant and not enough is done to protect that investment and make certain it remains through maturity.

The price to recruit and train new people is substantial and lost productivity while new hires are in the learning mode is costly. A generally accepted measurement of the cost to a company to replace an employee is 30 per cent of the employee's annual salary.

Let's examine one case. The company has to replace about 300 employees a year. If each one earns $20,000 per year on average, the cost would amount to $1.8 million ($20,000 x 30% = $6,000 x 300 employees = $1.8M). That's a lot of money for which the employer gets absolutely noth-

It's A New Economic World

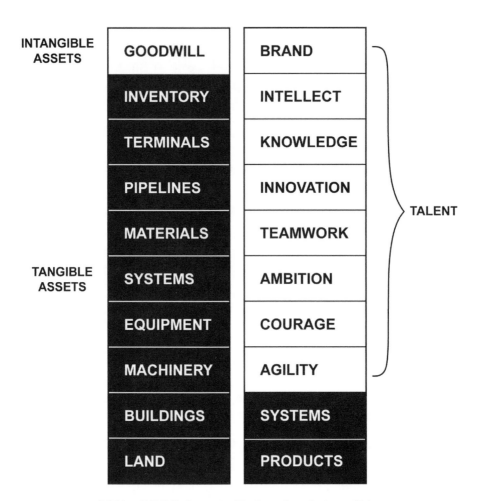

80% of S&P Assets Today Are Intangible

ing but headaches. But lost productivity and a big bill for Advil weren't the only downsides. Consider the tremendous drag this created on the organization's quality of service. It takes time for newcomers to get up to speed. The more that people do a job, the more experience they have under their belts, and the better they get at it. The truth is, new people are likely to make mistakes because they don't yet know the ropes. High turnover creates a limited pool of talent for promotion and makes business continuity a real challenge.

In most cases, money isn't the primary reason people leave. According to one expert, Michael N. Abrams, Vice President and Managing Partner of Numerof & Associates, Inc., what departing employees would term a "difficult" boss coupled with a lack of empowerment are the top reasons employees leave their job in the United States. People simply don't like serving at a boss's whim. And they don't like to lack information or a sense of control. People spend a lot of time at their places of employment, so perhaps it's no wonder an agreeable and pleasant work environment can be a major factor in keeping employees happy. Without one, they are likely to jump at the chance to hurry off to greener pastures.

Boosting Employee Retention

When the issue of employee retention is considered, management often focuses solely on why employees leave. Exit interviews, for example, are widely used. While there's nothing wrong with finding out why someone decided to go elsewhere, this can mean the statistics used to measure employee retention show only the negative side of the equation — the number of people who leave and why. Laurie Friedman, a talent management consultant, suggests that it also makes sense to ask, "Why do employees stay?" When it comes to boosting employee retention figures, understanding what employees like about working for a company can be a good place to start. If the company is doing things right for some, can these things be done even better? Can other attractive workplace offerings be added to what already exists? Friedman says making an organization "an employer of choice" in today's competitive labor market is a lot like positioning products so they will sell well. In addition, understanding the positive things about an organization from an employee's perspective helps management understand the types of employees they should be working to attract.

How can an automated time and attendance system help in keeping employees on board? One way may be to involve them directly in scheduling the shifts they work. This will give them a measure of control over their lives and a sense of involvement. As Michael Abrams said, empowerment is an appealing aspect of work life.

How does this work?

Some software applications allow employees to go on line and enter their names on the shift they wish to work. If tenured employees have first dibs, the system can be configured to grant those with seniority exclusive access to the process during a specified period of time. Workers can also register their preferences for working certain schedules. This communication allows the employer to be a better "fit" for the employee's work-life schedule. As everyone knows, both parents work in many families, and there are more and more single parent households. It's no wonder a work schedule that conflicts with family needs can be much more than inconvenient, which is why a scheduling system that takes into account an individual's availability gives that employee a sense of control and respect. Earlier I mentioned that a difficult boss is the biggest reason people give for leaving a job. It seems to me, not liking a boss may have a lot to do with the boss expecting you to work at times that may cause difficulties.

Several strong products have been introduced to the market in recent years that provide robust, flexible staffing solutions that are integrated with time and attendance software. All the major vendors offer a scheduling module with self-scheduling capabilities and templates for building schedules based on business needs. Each have various "bells and whistles" to answer the market's demand for intelligent scheduling. Some of the underlying functionality differs, however, so purchasers need to be sure to understand their company's operational needs before watching a vendor's demo. These programs are not all alike; each offers a unique package of features. Knowing what to look for will allow a prospective purchaser to stay in the driver's seat and understand the differences.

The management of a large hospital network in the Fort Lauderdale area decided to go with API Software's ActiveStaffer solution. In spite of being in an industry plagued with high turnover, this particular organization had a very low turnover rate. I believe part of the reason could be due to its use of automated self-scheduling. Schedules at this hospital network are electronically posted, and employees have 45 days to sign up for shifts. Four years ago, when management elected to go with an automated scheduling solution, one hospital was using ANSOS nurse scheduling and two facilities were still using paper systems. None of these could be integrated with other workforce systems. All required double entry, were difficult to compile, and were not user friendly. No wonder schedulers were happy to have the benefits of a new system that eliminated those issues. The new system also was able to project when an employee would begin earning overtime, so that managers could now minimize overworking employees

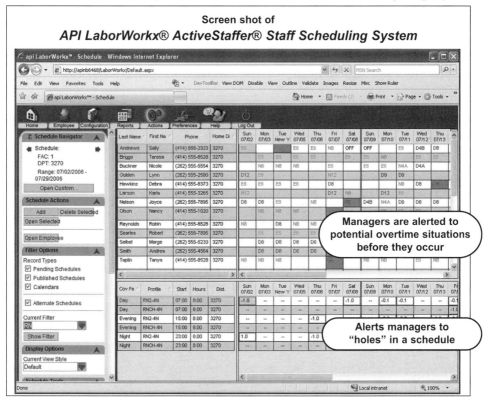

and level the workload. Nobody likes bearing the burden of working more than everyone else, so it's easy to see how this solution brought more satisfaction to workers.

When Kronos engaged Nucleus Research to study the impact of Kronos' workforce technology, Nucleus found that when nurses were given the ability to self-schedule, total absenteeism went down by 25% and turnover dropped by 20%. This shows the power of such a system and the advantage of investing in one. Attendance and retention were significantly boosted just by giving employees a greater measure of empowerment.

Some software vendors are now considering offering competitive shift bidding systems. This technology would allow employees to compete for shifts by offering to work the shift at a lower rate. An employee may prefer to work the eight-to-four shift so much, for example, she is willing to take a lower rate of pay to get it. Say, an individual makes $18.00 an hour. She might bid $17.50 to get the shift she wants.

Another concept being considered is to automate a bartering process. This would give employees and managers the ability to negotiate shift patterns, time off or other benefit allowances.

Maybe bidding for shifts seems a bit extreme. But why not at least allow employees to enter their preferences into the computer and have the computer schedule people according to these preferences — at least to the extent this is possible? A worker may not want to work Saturday nights because she cannot arrange child care. Or perhaps a person actually likes the graveyard shift. Seniority can be made a factor in scheduling, so that people are encouraged to stay on board, knowing that eventually they will arrive at a place where they will have more personal control over the hours they work. It seems reasonable to assume that if they are about to reach a point when they can pick and choose the shifts they want, they are not likely to move to another job where they will have to start all over at the bottom of the ladder.

In addition, putting the scheduling process into an automated system removes some of the bias and politics that can be a part of a manual setup. Fairness and opportunity are benefits of using workforce technology to assist in the scheduling process.

Letting People Set Their Hours

One company in the business of transcribing medical records lets employees set their own hours. Workers can do this job from home, interacting with the company via the Internet. I discussed this with the company owner. He said his employees don't brag about how much they make an hour, but they do like to tell people they can work whenever they want. They are completely free to schedule their time.

A major reason employees take this work is that they can do it when they want. This benefit costs the company nothing but nonetheless pays a dividend in the form of a fairly stable staff at an affordable price. Workers like the arrangement because they can stay up until midnight working if they want, then take the next day off.

Of course, this is not going to work for most businesses. The point is that more and more people want to arrange work around their lives rather than the other way around, which is not surprising. It's often difficult to take a job because it conflicts with the children's school schedule, a husband's job, or a class a person would like to take. Maybe someone's not a morning person. People want flexible scheduling. In heathcare industries in particular that operate 24/7, more and more companies are finding ways to implement flex scheduling because it can be a win-win solution.

With an interactive system, a manager can monitor these self-scheduled shifts — even remotely — and insure the work will be completed or the work site adequately staffed. If the load isn't going to be right he can make reassignments or pull in extra resources. He doesn't have to keep his fingers crossed to find out at the end of the week what got accomplished or missed. He is assured the supply of workers meets his needs and his crew gets to work at their preferred times.

What to do about High Employee Turnover

In what other ways can automated time and attendance help in the area of retention? Labor activity can be tracked against turnover to find out what's causing employees to leave. For example, is there a higher incidence of turnover in certain jobs? Do certain shifts seem to turn workers away? Does being forced to work more than 40 hours? Does retention improve at certain wage levels? What's the effect of having to work weekends often? Is there a higher incidence in certain jobs, skills or demographic categories? If so, is the company hiring the right people? Maybe those who do the hiring aren't selling the job correctly, and when people come on board they find it's not what they expected.

What financial incentives work at reducing turnover? The chart below illustrates some of the contributing factors to improving employee retention.

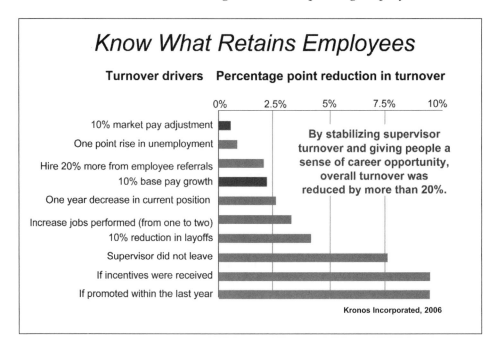

Treating Employees with Consistency

We seem to be born with an innate need to be treated fairly. If you have children, you know that the "fairness meter" turns on very early. Everybody is measuring how they are treated versus anyone and everyone else. An automated system delivers consistency in how people are handled. This can lead to fewer disgruntled employees and in turn to a higher rate of retention. Why? The technology makes it difficult for managers or supervisors to play favorites by giving breaks to people they like. And it's hard for them to make things difficult on those they don't care for.

Human interpretation, or bias, almost always comes into play in a manual system. People's intentions may be good and honorable, but it's human nature to treat our buddies one way and those we either don't know, or who rub us the wrong way, another. Not only can this cause morale problems but the company is at risk of overcompensating some workers, or of suffering through grievances for inconsistencies in how different employees are handled.

In the chart on the left, the number three reason employees stayed with the job was "supervisor did not leave." Obviously, the supervisor is liked and probably doing a pretty good job of treating everyone equally. WMT makes every manager "the good supervisor" by standardizing practices. A WMT system isn't something that will walk out the door with supervisors when they quit or retire. It can be a stable and favorable aspect of the employee's work environment and job satisfaction.

Let's look at an example. An incentive program named after and attributed to Baylor University Medical Center comes to mind. As the story goes, management instituted a bonus program for clinical practitioners to encourage people to work on weekends. Nowadays, "Baylor Pay" commonly refers to a pay program designed to give employees an incentive to work difficult-to-staff shifts, typically on the weekends. In its current form it may differ from what was actually used at Baylor but today such programs work by rewarding employees who work a combination of specific shifts with a set amount of hours during a pay period. The programs are designed to meet business needs and minimize staffing issues. They stipulate the number of shifts, the shift durations, the number of bonus hours payable and sometimes include qualifiers that penalize employees who are absent during a period of time before or after the Baylor shifts. They may also require a set number of worked shifts over an extended period of time in order for a worker to be eligible to participate in the program. The idea is to encourage good attendance and a commitment to working less desirable schedules.

Here's how one such program worked. Provided an individual worked two twelve-hour shifts on the weekend, that person was credited with eight hours of additional time.

But, as everyone knows, life happens and sometimes employees fail to meet the letter of the law. When a manual system is in place, it's easy for the system to break down because there are often people around — supervisors — who will try to "fix" the problem.

Suppose a person works one twelve-hour shift, and then only eleven and a half hours because her child gets sick. This person would not be eligible to receive those bonus hours, would she? No. But what do you suppose is likely to happen in a manual system? The supervisor might look at the situation and say, "Gee whiz, look at this. Greta is a half hour short. Old Greta's a great gal and a loyal worker. It wasn't her fault her son got sick at school and had to be picked up early. I'll just add that half hour."

Or maybe a supervisor doesn't like Greta or is displeased with her performance in some other area.

"Sorry, Greta, but here's the policy in black and white. I simply can't add an extra half hour. Uh-huh, no way. I don't care if you will work three extra hours on Monday. I can't go against company policy, Greta. You know that."

Unfortunately for the supervisor and the company, Greta and her coworkers talk. They talk a lot and they talk about what they get paid. Greta knows full well the same thing happened last month to Suzy and she did receive the bonus hours despite her shorter shift. They also know the supervisor will come up with a good explanation for this and that complaining will do little or no good.

After this happens, where do you suppose Greta is going to fall on that continuum we discussed earlier where employees are positioned somewhere on a line that runs from "engaged" to "disengaged"?

The message is an automated system insures consistency. It removes the discretionary nature of manual pay programs. Consistent programs establish stability in the workforce. Stability means less turnover.

Compensating for Management Styles

Automated scheduling has all kinds of flexibility, which makes the institution of best practices fairly easy. But what if it turns out that scheduling methodology is not the reason for the difference in a department's performance? Another question to be answered might be, "Do these managers have different management styles?" You may recall what Michael Abrams said. "People don't leave companies, they leave bosses." Autocratic managers, for example, often have trouble holding onto employees. Customer service may suffer and other problems may persist because the employees under an autocratic manager are reluctant to make decisions that may incur the boss's wrath. In other words, they are not about to stick their necks out, and are quite likely to take a hike when the opportunity arises. A computerized scheduling system may help mitigate the negative effects of such a manager. It may even lead to fewer no shows, fewer late arrivals and a lower level of schedule disruption overall.

How so?

Not only can a scheduling system be set up to allow people some flexibility in scheduling themselves, as previously mentioned, but it can empower employees to find their own replacements when they need time off, giving them a measure of control and empowerment. A system can, for example, be set up to allow schedule swapping. Automated "shift swapping" is gaining popularity. The system allows employees to identify their own replacement, submit the request for time off along with the suggested replacement — who also registers his approval or request for schedule change — and receive an automated notification of the supervisor's — or the system's — acceptance of the change. The supervisor's approval action will then automatically update both workers' schedules and notify them of the approved schedule change.

Let's say I don't want to work a particular shift because I was the fourth caller to the local radio station with the correct answer and won a ticket to the Rolling Stones concert. My friend Tim has the same qualifications I do and can work my shift. I can go into the notification system, report that I'm going to miss the shift, and that Tim will replace me. With automated workflow, the system will notify my supervisor, who will approve the switch, an electronic notification of the approval will be sent to Tim and to me, and the schedule will be automatically updated.

What happens if Tim wants to come with me to the concert and I can't find a another replacement? I could still indicate I will not be able to make the shift. A notification would be sent to the supervisor but could also be posted for all employees to see so that anyone interested in picking up that extra shift could put in a bid for it, or schedule themselves as a fill-in.

These systems update the supervisor periodically about any open shifts. If no one signs up, then the manager can go through the normal selection process. If everyone is online, then no paper or phone calls are required. If not, at least the only call the supervisor or scheduler needs to make is to the employee he already knows is willing and capable of working that shift.

There are a number of benefits to this arrangement. There's less likelihood of an interruption in labor supply, the employee did not have to complete any forms or contact the unpleasant manager directly, the manager was prompted to adjust to the schedule change as needed, and the entire staff had the opportunity to bid on additional work opportunities. And most important, employees in this situation enjoy a heightened sense of autonomy and control over their work life. In an area with an autocratic manager it's one less situation in which these employees feel powerless.

Building a Team Environment

An upcoming chapter that goes into detail on data collection will discuss the need to record exempt employee time. Beyond the reasons to be covered there is an additional benefit to including exempt employees in the time and attendance systems and processes. Companies promote a collaborative, team environment by treating salaried managers and hourly workers alike. After all, both can be required to log into the time and attendance system. Making the practice of exempt employees reporting their activity visibly may help dispel notions that hourly employees are being treated unfairly or that "Big Brother" is watching only the lowest-paid workers.

That Big Brother is watching is often the reaction of the least productive employees. Obviously, they don't like what they view as an intrusion into their daily lives. Those using this as a protest may be hopeful that their assertions will somehow overthrow the company's initiatives and put an end to the new system. They fear the new system will uncover their inadequacies, and rightfully so. It may well catch them goofing off.

The Big Brother theory can be diminished, however, with a good communications plan that educates the workforce about the business needs for the new technology and the overall positive impact it will have on the health and longevity of the company, as well as to the jobs they hold. Productive, engaged workers will embrace the new capabilities and support the changes. Average employees should buy into it and give their support once they recognize the company is serving their interests by making the organization more competitive and financially stronger. More will be said about ways to manage attitudes about a new system in the section on implementation considerations.

Talent Management

Time and attendance and scheduling solutions deal with employees already on staff, but a new field known as "talent management" works to insure that the right types of workers are brought on board in the first place. The process of attracting, developing, and retaining labor resources is a growing area of workforce management, and software vendors offer a number of products in this area. Clay Ritchey, Senior Product Manager for Kronos, for example, boasts that Kronos applications actually get smarter over time as data about an organization and its staff builds and the record grows concerning how well employees perform, how long they stay, and so forth. In addition, hosted solutions offer the advantage of leveraging this accumulation of data across an industry or a region. The data can then be shared by each Knonos customer.

Using this data, companies bring on board employees who are a good fit and keep them longer. Money is saved because less training is required, productivity will be higher, and turnover lower. Better employees — those who fit the organization — are absent less and more productive, lowering the amount of overtime that might otherwise be required and generating greater outputs in volume and quality. This being the case, why wouldn't an organization work to improve its talent management?

Chapter Seven: The Many Benefits of WMT Scheduling

A scheduling module is essential to getting the most meaningful data from timecards and to effectively managing labor resources vis-á-vis business needs. The transition to an automated scheduling system may be difficult and time consuming for a short period of time, but it should lead to better decision making, as well as more time in the long run for managing and evaluating. It will also allow managers to more easily forecast needs and costs and make adjustments to meet budget and staffing objectives.

Software now available will allow employers to build a schedule based on the actual work volume and allow front line managers to override built-in restrictions if senior management decides they want this to be possible. Volume is what drives scheduling regardless of the industry. In manufacturing, the metric is production capacity. In retail it's customer traffic. In healthcare it's patient census and acuity. In consulting it's project workload. The requirements of a product or service dictate the type and number of workers.

Automated scheduling follows a logical process, but it needs to be kept in mind that workers are not machines. Some are better than others, some work well together and others don't. Some want to work weekends and some want to work nights. Workers take vacations, go on leave and call in sick. Sometimes they don't show up. All of this means the human element has to be factored into the scheduling process. A supervisor may look at a schedule and decide quite logically it needs to be adjusted. Mike and Mildred are scheduled on the same shift, for example, and Mike and Mildred are currently going through a messy divorce.

Often, a balance needs to be struck between financial goals, operational needs and human nature. It may cost more in lost productivity, for example, to run the line with one less person than it would to pay Bob at his overtime rate because a set number of workstations need to be manned to keep the takt rate at the desired level.

For these reasons, it's not likely automated scheduling systems will ever fully replace the scheduler role. But the technology will institutionalize good business decisions and make schedulers accountable.

Scheduling systems can have whatever degree of restriction may be needed in a particular situation. If scheduling parameters aimed at managing costs, skill-match, preferences or any number of variables, are violated, the system can flag, warn, require a manager override or completely prevent the assignment. The system is doing its job by providing visibility into what is about to happen with labor utilization and cost. And to make sure the best course of action is being followed, the process can require the involvement of multiple layers of management so that staffing decisions are validated and approved.

The famous line in the movie *Field of Dreams* was, "If you build it, they will come." In the workplace, if you schedule them, they will work, and the company will pay them. Workers should not be treated as fixed overhead. Demand should be evaluated and supply chosen carefully. A schedule should be built and rebuilt as needed, and managers should be held accountable in this process. The WMT solution is the best way to insure that managers are held accountable. In the world of Six Sigma quality control, people are fond of saying 'you cannot expect what you do not measure.' In the same vein, one cannot expect smart scheduling from managers when the results aren't measured. Technology is a tool. It builds the ideal model based on available data, allows managers to tweak it, provides a trail of what occurred from employee absences to under and overstaffed shifts — to every change employees and managers make throughout the process. What occurred can be seen and evaluated, and this means it can be managed.

How a Scheduling System Accomplishes Its Goals

When a work schedule is put together, it is typically done for a set period of time such as a week, a month, six weeks or whatever the company's defined "schedule period" is. In a manual system, who is to work on a given day at a specific time is written down. This process is repeated for each "period." The manager sits down, looks at the calendar and starts putting together a schedule, just as he did six weeks before. He has to think about who is on his team, who might be taking vacation time, who

146

likes to work on which days, perhaps who works well together and who gets the work done. He may look at last period's schedule and start from there. Or he may start with a blank page. He may be able to fill in 75% of the schedule without checking with anyone, but then the phone calls, cajoling, wrangling and negotiations must begin. This is time the manager could use to review patient status if he is in heathcare, oversee production outputs in manufacturing, help customers in retail, or engage in other, more productive activities no matter what type of organization he or she is in.

In an automated set up, a number of tools exist to make this process faster and easier. Scheduling systems can fully automate the process, assigning staff to shifts as the anticipated workload requires. Alternatively, such systems can provide a tool kit of templates and repeating mechanisms that simplify the building of a schedule but still allow the manager to use his own judgment.

Full automation allows a manager to enter business data that reflects the volume of work, such as the number of parts to be produced in manufacturing or the anticipated volume of customers in retail. The system will be pre-configured with a set of custom criteria that use the volume data in combination with parameters for selecting staff in order to build the schedule. Selection criteria can include settings that tell the system to select the employee with the lowest base pay rate, or the fewest hours worked, or the best job skill match, or those who prefer to work a particular shift. A company can establish criteria that are unique to the organization. Parameters are limited only by what data is stored in the system and the ability to qualify an employee based on the characteristics. For example, if management wanted to select employees based on their hair color, this could be done — it simply needs to be identified in the system.

The system evaluates needs. It's demand-driven workforce management. A retail outlet that expects a high volume of customers at a work location — whether it's a car wash, department store or even an amusement park — will have to have a number of car washers, stockers, salespeople, or entertainers and cashiers to handle these customers and to generate the maximum sales.

There are varied levels of automated schedule deployment: full, partial and assisted scheduling automation. In full automation mode, the automated schedule can populate employees into the work schedule for a specific period of time, or it can do so indefinitely into the future. For some categories of workers, such as nine to five office types, this works very well. Their schedule is generated once and is automatically repeated into the future. Temporary changes, such as for vacation or special project work are handled by editing the specific dates from the master schedule. This also works well for schedules that rotate staff in patterns such as seven days on, seven days off. Such programs are sometimes put in place for workers who commit to work in a particular program for an extended period of time, say six months. In these cases, the automated schedule works nicely for the pool of 7 on/7 off workers and is populated on the master schedule well into the future.

The automated schedule also works well when creating a schedule that is quite complex due to the many variables that determine what workers are needed and which workers are the best match. Manually constructing such a schedule can be hard work. It also requires getting it right. If the workers who show up have the wrong skills, that's a big problem. Allowing an automated system to use built in workloads and parameters frees the manager from what can be a time consuming and possibly unrewarding task.

In partial automation mode, the scheduling technology can be used in tandem with management input. A system can be designed to provide the manager with templates of common shifts, such as 7a-3p, 3p-11p, 8a-4:30p and patterns such as Monday through Friday, Saturday and Sunday, Week 1: Mon, Wed, Fri & Week 2: Tues, Thursday. A manager can use such as system to select the best matched employee according to job requirements. The system can then display a list of top candidates, ranked in order or according to preconfigured selection criteria. The manager can then choose workers from a list that gives him excellent business intelligence concerning the most qualified and willing workers. The manager can add the "human factor" — his personal preferences — in making the final selection.

The assisted mode of scheduling technology can be deployed in an even more basic manner — a computer-based spreadsheet on which the manager makes all schedule assignments "manually." This solution doesn't take full advantage of the available technology, but it does preserve older processes. More importantly, it moves the company forward in scheduling integration by supplying the time and attendance system with schedule data and providing greater access and visibility into what individual managers have scheduled for their areas. The manager may experience less time savings, but he will gain significant benefits in meaningful labor activity data and reporting. The schedule can also be distributed and shared more easily because it is no longer on a single sheet of paper or within a stand-alone computer system.

It's important to mention that in today's work culture, the employee work schedule almost certainly will change. Whether the schedule is generated from a fully automatic process or is handwritten by a front line supervisor on a paper napkin, demand for labor, and employees' ability to provide it are going to vary from the original master schedule.

Companies must operate efficiently. In the recent decades, a dramatic surge has occurred in cost conscious business processes such as lean manufacturing and just-in-time supply chain operations. Labor supply is part of this. Companies must acknowledge that the demand for labor does not remain constant. Highly competitive organizations are waking up to the realization that to keep labor costs low while meeting production demands that fluctuate, they have to be agile in the scheduling of employees. Using scheduling technology within the time and attendance suite of applications provides the responsiveness needed. Changes in the schedule come from either a shift in supply (workers) or demand (work volume). On the demand side, if production plant A has a shutdown and plant B has to pick up the slack immediately, management needs a tool to help determine what should be done. If a hospital has an unexpected influx of critically ill patients, the right staff in the right number needs to be called in immediately.

On the demand side, if half the student population at a college comes down with an epidemic of flu or food poisoning, campus student workers will be in short supply. Scheduling to meet this type of change in a manual system efficiently is extremely difficult.

Workers also experience unexpected events that prevent them from working a shift. With more parents working these days, when a sick child has to be taken care of by one of the parent-workers, one will have to call in and take the day off. Personal business such as closing on a new home may result in lost work time and an interruption to the set schedule. Management needs a tool to use to work these changes into the schedule.

There's nothing new about changes. Someone once said that change is the only constant. What's new is that instead of relying on managers to handle these business needs in an ad hoc fashion and with little oversight, smart business people are using scheduling technology. So, instead of allowing Johnny Laidback, supervisor of the shop floor, to scramble around and fill an opening with his favorite buddy — once he finally gets word from someone on the production line that Amal Tired didn't show up for work today — the scheduling system will generate an immediate alert that there's an absence because Amal Tired didn't punch in. It will simultaneously identify the most suitable replacement, using best practices and cost-conscious factors and notify the supervisor and replacement employee by e-mail, or pager, thus fixing the problem in short order.

This scheduling repair process is possible because a schedule will have been entered into the system. Having a populated schedule in the computer makes attendance notification a no-brainer. Not only are these urgent situations more effectively managed, integrating schedules with time and attendance allows for attendance tracking over time, and tracking data can be used to better manage the business. For example, the number of arrival and departure exceptions can be tracked. The tracking can be done by specific employee — counting the number of times the employee is late and indicating how late the employee arrived each time. Attendance can also be tracked by group, showing attendance trends by work area, supervisor, job category, tenure, shift or whatever makes sense for the business. The ultimate goal is to manage attendance better. To do this, a manager must know what, where and when attendance issues are occurring. Schedules allow labor activity to be evaluated, measured, and characterized. A timeclock will record when employees arrive and depart and how long they work, but it alone will not paint a picture showing how the activity should be interpreted. Trends can be developed from this data. From trends come predictions that allow the scheduler to anticipate and forecast the variances in supply and time. Of course, not everything can be forecast 100%. Scheduling systems tell the manager about problems *as they occur.* Unlike managers, scheduling systems don't take vacations, call in sick, or go to meetings. So schedule repair can be done consistently, immediately and wisely at any time.

These systems also work well under pressure. What if the demand for labor spikes and many employees need to be called in at once? The scheduling system can probably handle an increase in the volume of work more easily than Johnny Laidback. In addition, increased efficiency, more meaningful data, automated processes and good business practices will ultimately impact operations in a positive way.

Earlier I mentioned some common objections to automated scheduling systems people typically raise. Some people will object to the implementation of a new system because they are used to doing things the way they have been doing them for years. There are ways to implement the technology even when an audience isn't entirely ready to make the change. The beauty of these systems is that they are flexible enough to allow the customer to implement "in degrees" and to have the technology turned on "low, medium and high" in different locations throughout the organization.

Take a hospital, for instance. Automated scheduling software has been used for years in clinical areas. A recognized need for the technology existed in these areas long ago and vendors provided stand-alone scheduling packages designed to meet it. It's not surprising, then, when hospitals upgrade their time and attendance systems and include a scheduling solution in the implementation, that clinical areas in an organization can be very enthusiastic about getting a new scheduling system. At the other end of the spectrum, usually areas in administration, managers can be quite resistant to going to an automated scheduling system. Often, they simply don't see the need.

To accommodate this difference in buy in, scheduling systems can be rolled out to some areas in a phased approach. The new system can be turned on full blast in a clinical area that welcomes an integrated scheduling system. After all, it will eliminate the need for double entry of data as well as the disconnect between timekeeping and the stand-alone schedule system. Immediately upon implementation, managers in these areas can have full access to all the system's capabilities. Typically, they can be expected to begin creating complex, unique, repeating schedules and to keep these schedules up to date on a daily basis.

For areas such as dietary and housekeeping, which may be lukewarm to the new system, scheduling can be implemented on "medium." Managers in these areas who have not been operating on a computer-based scheduling system but have somewhat complex schedules and fairly volatile change activity, will be expected to create a master schedule in the system for all employees and make changes on a less frequent basis. This might be done weekly or every pay period. In this way, more time is given managers in these areas to get used to the new processes and to learn the benefits without the expectation of intense usage hanging over them. Over time, these areas will be expected to begin using the system fully.

For administrative areas that refuse to be convinced of the need for automated scheduling, the system can be turned on "low." The expectation for these areas is that the master schedule will be created for all employees once. Managers are not expected to update the schedule. Exceptions that occur when work assignments change are dealt with in the timecard, and the schedule is a loose image of the work schedule. Only when an employee's job or permanent schedule changes — such as when he switches to the night shift — is the schedule updated for an employee. These areas may never go to full scheduling usage unless a business need is identified that necessitates a more accurate schedule picture.

The benefit in allowing each area to use scheduling at a different level of involvement is that all areas are on the system, and management throughout the organization has the opportunity to work with the technology and evaluate the benefits and costs. This reinforces the importance of the objectives that were identified when the system mission was established. Requiring all areas to use schedules lets everyone in the organization know that schedul-

Common reasons people resist automated scheduling:

1. Takes too much time. It's true that the processes are new and may seem like additional work. However, the time spent is "smarter time" used to set up continuous schedules or to provide more visibility into scheduled activities. The time spent creating and managing schedules may eliminate time spent reviewing and correcting timecards, requesting manual checks, revising schedules due to poor scheduling, identifying and locating personnel, and dealing with employee dissatisfaction or payroll errors. Changed processes frequently seem more difficult than the old way. It is often the case that only the transitional period is difficult, and in fact the new processes are more efficient.

2. Our schedules change too often to maintain in a computer system. Supervisors often manage a volatile schedule due to employee absences and varying consumer needs. The systems are flexible enough to allow managers to decide how much will be involved in keeping the schedule up to date. Some managers may be able to keep their scheduling systems up to date on a daily basis. It may be reasonable to expect others to update them only periodically throughout the pay period. In extreme cases, a system can be built around fixed schedules. Managers may be eased into the process by choosing the lowest level of maintenance until they are comfortable with the system, recognize the benefits of the automated scheduling system, and can handle more maintenance. It should be noted, however, that each level of maintenance provides a different degree of credibility based on how up to date the schedules are.

3. Scheduling is a personal art form. Or "my system is not broken." Often managers are committed to "their" way of scheduling including their tools and personal timeframes. They may be concerned that an automated system will be less effective than their accustomed method and restrict them because of system limitations. But the system features do *allow managers to duplicate their manual practices* and create templates for recurring shift patterns. An automated system also *institutionalizes their expertise* and allows for training and proxy sharing of their scheduling know-how. Although scheduling is an art form, it is also a logical, repeatable task that can free up manager time.

4. Scheduling forms relationships. Without standard methods or processes, managers devise their own systems and identify their key resources for staffing. They cultivate individuals who are willing to fill scheduling needs. Introducing an automated system threatens to upset established relationships — for better or for worse. A relationship-based scheduling methodology often has little to do with business objectives, such as holding down costs or insuring operational quality, and a great deal to do with employee or personal preferences. On the other hand, automated scheduling systems provide consistent, cost and quality based management of schedules. They draw on the entire employee pool based on employee skills and business needs. The system also tends to level out the hours worked among employees while at the same time reducing overtime and preventing premium stacking.

ing is an important part of the organization's human capital strategy and that using this piece of the technology is key to its successful use.

Human Capital Management and Scheduling

In the continuous pursuit of improvement, making comparisons and modeling the best practices of labor management and scheduling can be important. With the right time and attendance system in place, it will be easy to see what a particular department budgeted, what was scheduled, and what actually took place as the schedule played out. This can aid in planning future schedules, and it can be helpful in leveraging internal sources of excellence thereby spreading the KSA (knowledge, skills and abilities) of top performers throughout the organization.

As in the example in Chapter Two of the retailer that used its labor management implementation as a device to boost sales, companies are wise to identify the experts in labor utilization they have in-house and to study what they do in order to thoroughly understand how these experts go about effective labor scheduling. It may take time and a degree of analytical technique to document who has the best scheduling practices and to define those practices. But the effort will be worth the time and the cost if those practices can be applied throughout the organization.

Internal experts are individuals who forecast staffing needs accurately when they request their labor budget. They live within their allowance while operating a highly productive business unit. It's true their success may result from many factors, including that they create a positive work environment which results in low turnover and consistently draws employees to work. Documenting what creates this environment and empowering others to do the same is important. Nevertheless, the focus for scheduling best practices needs to be on the creation and management of schedules. For example, what goes into deciding how many workers are needed, when they will be needed, and what type of skills they must have? How are the workers selected for particular shifts? How are adjustments made to changes in demand and attendance? The answers will provide repeatable processes that can be systematized.

Remember the ad campaign for Gatorade that used the phrase "Be Like Mike" — meaning play basketball like the extraordinary winner, Michael Jordan? When it comes to scheduling, the campaign might be "Be Like Stu" because the record shows Stu is the best scheduling manager. The company can institute Stu's practices across the board so that everybody performs like Stu when it comes to scheduling.

This doesn't mean managers become robotic. The technology allows for the human factor — the ability to assess the environment and personalities on a given day and make appropriate decisions. It's always possible for exceptions to be made. It's important to know, however, that variances from the best practice will be visible and may be called into question later for review and justification. And it could well be that an even *better* internal expert comes along who improves on the process.

With data continually being entered into a computerized system, the organization has an opportunity to improve continually. Remember that with lean strategies improvement is not an event, it is a continuous process. However, the initial assessment process need not be repeated each year. Audit capabilities and benchmarking of scheduling practices make continuous improvement a natural byproduct of the system. The end result should be that managers become highly skilled schedulers because they are using a system with built-in expertise and abilities.

The Friendly Schedule Ghost

Just about everyone is happy when someone takes care of something for them, especially when they don't have to ask. The other day, for example, my son and I had lunch at my parents' house. After my mother and I went into the other room, my thirteen year old got up, cleared the table and began to wash the dishes. My mother and I came back into the kitchen and surprise! Everything was cleaned up. Who did that? Boy, would we like it if someone did that every day.

Automated schedules can be like this, doing unexpected things for employees. When schedules are integrated with time and attendance, data from the schedule carries over automatically, without the employee having to do anything. These are called "ghost punches." For example, a schedule can include a chain of work activity events that are expected to occur throughout the employee's shift. The employee may begin work at one location and be scheduled to move to a different location three hours into the shift. When the employee arrives at work and logs into the system — it doesn't matter whether by timeclock, web, or telephone — the data goes into the timecard. The schedule in the background recognizes that data as the in punch and tells the timecard "I know what this employee is going to do." The employee goes about his day and completes his shift. He goes to the system and logs out, which is his second and final entry that day. The timecard registers the out punch and the schedule fills out what the employee did during that shift. The transfer to the second location appears in the timecard as a "ghost" punch, allocating the employee's time to the two different work locations. No effort whatsoever is required on the employee's part. The less time spent going to the timeclock, the less chance there is of entering the wrong data or forgetting to enter the transfer. That ghost works hard and he's nice to have around. For management, he has properly allocated labor expenses.

More can be done with schedule data ghosted into timecards — changing jobs, changing rates of pay for specific scheduled labor activity, scheduling time off such as vacations and leaves of absence — far in advance. All this sort of thing can be entered when the schedule is put together, and at the proper time, the data will go into the timekeeping module for payment.

Scheduling Systems and High Performing Teams

In many cases, creating a schedule is in effect putting together a team. For this reason, a scheduling system needs to be multidimensional. It ought to take into account who, when, where, and what. In other words, which employee should be scheduled for which particular date and time, which location where he will work, and which activity he will be assigned.

People perform within two personas — as individuals and as members of a group. To get the maximum benefit, both roles should be operating at peak performance. Becoming a productive team member can take time, and it often takes a while for a team to jell. But once a team does jell, it can be very effective — much more so than several people who have been thrown together on an ad hoc basis. This is because teams typically progress through stages. The first is "Forming," which is marked by uncertainty and distance between members. Then "Norming," occurs when the team begins to settle down to become an efficient unit, followed by "Storming," which is what transpires when conflicts arise. If everyone on the team sticks it out through the storming stage, the team will eventually reach the "Performing" stage, when a mature team can be counted on to deliver solutions and work together in harmony. For this reason, many managers feel a system should be programmed in a way that keeps teams together to the maximum extent possible, and it is certainly possible to do this.

Budgets and Scheduling in a Dynamic Environment

Budgets ought to be considered the approved plan for labor expenditures. They should be a yardstick for measuring performance, but not a straitjacket. Scheduling is, as some managers argue, an art form, even in a mechanized environment. Give managers the right information and the best tools, and value will be the result.

As production increases or decreases and demand for labor hours changes, the schedule needs to reflect this, and the budget may have to be reworked. This is why it's a strategic imperative to use a scheduling mechanism that can quickly and easily adjust to fluctuations in the amount of labor required to produce a projected volume of work. It would not make sense to prevent, due to budget restrictions, a manager from scheduling more workers if demand was up and the imposed limit would result in a production shortfall and, therefore, less revenue and profit. It's important to keep in mind that the cost of not putting more labor to work or not using the most expensive workers may be greater than the amount that would be saved by holding back. It may help to have processes surrounding mechanized scheduling that include a "sanity check" or override feature that gives the manager pertinent information about risks and negative impact factors.

Such factors might include winning a new contract, a competitor going out of business, or an important customer with a rush delivery that necessitates labor efforts above and beyond the norm. The result of not meeting the customer's demand for the product might be that the entire account will be lost — making the investment in additional labor expenditures for the extra labor worth the additional cost. This is where complete data integration becomes indispensable. Enabling a front line manager to assess how critical a situation is and to make important decisions about deploying his staff can be invaluable.

Daily and Hourly Schedule Fluctuations

A schedule for a company that builds complex machines to customer specifications might project that a particular machine assembly will be ready to work its way through the production process next week because that's when the subassemblies are due to arrive. So the machine is scheduled for production on a certain day. It's simple enough to determine the manpower and specific skills that will be required to complete this assembly, and thus, workers are scheduled.

What happens if there is a delay? Suppose it turns out a critical component will not be available? This sort of thing is bound to happen from time to time.

The scheduling system needs to be flexible and able to reschedule the number and location of workers on a real-time basis. In such a plant, a newly-refreshed schedule could be generated and posted hourly telling skilled workers where they are assigned and what they are slated to be doing as the day unfolds. The same sort of thing can and does happen in all kinds of business environments. In business people have to be able to react quickly and intelligently.

Staffing at a Level to Maximize Profits

No one wants to pay employees to sit around and twiddle their thumbs. But what's the right level at which to staff when history shows there are certain to be peaks and valleys due to seasonal fluctuations in demand? Lean manufacturers typically deal with highly seasonal markets by establishing production capacity in the middle between anticipated peak demand and the minimum demand expected. For one thing, it's almost always easier to expand capacity than to cut it back. As a result, many lean producers plan on hiring temporary labor or on adding shifts during peak periods. But there is also another way to deal with seasonality.

As most people know, inventory is a dirty word to lean manufacturers, and they try to eliminate it to the extent possible. Even so, it may make sense for a company that has a good idea what's coming in terms of demand to build some inventory in advance of seasonal peaks. This is done during slow periods when daily demand is down. The products built will usually be standard, off-the-shelf items, or in the case of build-to-order operations, units completed only to the point that customization can begin to occur. Then, during peak-demand times, standard products will for the most part be delivered out of inventory, and production capacity will devoted largely to keeping pace with custom or specialty product demand. In this way, a lean manufacturer is able to even out the peaks and valleys and get maximum value from the workforce he has employed.

Identifying best practices, measuring, fine tuning, and measuring again are made possible with WMT. The ability to constantly ratchet up performance in this way makes software-assisted scheduling an indispensable tool in the push for continuous improvement that's become so necessary and important for companies to remain competitive in today's global economy.

Chapter Eight: How Automated Systems Can Help Companies Stay on Budget

It addition to helping managers stay on budget by eliminating stacking and other ways employees may end up being overpaid for the work they do, an automated system can help eliminate the possibility of fraud. It can also help management spot areas of the business that may be wasting time and resources or not operating as efficiently as they should or could. So let's turn our attention to budgets, and ask, why are they often busted?

Historically, the budgeting process is an annual event. Labor expense allowances are projected and requested annually based on historical experience and an educated guess of what needs will be during the coming twelve months. Once a budget is approved and moneys are allocated, it is put to bed. It's not retired and it certainly still exists, but typically it's not used or referred to on a daily basis. Managers normally report labor expenses relative to the budgeted amount on a periodic basis. This information is after the fact and sometimes is accompanied by rationalizations to explain variances. Managers do not submit a work schedule and its associated costs along with these rationalizations, nor is the cost of labor that was scheduled overlaid against the budget for the period in question. This is the way things have historically worked. But suppose this way of working changed.

Imagine Supervisor Johnny Laidback walking into Manager Todd Tightwad's office for a midweek schedule review.

"Todd, I've put the revised schedule together for the rest of the week," Johnny says. "I called in my buddies, who are now going to be getting overtime on Friday, to fill in for call-offs. My department will be ten% over budget this week."

Would Todd Tightwad reply, "Whatever it takes, Johnny. The work has to get done." Or, might he say, "What, are you crazy? The big boss will blow his top when he sees these numbers!"

I think you'll agree, the reaction is likely to be quite different when management can see the cost of the absences in real time along with the projected cost of using the wrong fill-in workers and the cumulative effect on the budget. Perhaps even Supervisor Johnny might propose a different solution if he had to report the economic consequences along with his proposed schedule.

In another, more attractive scenario, Supervisor I. Will Getitdone arrives with the revised schedule that the system helped him complete. "Todd, here is the adjusted schedule. We had call-offs early this week but I was able to replace them with staff members who weren't already scheduled to work a full week and had lower base rates than the absent workers. I did play around with putting in Jeff and Ed (his buddies) who are always willing to work extra, but the system alerted me to the budget violation that would create. I didn't want to go over the budget so it made sense to go with the other workers. In fact, we're right on target."

Hitting budgets will happen when smart labor utilization is expected, projections are made, measurements are taken in real time, and budgeting becomes a part of the daily decision-making process. And it won't require Johnny taking the schedule and cost information in to show his boss. The boss will have access to this information any time, just by clicking a mouse.

Evaluating Staffing Levels

As technology has advanced, certain industries (such as heathcare) have become major investors in new machines and devices. When manufacturers market these new innovations, they typically indicate the number of workers it will take to run the machinery.

Recently, I talked with a human resources vice president of a heathcare organization about his staffing policy relative to equipment. He indicated that when expensive new equipment such as an MRI machine is added to a department, he generally accepts the manufacturer's suggestions about staffing. I asked him if he later evaluates whether the projection indeed represented the proper level, whether the ratio was valid based on his organization's actual machine usage. The information was available concerning actual machine utilization — how many MRI scans were performed, how many patients treated, and how much revenue generated. The operating and purchase costs for the machines were known as well. But how about the personnel component? Was an assessment ever made to determine if the right number of employees was supporting that equipment?

When I posed the question, he paused, thought a moment and replied with something like "Hmm, you're right. We don't look at staffing in that way." It was apparent to me he was thinking, "Maybe we should."

I pressed on. "What if you bought two MRI's and each required two FTEs (full-time employees), so you hired four new employees to run those machines. Somebody will have added four employees to their little kingdom down in radiology. Is it possible that having two machines doesn't really require two FTEs? Is it possible they could be handled by three resources pooled together, or a mix of part-time and full-time staff scheduled around peak usage? What kind of idle time exists between patients, or at slow times?"

Human nature being what it is, the person who runs the department isn't going to raise his or her hand and say, "Wait a minute, I've got too many people reporting to me!" And Management doesn't check. Up until now, too many industries haven't looked at labor as a trackable or manageable resource. In the past, it would have been very difficult to conduct a proper analysis. But with an automated time and attendance system and the proper configuration it can easily be done.

The same goes for space utilization. Companies occupy commercial real estate. Commercial real estate is all about location and square footage.

Commercial Space Utilization

A friend of mine owns a gift and novelty store, a Hallmark outlet of sorts. She told me that the first ten feet of space in a retail store is "dead space". She knows that those ten feet right inside the front door are like the "fly over" states. Customers pass through this area but they don't stop and they won't make the majority of their purchases from what is shelved in it. It's all part of the shopper mentality. Everyone wants to browse the store and no one is willing to gamble that what they see first is exactly what they want. Something more enticing must be in the middle of the store, or perhaps a sale item is on the back shelf. As a result, she knows that whatever she places in that area won't sell as well as the same item further back in the store. So she had better not put her highest margin product in that floor space. That's a pretty scientific way of looking at square footage. It's also a very smart way of doing business.

If I were her, I wouldn't assign a sales person to that area of the store, would you? To do so would be to waste labor dollars. Extrapolate that approach to physical space as having revenue generating and expense factors associated with it, into the larger business world.

A good WMT system can help an organization determine if it is using valuable space in the most efficient way. Let's say, for example, several thousand square feet of a medical center are devoted to radiology. How much does it cost to run that operation in terms of labor? What's the revenue? Would it be more profitable to use the space for a physical therapy facility? A health club might offer personal trainers for one-on-one services and yoga instructors for large classes. How is the space used relative to the income they generate? Do more personal trainers result in higher customer retention rates?

These are the kinds of "what if" games the technology will allow management to play.

Controlling the Kingdoms — Determining the Correct Staffing Levels

Labor data technology can be used to evaluate a manager's request for more staff by taking a look at the manager's record. What is his current labor utilization compared to the revenue his operation generates or the amount of product it produces? How does the staffing in this manager's department compare to others with a similar amount of work?

If the company is going to the expense of hiring new workers, will they be efficiently deployed, and will they come to work? What is the manager's record of employee retention and attendance?

Is the manager having trouble filling shifts with qualified personnel? Does this manager's department have a significant amount of overtime? Will an additional employee reduce this, and if so, will the reduction be sufficient to cover the new salary?

What if Bob's department gets the same amount of work done that Charlie's does, and Bob's department has ten people while Charlie's has fourteen? Obviously, something is out of balance. Adding more staff might not be the answer.

Eliminating Costly Employment Agencies

I believe a chain of car washes in the city where I live could benefit from WMT. There are half a dozen or so locations in different parts of town. My guess is attracting reliable people to work at these car washes isn't easy. The last time I had my car done, most of the workers were young men putting in time at a temporary job. Maybe it was summer break, maybe an after school job, or it could have been a job between jobs. Suffice it to say, not many of these guys are planning a career at the car wash. They realize the boss is more interested in whether they show up than they are.

Let's say a bright, sunny day comes along. The beach or the park or friends beckon, and several workers don't show up. The same sunny day inspires proud car owners to get their cars washed, and they head to the place in droves. So what does the car wash manager do? He calls a temporary staffing service called Agency, which is in business to provide last minute, temporary workers. Of course, Agency puts a big surcharge on a day laborer's normal pay, which is likely to blow the manager's labor budget to pieces. Instead of paying minimum wage or slightly more, the car wash is now paying perhaps $10 an hour for the labor. Not only are these workers probably less enthusiastic or productive than the permanent employees, quality may also be an issue. What a great deal — poor performance for more money.

If this happens on a regular basis, the extra cost can add up to a significant sum and reduction in customer satisfaction. It seems logical, then, that reducing the use of Agency may be a key to more profits for this organization. Finding incentives or ways that are effective at getting people to show up for work should be a top priority.

One solution might be to stop operating each car wash location as a separate and independent unit. Since it has a number of locations around town, the company might consider establishing what in effect would be its own temporary employment agency by considering all the employees at all its locations as a single pool of labor. Using a WMT system, trends could be studied to determine how many positions are likely to be needed on a given day. Weather might be factored in as a variable. A certain number of floaters could be hired. Then the scheduler, using the WMT system, could assign the floaters, who would be deployed to the locations as needed.

If the company wants to keep scheduling in the hands of each location manager, another approach would be for each to schedule his location using primarily his "home" workers. For peak periods, heavy customer traffic or call-offs, however, the manager would have access to a database of all available in-house workers or floaters. Some of these might be "on call" or "per need" employees who are paid a slightly higher rate when they work — but significantly less than the agency rate — in exchange for being available for last minute assignments. As in other industries, on-call staff might even be paid a minor stipend for their on-call time in order to compensate them for being "at the ready."

In the airline industry, crew members have certain days that they are required to be ready to come in to work within one hour. It surely takes a flight attendant more time to clean up, pack up, and get to the airport than it does a guy who needs to pull on his jeans and drive over to the car wash. It's a win-win It enables employer and employee to handle the realities of supply and demand in the labor market with adequate flexibility and reward. The manager has a larger pool of trained, in-house labor to draw upon and employees benefit from some "paid" free time and higher rates for coming in on short notice. Who doesn't want to make more than the guy working next to him?

Managers might use the technology to recruit the best candidates. If a manager knows he needs a lot of "early risers" to fill the 6 a.m. shift, then schedule around employees' preferences for when they like to work and recruit employees who fit the need.

The technology might also shed light on how to drive the business around the available labor. Perhaps customers could get a discount for having their cars washed at night or early in the morning when workers are more willing to work and cost the company less.

When I worked in the airline industry, the company and crew members agreed upon a scheduling methodology that replaced the typical calendar model. Each month includes 8 or 9 weekend days (Saturday and Sundays). On average, most people expect to have these days off, or about two days a week. So each crew member was allotted eight or nine days off a month, but not necessarily on weekends. The airline called these "G Days." A G Day is a guaranteed day off. For a business that operates 24/7 and transports its workers across the country, preventing them from going home every night, this program suited both the needs of the schedulers and the crew. For airline workers, weekends might be thought of as floating holidays. They don't enjoy the routine of having off every weekend, but they do benefit from their G Days and are often able to put several together for an extended "weekend" that could fall anywhere in the month. This G Day structure freed the company from having to schedule around employees who needed to be back home every Saturday and return to work on Monday. That simply didn't make sense in the transportation industry.

The airline I worked for was primarily a charter company. Charter contracts were never the same month to month and new flights were added at a moment's notice. One of the airline's sweet spots was filling in for the major carriers when they needed a replacement aircraft or filling in for the military when they needed to move troops. These contracts came up very quickly and crews had to be assembled in a short amount of time. The people in scheduling looked at who was available to assign to these flights. First, they considered anyone who wasn't flying at the time. Since they were only obligated to give the employee eight or nine days off a month, employees could be scheduled to work without any additional cost if they weren't already assigned.

Crew members could have more than nine days off. The G Days were just the minimum number of days promised. Crew members were paid a monthly salary. If their total flight time — block time, it's called — exceeded a set amount, they would earn overtime. Because of this, a crew member who was not scheduled to work on a particular day could be called in without adding additional cost, provided the added flight did not push him into overtime.

As a last resort, the scheduler could look at crew members who were at home on a G Day. In critical situations, these employees could be called in and paid a premium for working on their "guaranteed day off."

The G Day program created a pool of labor that could be scheduled at a premium. This was crucial because an airline can't call in car-wash types from the local staffing agency. Any firm that uses highly skilled and regulated workers has to have the ability to fill their staffing needs internally.

Earlier I explained how the Crew Activity Notification (C.A.N.) Reports could help the airline project labor costs. You can see now that sales could contact scheduling and request an estimate of any additional crew expenses if a flight was added to the schedule. The scheduler could easily determine if he was likely to have to call in G Day personnel or put crew members into overtime to staff the flight.

The benefits to the employee were flexibility, premium pay for working extra, and a guaranteed base rate. He also had his days off each month. He, too, could use the C.A.N. Report to project his earnings against the scheduled activity and call-in flights. In addition, the G Days could be adjusted as operational needs changed over the course of the month. A worker getting the third Tuesday may be willing to switch it to Wednesday or the Tuesday of next week, or pair it up with another G Day for a longer break. In the travel and hospitality field, the mentality about weekends isn't the same as it is in the nine-to-five business world.

One of my large heathcare clients also used a temp agency service to supply nurses when a shift came up short in a clinical area. The client had thousands of employees and a number of facilities in different locations around the area. When it came to staffing, each of the major facilities operated somewhat independently, however. Some of the facilities were already using automated scheduling software to help with the complex task of assigning shifts. But these stand-alone systems were not integrated, meaning they didn't include the entire staff in all locations. When shortages occurred, hospitals called the temp agency for replacements. Management recognized this inefficiency and unnecessary expense and implemented a WMT system that integrated time and attendance with an advanced scheduling module. The intent was to rely more on internal resources to the extent possible and to reduce the use of costly temp workers. The WMT system enabled schedulers to look at a much larger pool of qualified workers and to "borrow" staff that were not being used elsewhere. The system showed who was qualified, who was available, who wanted to work that type of shift, the total hours worked thus far — in order to avoid calling in someone who would then be pushed into overtime — and how to contact them. When people were assigned shifts in non-home locations, the employee's primary supervisor could see the additional assignment as well. This prevented double-booking.

The end result was lower labor costs and greater utilization of current staff. This translated to more revenue per employee, which was a bigger benefit than one might imagine since each employee costs a company overhead in the form of worker's comp, insurance, unemployment, benefits, training, and so forth. In addition, more reliance on internally trained and vested employees can lead to higher quality service and improved team building because workers become used to working together. Higher quality service can mean better patient outcomes, such as improved recovery rates, better heathcare rating scorecards, reduced risk from poor service and a better reputation. This can in turn lead to a competitive advantage in the labor market by moving the organization closer to its goal of become the "employer of choice." In addition, more satisfied patients results in more business, which equals more revenue.

How One Post Office Got on Budget

My husband has a long time friend from way back in his college days. Everyone in his circle of friends had a nickname — Duds, Shags, Teaz — this guy is affectionately known as "the Gas" because there once were three guys labeled Liquid, Solid and Gas. Gas always has a funny story to tell, especially about work situations and his travels. He told me one of those funny stories about going to this little, tiny post office. He went up to the first window where an older gentleman was stationed and told the man he wanted to mail a package. The man said he'd have to go to the window around the corner where parcels were serviced. The Gas dutifully stepped back and walked around the corner to the next window. When he arrived, he realized that the man behind the counter at this station was the same guy, but he now was literally wearing a different hat. As though he'd never seen the Gas before, the guy asked "May I help you?"

Jolted a bit, the Gas replied, "Um, Yes, I want to mail this package." The older man weighed the package and calculated the postage. When the transaction was complete, the Gas said to him, "I'm sure glad you waited on me. That *other* guy working here is a real jerk."

I wish I had such a quick wit.

The point of this story is to know how much labor a business can support and to staff accordingly. The management of this post office had obviously figured two roles had to be filled — regular mail and package delivery. Both needed to be serviced at all times. There wasn't enough customer traffic, however, to justify two workers. So they improvised, albeit in a somewhat comical way, and put workers where needed. Real-time demand for labor was met in this way. If the guy had told the Gas they didn't do parcel packages until three o'clock, my friend might have walked out the door and across the street to UPS. That is what happens when labor cannot meet customer demand. Business walks out the door, and the parcel post window doesn't generate revenue.

It would have been a problem in this post office if the person scheduled to work could only process mail. Every work environment has associated tasks. Every worker has skills. When more than one location and employee are involved, location and task-skill match are important. That particular post office employee was the perfect person to have in that office because he could wear two hats. In large organizations that pool resources, knowing where people are needed and what kind of skills they must have is critical. Not only is it important not to under- or overstaff relative to date and time, it's important to have the right mix of task skills in a location. In addition, knowing what the right ratio of revenue to workers is by location will impact overall success. Business people know this intuitively and vendors of scheduling software have caught on.

Scheduling the Work Around Labor

Technology has delivered the ability to bring work and employees together in new ways. Telecommunications, including local area networks, WiFi (wireless internet) and satellite communications all allow people to work together without being in close proximity and to collaborate in different media simultaneously — not just voice or sound, but on the same design or engineering project. No restrictions need to be placed on when and where the work gets done. The ability to employ off site workers as well as those who prefer to work off hours gives employers flexibility with respect to the labor pool they can draw on. A production-oriented business may benefit from scheduling the work around the availability of labor, rather than scheduling the work first and attempting to get enough workers to run the line. And why not? Supply chain management and lean production innovations often are driven by material and equipment-focused systems. New technology allows a business to turn that model on its head and look at supply and production schedules driven by a labor-centric system.

Part Three
Workforce Management Technology Systems and Installation Considerations

Chapter Nine: Adding Value to Data through Collection and Distribution Techniques

What are the three biggest things to consider when buying a house? Location, location, location, of course, and it's the same when it comes to collecting and distributing workforce data. *Where* the data is collected, *where* the employee performed the activity, and *where* the data goes after it is reported by the employee are crucial to the value and integrity of the information and the ability to control the labor activity being reported. Payroll data has historically been simply a matter of capturing *who* and *when*. Processes collected the names of people who worked and when they worked. In some cases, it might have included *what* the employee did. That was all that was needed for payroll.

But operational activities don't exist in the two dimensional world of only what and when. Operations take place in a location. People work in teams, on wings or floors or in units. They are assigned to equipment and production lines, buildings and geographic zones. If the work is more conceptual than physical they are assigned to projects, cases, or clients. The point is, their work relates to a third dimension of data that historically hasn't been an issue in the Payroll Department. That third component is what relates their work to the organization's products and services. It is the connection between an employee's work contribution and whatever is being sold. When an employee is in the correct location, doing his job, his work should be adding value.

Management should want to collect time, location, and task-related data with a new system because it will help them better manage human capital. Having an employee go to a particular spot to report on and start an activity is a crucial element in collecting value added data. A phone might be located there, a PC, a bar code reader or some other device.

An employee might be required to clock in when he begins an activity and to clock out when he finishes. This isn't limited to any one type of company. This sort of information can be extremely helpful to companies that bill clients for the time people spend working on their behalf.

Lawyers and management consultants are two examples. My editor recalls that when he worked in the ad business it was imperative to have time records to justify client billing. Yet, he and other executives might not fill in manual time sheets until the end of the day. More often, it was at the end of the week — in the last half hour before time sheets were due. As a result, many were based primarily on memory.

How accurate do you suppose they were?

How much legitimate, billable time do you suppose was lost?

I'm willing to bet that over time the accumulated effect was substantial.

For the most accurate picture, then, of an employee's labor cost and the value it adds, data collection ought to be done at the moment closest to when work actually begins. This is why improving the ability to collect data at the precise moment productive work begins should be a goal when time and attendance data collection is being automated. The ideal setup is for the employee to report his beginning time at the exact minute and location an activity starts. And you know what? That setup is usually not a timeclock by the entrance door or next to the break room on the other side of the plant. Fortunately, technology now provides the opportunity to locate collection devices in proximity to work locations.

Locating the collection devices in actual work areas insures that compensated time is productive time, supervised time, engaged time. It lessens the gaps between the time employees *report* to work and the time they actually *begin* to work productively. It may not seem like much of an improvement, but small savings repeated day after day add up.

What's really exciting is that the technology is rapidly evolving in a way that will make "location" of the device a non-issue. Collection and reporting devices will go with the worker, be everywhere unencumbered by cables, power cords, a wall to hang on, or a desk to sit on. By the time this book reaches your hands, it's likely that relatively inexpensive devices for this will be available. Cisco, for example, has one in the works. Think cell phones and you'll begin to see where data collection devices are headed.

Enabling workers to report their activity as it occurs also reduces errors and omissions. Filling out a time sheet at the end of the week, relying on memory, is prone to mistakes and honest omissions. It is also ripe for unscrupulous workers who may choose to fill in the blanks with data that is not representative of their true work activity. The more this type of waste, fraud and abuse occurs, the more entitled workers feel to continue it, and the more money employers lose.

"Fred never gets here in the morning till 8:30 a.m., and I'll bet he doesn't mark that on his time sheet. So I'm not going to put down that I left 20 minutes early yesterday. It's only fair."

Types of Collection Devices

Many workers use computers in their jobs, and a growing percentage in many businesses have them on their desks. When an employee arrives, all she has to do is sign in, and the system knows she's there. The employee can also use the computer to access information about herself, such as how many days off she has earned, year-to-date, or hours she's already worked this pay period.

It might be more practical for telephones to be used in some locations. This is particularly true in large locations, such as a medical center that may be spread out and have a number of entrances and exits. Timeclocks can cost $2,000 or $3,000 apiece, and not everyone who works in a medical center has his own computer. Using telephones is an excellent solution because they are ubiquitous in most workplaces.

Telephones can also save time. In a large building or an office complex, the nearest clock might be ten minutes away from the employee's workstation. A phone is usually right at the workstation, or at least nearby.

Using a phone the employee might call in and punch a code, perhaps his or her social security number (although companies are moving away from using SSN for privacy concerns), an employee ID, or a PIN (personal identification number). Voice validation is also a possibility. Whatever the case, the computer on the other end knows which device was used (based on the device's electronic "address" or the phone number), the time of the call, and who is on the line once the code is entered. The computer might prompt the employee to punch in another code that will enter a specific activity. When the employee is finished signing in by phone, he or she doesn't have to hang up if someone else is waiting to check in on the same phone. She can simply punch the pound sign and then hand the phone receiver to the next person.

The collection device can also be set up to give employees information if they want it, such as how many hours they've worked this week, the next shift they are scheduled to work, or how much paid time off (PTO) they have coming to them.

It's important to have this capability in a paperless system because people will want and need it. To keep a system from being overloaded at peak punch times, however, it may make sense to limit the hours in a day this type of information can be accessed. Many systems can be set up to do this. Otherwise it might be necessary to add servers and other IT infrastructure in order to accommodate high traffic — lots of calls or entries — at peak times.

The amount and type of information a particular person can access can also be limited based on an individual's position in the company and what he needs to know for his job. Collection devices readily administer "security" profiles that tell the device what each employee is allowed to do at that machine.

In addition to telephones, PDAs (personal digital assistants) can be used to enter and access data. So can the types of devices UPS and other delivery companies use to track packages. As noted above, Cisco is working closely with WMT vendors such as Workbrain and Kronos to develop devices that will be available soon, perhaps by the time this book gets to market, designed and manufactured specifically for the purpose of WMT data entry. One resembles a memory stick and is about that size (2" x 1" x 1/4"), making it easy to wear around the neck on a lanyard, clipped to a belt or lapel, or to put on a key chain. The cost is expected to be relatively inexpensive — less than a cell phone. To check in, an employee simply will have to press a button, state his name, and give other pertinent information.

"This is Jane Smith, reporting to work in sporting goods."

In addition, the employee will be able to use this device to give and receive information such as an upcoming work schedule or how much

Kronos Incorporated, 2006

paid time off he or she has accumulated, initiate a message to another manager or employee or to instruct the system to take an action like run a report.

Either with global positioning technology or by noting the point of entry into an ethernet or cell phone grid, the device might also keep the system informed about the approximate physical location of the employee. This will come in handy when trying to track someone down— a doctor in a hospital, for example — although this level of sophistication may not be available quite as soon as more basic models.

Finally, there is the time-honored timeclock. But these aren't your father's timeclocks. They can do much more than punch a card. As with those that have been around for decades, timeclocks are usually positioned near an entrance or a high traffic area. But today's clocks are connected to a computer network or system. Once the clock is punched, data enters the system and is instantly available. This allows management to see who is working and where at any given time.

The clocks can be preprogrammed to automate sign-in to special categories of work and compensation such as Call-In, Extra Shift, special premiums, temporary supervisor or line leader rates, and so forth. "Timeclock" has really become a misnomer for these devices. These data collection devices are now tools for two-way exchanges of much more than time related information.

Exempt from the Clock?

An exempt employee is an employee who, because of his or her duties, responsibilities and decision making authority, is exempt from the overtime provisions of the Fair Labor Standards Act. Exempt employees are expected by most organizations to work whatever hours are necessary to accomplish the particular goals and deliverables of the position they hold. Unlike nonexempt or hourly employees, exempt employees usually have some flexibility in their schedules and can come and go as necessary to accomplish their work. Employers cannot simply label a job as exempt to avoid paying overtime.

Let's say a number of workers on staff meet the exempt requirements. Although salaried employees are exempt from overtime, management may still want to track their activities for reporting or cost accounting purposes,or to provide information that will be used to bill clients for services rendered. Certain service sectors have strict guidelines as to the number of staff required relative to the number of "customers" — i.e. patients, residents, clients. For them, tracking exempt time is a critical operational need. They need to report and prove that they staffed adequately for a particular case load. In many situations, exempt employees should also be included in time and attendance data so that the figures management uses to make decisions, provide service and bill clients will be representative of the whole.

But this can be problematic. Exempt employees aren't being paid by the hour and are often considered "professional workers," so they typically don't punch in and out at a timeclock or report their actual arrival and departure times in time reports. Often they record a duration to represent their day such as "8 hours". They are, of course, expected to work a full week but technically their pay cannot be reduced if they leave early every now and then or don't work a full 40 hour week. If it takes more than 40 hours to get the job done, they are expected to put in the hours necessary, but their pay does not change. Therefore, because exempt employees actual time worked and pay are not related, many companies have historically not closely tracked the time they put in. Businesses that did may have been scrutinized by regulators for their classification of these workers and even been fined for wrongdoing. The result is that many companies are reluctant to track exempt employee activity. They don't require them to punch, and they don't have them call in.

But times have changed. Technology has introduced data integration into management's tool box. Workforce management technology systems now deposit labor data into the corporate data warehouse and parse it into reports that are used to make business decisions. Omitting exempt labor data would lead to an incomplete labor activity picture. Suffice it to say, the old principle that recording exempt employee time equates to tracking time for hourly employees isn't true in today's info-centric business environment. So long as the data isn't used to compute salaries or earnings on an hour-for-hour basis, companies are safe to collect the information.

There are numerous ways to record exempt employee activity. Some companies are satisfied with manual processes that allow exempt employees to report their time on a weekly basis. Some require salaried personnel to allocate their time to cost centers, projects or customers. These processes do provide some sense of exempt labor activity and cost but fail to provide real time data and are not as accurate and verifiable as those for hourly employees who use a data collection device such as a timeclock or computer.

Solutions for the Salaried

There are some considerations when planning to track exempt employee time in a new workforce management system. For consistency and reporting purposes, it may be preferable to have exempt employee hours come from the same system as hourly employees. A problem may arise, however, because an exempt employee may work less than 40 hours, or he may work more, but his or her pay should not change accordingly. In other words, actual hours worked may vary each week, but the employee's earnings do not. I have encountered systems that are easily configurable to limit the number of hours passed to Payroll for an exempt employee, thus eliminating the potential problem that excess hours pay might be automatically generated. A problem I've run into is that the same systems sometimes are not equipped to guarantee the weekly minimum hours to support the salary payment, which might result in an underpayment. Turning on an "auto-pay" isn't a great solution because it doesn't take into account benefit time and actual instances where the employee should be paid for less than a full week, such as with a termination or leave. I strongly recommend including exempt hour tracking requirements in the technical specifications when selecting a system and verifying that it can support the payroll system side of the process.

One configuration solution is to set up the labor management system to recognize "one punch" as a valid entry per day for an exempt worker. If an employee calls, punches or checks in at any time during the day, or his supervisor validates that he worked, the system will log in a day's work — eight hours, for example — for that employee. At a minimum, this can help keep track of days worked so that paid time off is taken appropriately. If the system registers no punch at all, then a manager has a right to question whether an absence occurred or paid time off should be applied. The one-punch system also allows the exempt employees to be included in "on premises" reporting so that management knows who is physically on site in real time. It can also verify coverage in work environments that require specific staffing levels, because the employee's "punch" can be used to validate her identity and location. As the section on scheduling previously explained, a schedule in the background could be referenced to provide more detail about when the employee worked that day.

Auto populating punches from a schedule can also work to get exempt employees into the system without the need to track their work day in real-time. This way the timecard shows the employee's planned work schedule while generating the hours that must pass to Payroll for payment. Systems that employ auto-populated punches from schedule don't require the exempt employees to clock in. This also accomplishes more accurate cost accounting than would otherwise be the case by attributing the exempt employee's wages and costs to the business activity in the same way hourly employees' time is recorded.

On Premises Notification

A number of ways can be used for the system to know who has punched, who is on premises, and who has failed to arrive as expected. A person might have a badge with a magnetic strip that's swiped. Some systems require a PIN in addition to this. More and more, however, employers are using biometrics. All an employee has to do is touch a pad on the clock with a finger, and the system will identify her. In these ways you can know to varying degrees of certainty who is at each location.

What happens when someone forgets to punch? The system can be programmed to generate a list of those employees with missed punches or who fail to show up and provide this to the appropriate supervisor. Call this the "work flow" component. In selecting a system that's best for your organization you must know how the information needs to get to the manager. Some systems will generate an electronic page to cell phones or PDAs. Others provide the notification only within the application requiring computer access. On premises can be a powerful tool. The key is to purchase a system that adequately delivers this information to the right individuals, at the right time and via the available technology.

Where the Data Goes

Collecting data from an employee at the time and the place it occurs provides real-time data. What makes it even more valuable is that this data is visible and accessible. Where can the data go? Wherever it needs to.

Data should travel on a need-to-know basis. Does Payroll need to know on a minute-to-minute basis who has reported to work or ended a shift? No. Pursuing real-time data is for operational purposes. The immediate dispersal of the information collected is to provide a tool, a window into today's activity.

As the saying goes, "You cannot manage what you cannot see." So who should the data be for? It's for the Subway Shop scheduler responsible for ensuring that each of the five stores he or she manages in a ten square mile area is staffed at all times. Obviously, this person cannot physically be in five locations at once. But the WMT system can tell her who is at each location and who has not yet arrived. It's also for the foreman on the shop floor who gets the production line ready. It's for any scheduler who needs to make certain the entire crew has reported to work so that the work can begin on time. It's for the retail store manager who expects a rush of holiday shoppers and needs to direct staff to high traffic areas. And it's for the business owner who must control costs and wants to be alerted to workers about to go into overtime.

Collecting data at specific locations provides immediate visibility into what is going on, where it is happening. Data can also go beyond schedulers and front line supervisors. That's the beauty of a technology that collects data on everyone. It is of interest and value to other levels and can be made available to them via these work flow notifications, on-line workspaces within the application, traditional reports mailed electronically or printed hard copy, or sent to the data warehouse repository. You decide where the data goes and when.

Capturing Activity Specific Time Spent

Let's say a factory produces complex machinery that needs to be customized to customers' specifications. An example might be a heating and air conditioning system for a large building or a shopping mall which is made up of valves and controls and air handlers and different length ducts and vents and so forth that curve this way and that. Each person who performs a task in the building of that system might clock in at the beginning of an operation and clock out at the end, perhaps by swiping a barcode with a wand. In this way the actual cost of the labor it took to build a particular custom HVAC system can be determined, rather than simply estimated by the seat of the pants.

Accurate information about how long it takes to perform different tasks can be extremely valuable to manufacturers who want to run a lean operation. It's information they need so they can schedule items through production in the right sequence with the right number of workers deployed in the various activities in order to maintain a predetermined rhythm of production and eliminate as much worker downtime as possible.

Collecting Product and Job Specific Data

How is information collected about how much labor went into a particular task? We've mentioned timeclocks and telephones. Another way is to use barcodes. Visualize a laminated sheet attached to a clipboard with rows of barcodes on it representing different activities, jobs, parts, and so forth. A barcode-reading wand can be positioned nearby. As a product moves into a workstation for a subassembly to be installed, the employee simply scans the appropriate barcode. When it's done, he scans another. The product moves to the next workstation, and this is repeated.

This may already exist in an ERP system in some fashion. What's new is relating the data to a specific worker, the cost of that labor, and other trackable data about who is doing what.

The information this produces can be used in several ways. It can be used for cost accounting as described above. It can measure a particular individual's performance against others who perform the same task. It can help establish the interval of time required for a particular operation. Or it might be used to calculate the pay for individuals who are compensated on a piecework basis. It can be used to track quality and output — who is the most productive and proficient. The data can reveal the skill gaps that are hidden in a fog of general information.

Maximizing Care and Revenue

An automated time and attendance system can be used to integrate time and activity with billing. Many heathcare providers, including nursing and rest homes, are remunerated by Medicare, Medicaid and state agencies based on the actual services provided each patient. Let's say there's a house with five residents in it. There might be two workers on staff. Employee A might be in the activities room with Clients 1, 2 and 3 while Employee B is giving physical therapy to clients 4 and 5. Client 4 may finish physical therapy and go to the activities room, at which time Client 1 may go to physical therapy.

Sound complicated?

Agencies footing the bill require that billing reflect all this. In other words, the billing must identify the patient served and the activity. Obviously, record keeping in such a situation can be problematic. An older time and attendance system may only collect information about who worked and how long, so a separate system would be needed to record activities by individual patient. Sometimes it's hard to reconcile the two because the timecard may say a person worked eight hours while the activity sheet adds to 12 hours or more. How can this be? Two or more patients may have been served simultaneously.

An updated time and attendance system can bring these two record keeping activities together, simplify the process for those keeping the records, make it possible to reconcile patients served and time spent on the job and at the same time automate the billing of services rendered.

Respite service is another area where this way of working can pay dividends. This service is rendered when a professional heathcare provider comes into someone's home to provide "respites" for family members who are caring for someone who is physically unable to care for himself For example, think of a handicapped adult who still lives with his parents. Medicare allocates a certain number of respite care hours it will reimburse per month per individual. The idea is to give the primary caregivers a break for a weekend, or to go shopping, or to just get out of the house for a couple of hours.

Let's say Medicare or the state will pay for 25 hours a month of respite care for a particular individual. A heath care provider should consider this as a purchase order. But how do most companies know whether they have delivered all the care they are entitled to deliver? In a manual system, the cumulative number of service hours is probably not known until the last timecard and activity reports are submitted for the month. Whoa! That's way too late. But with an automated system it would be relatively easy to make sure none of this potential revenue falls through the cracks. Approved-care hours provide a "budget" for that patient. The hours could be scheduled over the course of the month and direct-care staff assigned to the schedule. The system could be scheduled to give periodic reports and to highlight those who are in danger of being underserved. As the nursing aides work their assigned shifts, they report their time to the system — including the patient information. If an employee misses a shift or the patient is unable to be served on a scheduled day, the balance of hours would indicate that additional hours should be assigned to replace the missed shift. Periodic reports of budgeted versus actual hours would alert management to situations where revenue is being lost.

How does this work? Kronos has a product called TTE Homecare. TTE Homecare is a telephony-based solution that allows employees to use a telephone to report their work activity. They call a number, the computer answers, the worker identifies himself with a PIN, and the computer leads the employee through a series of prompts, such as which patients were served and what the activities were. Unlike previous telephony systems, TTE Homecare is configurable to allow users to program the system in order to collect the required business data along with time and attendance information. TTE Homecare enables customers to set up a system that will prompt the employee to provide the patient-related information they require. Workers can listen to different recordings based on their job or work location. The system then exports the data to a WMT database — Kronos' Workforce Timekeeper — and to the company's billing system.

This is one way a vendor has answered its customers' demands for a system that allows the employee to report activity in multiple formats and to include critical business information as well. Time must be reported for payroll reporting, but equally important, client-based activity — including customer numbers, service types, activity durations and concurrent events — needed to be collected. This program allows it to be done in a simple and cost effective manner.

Telephones are about as basic as hardware gets these days. They are inexpensive, easy to use and readily available. Even cell phones can be used. Phone lines are also inexpensive and reliable. 800 numbers can be used for multi-state operations and T1 lines can provide enhanced bandwidth and speed. A reporting pathway must have very little down time, and telephony systems are very reliable.

Evaluating a System's Components

Technology today provides a variety of functional options, types of devices and channels in response to the needs of different business processes and data sharing requirements. There are considerations for selecting the type of devices to be used, the infrastructure and the processes that carry the data from employee to paycheck to business manager.

Cost will certainly drive what your organization can afford in terms of sophisticated technology. Knowing what you can spend before you shop will allow you to focus on what you can afford. Workforce management

---

Cost

Cost of the devices (hardware and supporting software)

Cost of device infrastructure (networks)

Installation costs

Replacement costs & device life cycle (based on use; how long will the system last?)

Cost of system support (personnel to manage & maintain/repair the devices and systems)

---

technology when used as suggested by this book will deliver cost savings and a return on the investment. The only question is, how much? That's why the process of selecting the appropriate data collection devices should include a cost-benefit analysis.

You'll notice the list of costs includes more than just new equipment. The vendor should be able to provide guidelines as to how many FTEs will be required to manage a system of the size and complexity you are purchasing, or how many hours of administrative oversight the system demands each week. Have the vendor verify the ratio of FTEs or administrative hours to your system with actual examples from customers. It's a good idea to talk with current users about exactly how they are using the system in order to make certain the comparison is appropriate. It's not just a numbers game. Fifty clocks installed at one plant all doing the same thing are not the same as fifty clocks installed at fifty different locations in three time zones configured ten different ways. Understand your level of standardization because system complexity will determine the economies of scale.

In addition, all FTEs are not alike. Your implementation may entail a significant staffing component. Employees will have to administer each piece of the system. Their duties and skill sets may vary widely, and their labor cost must be considered. The RFP process should include obtaining detailed job descriptions and salary estimates for the new system's support staff. The guys down in the Information Systems (IS) Department who run the HR system today, may not know anything about overseeing a sophisticated telephony system or patching PDAs into the network. And the Payroll coordinators who will no longer have to use their adding machines to tabulate paper timecards may not have the foundation of knowledge required to learn how to configure a new computer application.

Security
User/employee validation
System Administrator security
Tamperproof
Protection of confidential data

Ensuring the data is legitimate and protecting the data once it is collected are two things crucial to providing credible data. For this to happen, you need to know in what locations you need the system to be a security guard and where opportunities exist for employees to use "the buddy system."

The buddy system is when Bob says to his coworker, Charley, "Hey buddy, punch me out when you leave today. I'm going home early."

If it's important to know it was actually Bob who punched out at 5:00 p.m., then make certain the technology has some sort of user identification validation. Phone systems can enforce voice identification or caller ID. Also, ANI (Automated Number Identification) is provided today on most telephone lines. Telephony systems can compare the incoming phone number against a list of authorized phone numbers — restricting callers from attempting to call from an unidentified or unauthorized phone number.

Biometric technology allows customers to verify an employee's identity via fingerprint scanners, palm print readers and optical retina identification. Then, once the system has approved the user, the data must be protected from manipulation or disclosure except by authorized personnel. If edits are allowed, the original data should be archived as well for backup and not deleted or overwritten. A number of systems that collect call information will overwrite that data when a supervisor makes an edit. Is that important to your organization? System security includes maintaining an audit trail of all data inputs — showing who entered what, when, and offering the user an opportunity to attach a comment or flag notation concerning why a change was made. Employees who are working the old system will constantly seek ways to outwit the new system and avoid detection. That's why when security is evaluated, it's important to think like someone who wants to circumvent the controls in the system.

There are some basic security issues to think about as well. If employees must enter an ID number on a key pad in a common, unsecured area and the keypad is visible to passersby, the question needs to be addressed, should that ID number be kept confidential? It's not uncommon for employers to assign employees' social security numbers as their login ID numbers. Punching that number into a keypad for anyone to see could be risky. Asking the vendor if the display can show only an asterisk (*) instead of the actual numbers may be all the security that is needed. For phones , the same numbering convention might allow the next caller to hit the "repeat" button on the phone and view the last employee's ID number, which might be his social security number.

PINs are also a concern. Such a number is only as secure as the employee wants it to be. Relying on the employee to keep his PIN number private and using it to verify his identity is potentially fraught with trouble. Again, the "buddy system" can come into play when Bob shares his PIN number with a coworker to punch in for him. Also, PINs are often forgotten and require continual reassignment. That assignment process opens up yet another opportunity for abuse when system administrators change an employee's security settings and must use some other means of verifying the employee's identity. Any number that identifies an employee in the system must be guarded. Screen views, reports, displays and playbacks are windows of opportunity for unauthorized users to gain access to employee records.

In your evaluation of systems, ask vendors to explain how they view the security issue. Make certain the importance of guarding data is clearly understood.

It goes almost without saying that the system you want needs to be

---

Ease of use

Employee/end user usability

System administrator — complexity of setup and management
of multiple devices and the underlying infrastructure

Scalability — ability to add devices, change configuration, and
so forth.

---

easy to use. The process should not be overly complicated or time consuming for employees to identify themselves to the system and enter their data. Obviously, it shouldn't impede their ability to get to work, and it needs to allow the next person in line to do the same. For many systems, administrators are able to customize prompts so that employees are given specific step-by-step instructions as data is entered in the system. These prompts may also be designed to "retire" after the employee gains proficiency and no longer needs the extended version of prompts or explanations he depended on when he first began using the system. The system should also have the ability to cancel or back up (the old "do-over" key) when a user makes a mistake or "fat-fingers" an entry. Accurate data is crucial, so people need to be able to correct their mistakes or abort before the system collects erroneous data. Systems that confirm (repeat back) the information entered are even better — assuming the process is not overly time consuming.

I often suggest that during orientation employees be given a "cheat sheet" the size of a business card with instructions covering basic steps for reporting activity, or even for more difficult tasks. Posting instructions by the collection device is also a good idea. Including the phone number of the software company's Help Desk can be helpful too.

More than end users should be considered in your evaluation. System administrators will benefit from technology that's easy to work with and maintain as business needs evolve and the system undergoes minor modifications. A configurable system — one that requires an administrator to be proficient in a common computer language or proprietary tool kit generally displayed in a GUI (Graphical User Interface) on screen workspace is preferable to a programmable system because it will be easier to learn how to use, more stable and require less skilled and less-costly personnel. Plus, rewriting system programming may require extensive system testing and validation before changes can be put into effect. Configurable systems limit what the system administrator can change in the underlying platform and should be fairly goof-proof as far as overall system stability is concerned. The desired outcome might not come about when an error in configuration is made, but the system is less likely to crash due to a configuration mistake than it would from a programming change.

Ease of use also translates into ease of growth. Over time, it is likely your business will grow or change, or both, and the system will need to expand. As a result, vendors ought to be queried as to how many more devices a system can accommodate before more hardware or network infrastructure is needed or an upgrade is required. The architecture you are sold will be based on your current size. It's good to understand where you will max out that landscape as your employee base or device inventory grows.

Functionality

Options for data collection — type of data that can be collected and frequency

Data Transfer — interfacing with other systems

System Performance — sizing the system for the appropriate volume of data inputs and outputs

---

Understanding what the data collection technology you select must be able to do can be more daunting and involved than you may imagine. The best way to define functional specifications is to diligently investigate what current systems in your organization do today.

It's best to first determine if procedures and processes are standard throughout your organization. There are several ways to do this through a sampling of data, or perhaps an all-inclusive survey of each business unit and employee category. On site observations and interviews conducted by a business analyst are even better. If your operations are managed centrally and policies and processes are strictly adhered to, you may be in a position to interview a small group of employees and managers. This would probably be the case if everyone uses the same forms and systems, the same numbering systems and naming conventions, the same reporting cycles and a similar organizational hierarchy.

Another indicator of standardization is locality. If all operations are in one city or state, it's more likely processes and procedures are standard than if an organization is spread out across multiple states and localities. A single line of business or homogenous customer demographics also lessen the chances a system will have to handle a lot of complexity.

Companies that grow by acquisition and allow new business units to continue existing practices instead of converting to corporate standards are likely to require different system features than those that have standardized. Organizations that have been in business for many years and have expanded over time may be fairly conservative in their current practices but on the verge of benefiting from more advanced data collection features. Having a wide variety of worker types, including everything from commission-based staff to exempt and project-oriented employees and hourly, per diem and piece-rate workers, indicates a need to thoroughly explore the functional requirements.

Once the type of discovery process (sampling, survey, site visits, and so forth) is identified, and whether it relies on a sample or is inclusive, the investigation should include what the system does today, what works, what doesn't work, what it should be doing and what it should not do. The resulting functional specifications may even include levels of required functionality:

Level I: Basic/required,

Level II: Enhancements, and

Level III: Optimum features — the gold plated faucets you'd love to have but probably can't afford unless they come standard

The important point to keep in mind is that it's imperative to know what your system must be able to do. You must uncover the full set of detailed functional requirements. If one group of employees cannot use the system because it doesn't do X, then X is critical and cannot be overlooked. If you know your processes are complex, nonstandard or not well documented, the best approach is the most extensive discovery you can afford.

It's also important not to forget that paper time sheets are still a legitimate device and represent a process that may be the best workable solution for some organizations given the issues raised above. The most prudent exercise is to begin with an assessment of how current collection systems measure up against these considerations.

Scalability

If your organization plans to expand and you are looking at an automated time and attendance system, scalability is something that needs to be evaluated. No matter what your numbers are — whether you have 250 employees, 2500 or 25,000 — scalability is critical. The different aspects of scalability include hardware, network and software.

First, the software component should be evaluated. Some platforms are not designed to handle large databases or a high volume of inputs. Some vendor systems are designed on operating systems or database applications that are capable of handling only a limited amount of data.

I once discovered the hard way what lack of scalability can mean when working on a large-scale implementation several years ago. This time and attendance project included the purchase of a telephony system for data collection. Employees would use a telephone to call into the system, and the system would record a "time stamp" of their arrival and departure times, change of location, job or activity. The company had more than 25,000 employees across the country. Employees typically called into the system several times a day to report a change in work activity. The system was rolled out gradually, adding a few thousand employees every few weeks. The telephony system worked well for the first few months. But a point was reached during the implementation when the system became unstable.

Little had changed from the initial rollout except call volume. More and more employees were in the database, and an increasingly heavy volume of calls was coming into the telephony system. Suddenly, phone lines were down and the telephony database would freeze. Employees could not call in, and the telephony module could not transfer the call data to the time and attendance database. What had worked just fine for the first eight or nine thousand employees now routinely crashed. Field personnel were increasingly frustrated by what had become an unreliable system. Employees returned to their manual time sheets. Management was dismayed at the direction of the project rollout and upset with the vendor. The rollout was temporarily halted and some regions were taken off the new system in order for stability to be regained for the divisions that had been on the system for some time. Rumor had it that out in the field the project was now called the "time and chaos" system, instead of time and attendance.

I wrote a memo to the vendor detailing the state of affairs from a technical standpoint — how often the database had to be compacted and repaired, the occurrences of line outages, the volume of calls. I did not go into the soft-side impacts — the high level of internal frustration, the sense of being in crisis mode, and so forth — but even so the vendor contact called it a "toe-curling message." The problem rapidly ascended on the vendor side until it reached upper management.

The vendor did an outstanding job of pulling together what I would call a "Tiger Team" of its key developers and product specialists. The vendor team held daily calls with the customer team and created a test environment on their premises that replicated the customer's setup. The frailties of the telephony system were identified, the hardware was beefed up and the workload on the database was parsed out among a shared server network. The scuttlebutt internally, however, was most interesting, and provided a valuable lesson.

I had joined the team on this project long after the vendor had been selected. Apparently, the group that went through the RFP (Request For Proposal) process consisted of personnel from several areas including Finance, Human Resources Information Systems (HRIS), Payroll, Operations and IT (Information Technology). IT had apparently raised concerns about the platform on which the telephony system operated but it was eventually purchased anyway. The primary time and attendance application selected was quite capable of handling a 30,000 employee database. But the telephony piece was in a Microsoft Access database. From experience and accumulated technical expertise, IT believed Access would not be a suitable environment for handling the expected volume of data inputs. Of course, the vendor assured the customer that the system would perform as required. But we later learned that no customers that had more than 10,000 employees were on the Access based telephony module. This installation would be by far the largest database this telephony product had ever attempted to handle. *Scalability* — going from 10,000 to 30,000 employees was a significant factor that even the vendor underappreciated.

Like people, systems are capable of handling only so much. Systems have to fit. Just like people, if they can't handle the workload, they will fail and the work will not get done. On a very technical aspect of product suitability, the technical experts in IT apparently lacked sufficient influence in the company to insure that the appropriate product was purchased.

It's important to learn from this. If you are selecting a product based on technical requirements, listen to your technical experts, or require the vendor to certify or validate that their product will perform. It would be best to go on site for a demonstration to see the product up and running under the same conditions your company will impose on it. Stress test the product, take it for a test drive, see it actually do what *you* will need to have it do.

Beware of Potential Maintenance Nightmares

That's one aspect of scalability. There are others that can be more subtle, but just as deadly, or sometimes just a dead end. Marketing departments are great at identifying customer demands. Programmers can be terrific at designing solutions that answer these demands. And sales people can be geniuses at making every wish seem to come true if only the product they are selling is selected. But the old saying, "What you do for one, you must do for all," is very important in systems that are replacing manual processes for a large base of users. Managers of enterprise-size organizations need to be careful that the products they purchase were designed for an enterprise-size user community. Developers who are not designing for an environment that is constantly changing and growing — where system setup and user features must be applied to large numbers of individual users — can be maintenance nightmares. Worse yet, the demands of an enterprise-size user base can mean that certain features in the system simply cannot be turned on. The heavy burden cannot be supported at the individual user level if it is not designed appropriately.

An individual or manager's universe of employees and data in a manual system is quite limited. He or she only has access to what comes in on paper. But when these individuals become computer system users they are thrust into a much larger universe of data and functionality. In enterprise-size organizations, the data can be huge. The variety of functions needed can be vast, spanning the entire organization. Therefore, a system must have mechanisms for limiting what each individual user can see and do. If the vendor says a particular user will see only that individual's small group of employees, be able to do only what you want him to do, and have access only to certain data or reports, you must ask how this will be accomplished. If the system can analyze data and give users crucial alerts in real-time situations ask how that information will be distributed. In the military it's called logistics — acquiring and distributing supplies to the troops on the battlefield. The system must be capable of doing the same thing with the data. It must be able to identify who needs what, when, and how much, and it must provide an efficient means for delivery. In addition, it must be able to adapt to changes and work well for every business unit. Efficiencies in setup for large implementations are a must.

Let me give you an example. If you want a small group of individual users to have access to a query that shows them only the employees in a specific line of business, there should be a way to create the query once and assign it to that small user group all at once. In addition, if the line of business changes and the system data changes, the users should get the new information automatically. If a user owns access to a certain type of data — say employees in the south region — he should receive the changes to that data. If the south region acquires a new location with a new set of employees, then the definition of the "south region" changes and south region users should automatically get the newly defined south region data. You don't want to have to repeat the process all over again; the system logically should know that those users need the new information. This may have been incorporated into the system design. If not, and data set definitions change frequently, this could be a huge maintenance issue. The logistics or maintenance features built into the system — how changes are inherited or delivered — are key components of scalability.

Workload and Hardware Considerations

The last aspect of scalability we'll talk about has to do with workload and hardware. Vendors design products around assumptions about the product's utilization. Systems are built with functions and outputs — reports being a significant example of what is wanted out of time and attendance systems. Vendors offer products that are designed to operate under certain levels of demand for these functions and outputs. The customer must be able to quantify what demands for these functions and outputs will be and measure whether the product can handle the demand. No two companies are alike. What is sufficient output for one may not be sufficient for another. For labor management systems, the ability to access and use the data is crucial to enabling the technology to become more than a payroll reporting system. Some systems are remnants of applications designed basically to provide weekly or biweekly outputs. If their platform or programming has not been upgraded adequately to handle a greater demand for outputs, significant performance problems may be experienced when tasking the system to become a daily business tool. For the airline I worked for, the C.A.N. Reports worked well on the existing hardware because for payroll purposes they were only needed periodically, and for marketing, the demand was not exhaustive. If operations had decided to use the reports on a daily or hourly basis, problems most likely would have occurred.

I suggest you conduct a thorough analysis of the way your operations and support areas use workforce data before purchasing a new system Look at how needs may change and how having access to more information may actually increase the demand. The technology has two important jobs to perform — process information as it is received and manipulated by the users, and compile that information for generating tools, reports and actionable data for operational needs.

Each application relies on hardware — servers and the physical infrastructure of a networked system — to run the system. The software applications are just part of the package required. The servers are designed to handle the database, but their capacity to do so is limited. One server will support the application only to a certain size. If a potential buyer has 2500 employees, a vendor may sell the software and indicate one server will support the system. But if the buyer expects growth, he needs to know how many more employees that single server can support. Scalability in the hardware area means buying more servers or beefing up existing machines. If a user doesn't have the financial ability to purchase more servers, the system won't perform well. Scalability can be limited in terms of what is affordable and deliverable.

Chapter Ten: Mission & Communications

If the management of a company for which we are working wants its new system to help reduce labor costs, we consider this a mandate to configure the system to enable managers to do just that. "Mission-based configuration" is our terminology for a system that is set up to do more than simply pay people. It means approaching each pay rule, each user workspace, each system feature as a tool to be used to help accomplish goals. These tools need to be action-oriented. They should provide not just numbers but flags and meaningful information to be acted upon.

It makes me groan when I hear Information Systems (IS or HRIS) folks offer to spit out another report from their monstrous, data-loaded systems. Managers already have too much "information." As a society, we are trying our best to operate on the brink of information overload. One more spreadsheet filled with names and numbers isn't going to produce results. Managers still have to do something with that data — they have to interpret it in order to determine the message, figure out what should be done, and then take action. Usually, a report really doesn't provide a whole lot — they suspected they might have a problem in the first place or they wouldn't have requested the report. Providing just another spreadsheet relies too much on the abilities, alertness, time and motivation of each individual manager for something to happen. It assumes a manager will have the time to stop and analyze the report, then if he has the skills to do so, know what the appropriate action to be taken is and have the motivation to take it. In my book, that's too much assuming. A breakdown in the process is almost certain to occur a good deal of the time.

On the other hand, mission-based configuration interprets the data, identifies the action to be taken, and will go as far as management wants toward actually taking action. In the case of overtime, for example, a basic approach is for the system to be programmed to recognize when overtime is about to happen. The system might be programmed to flag those employees who are approaching a point in the current pay cycle when overtime pay soon will be incurred. A manager may be alerted to the flag because he or she routinely monitors the system for such alerts, or he can be automatically notified electronically — thus allowing him to continue his operational tasks without the burden of having to remember to check for flags.

Let's say the work week runs from Sunday to Saturday. Such a system might begin checking on Wednesday after the completion of the first shift. By that time, an employee who has already put in 30 hours, for example, is very likely to exceed 40 hours by the end of the week. The system will then check the schedule, determining how many more hours the employee is scheduled to work. Let's say it calculates that two more eight hour shifts which have been scheduled will put that employee into overtime with a total of 46 hours for the week. The system automatically generates a flag and perhaps an e-mail alert to the supervisor responsible for scheduling. The alert will draw the supervisor's attention to the probability that the employee will exceed the overtime limit if the schedule is not changed. The schedule could also be included in the alert and replacement candidates listed along with contact information. As my teenager would say, "How sweet is that?"

That's just one way to approach the overtime issue. Let's just say that the technology has been configured to prevent employees from being scheduled for more than a specified number of hours because that's the way management wants it set up. In the scenario above, an employee may not have been scheduled for more than forty hours but was called in to pick up an extra shift early in the week.

The mission should stay in the forefront of planning and setup for the new system. Scheduling software can be programmed to be an excellent manager of resources. With the right parameters and priorities set up, the system will select the best candidate to replace the overworked employee. It can determine who has the least amount of hours, who has the lowest hourly rate, who has the best skill set to match the position, who prefers to work that shift, and who can arrive at work the earliest. Mission based configuration builds business logic into the processes, replacing the idiosyncrasies of each manager's scheduling style with coherent criteria for making that business decision.

There are other ways to control the amount of overtime dollars spent.

Many times we find that compensation policies are loosely written and obligate an employer to overtime payments that are not required by law. As a result, either because those managing the programs don't understand the regulations, or because poor control exists over the way the activity is reported to Payroll, the company is simply paying too much. One example is "Guaranteed Shift" payments.

To explain this, let's go back to the Maytag repairman. He does take a day off every now and then. But invariably something breaks down at work and the maintenance man has to be called in. To reward the employee for this interruption to his day off the company agrees to pay him a minimum of at least two hours regardless of how long he actually works during that call-in shift. Let's say he comes in, pounds the furnace a couple of times with a hammer, pushes the reset button, and that old Trane unit kicks back into action. It may take him all of five minutes. Nevertheless, he was promised two hours of pay. Reporting this time as "two hours" invariably gets lumped into the regular time bucket, or "hours worked" for the week. Regular time is considered worked productive time and counts toward the calculation of overtime. But only five minutes was actually productive time that was "worked." In reality, the other hour and fifty-five minutes was "bonus time." Bonus time, like vacation or PTO hours, is not subject to the overtime requirements and does not have to be counted towards the weekly overtime limit. Nor is an employer required to pay bonus time at the overtime rate if the employee has already worked more than the limit. Let's say the maintenance man put in his 40 hours that week. The employer's obligation is to pay the worked time at the overtime rate, but the bonus time can be paid at the straight base rate, saving the employer considerably on the cost of the hour and fifty-five minute portion.

An automated time and attendance system can be configured to allocate these hours to the productive (OT) and nonproductive (non-OT) buckets. Overtime is reduced. The company saves. The worker still gets a bonus payment. The mission is accomplished.

The Need to Run in Parallel

Having a mission usually means things will change. But some things must stay the same. Testing is vitally important to insure that what needs to remain constant does so. This means a parallel test is in order.

What is a parallel? No, it's not a term referring to your high school geometry class, and it has nothing to do with your driver's test. (Remember parallel parking?) Parallel testing, running the old and new systems side by side, is a must when moving to any type of new system, especially when it involves employee pay. This insures that the new system mimics the old — and that it calculates time and benefits correctly.

There are various ways to accomplish this, and I'd like to share some things we've learned in doing so. Different degrees of parallel testing exist. The most extensive involves a complete end-to-end dual run of the new system and the old — whether the old system is a completely manual, paper process or one that involves an older automated technology. Employees, managers, system administrators and technical support personnel are involved.

I usually recommend selecting a small group of employees as a pilot group. Ideally, this group will represent a cross section of employee types and lines of business in order to test as much as possible. The pilot is not expected to be a 100% test of the new system. Rather, it is the first phase of the complete end-to-end testing. In organizations with big employee populations or covering a large geographic area, management may chose to roll out the new system based on a phased timetable since in complex organizations it can be difficult to orchestrate the training, support and logistics of an all-out "flip the switch" rollout.

During the parallel period, employees record their activity in both systems, (hopefully) creating identical data. Supervisors review and approve both systems. Related databases interface and update background data as normal, and everyone runs through the normal paces in terms of completing the reporting and processing cycle.

Ideally, a parallel will run for two pay cycles. The first pay cycle is often practice, or a warm up. It will generally have less than 100% participation. The data employed may not be identical to that used in the current system. The second period is a truer parallel, allowing the project team to review the results, tweak the new system and test the results. During the second period, the new system should generate output that's closely equivalent to the old system's.

It should be noted that this type of parallel is time-consuming and bothersome to personnel and not the most popular option in most field locations — unless the field is accustomed to corporate initiatives that are not well planned and prone to problems. In that case, the field may be the side rallying for a full system-proving period before a transition to a new system.

A less extensive parallel can be undertaken by relying on a "pilot" program to prove the system before "go live" rollout begins. In this case, the company can execute a mock parallel. Mock parallels take actual-time data from the old system and input it into the new system for a pay cycle. The only difference is that the data is put into the system via a mechanized process (import) or manually by project team members after the parallel timeframe is actually complete instead of by employees in real time.

The benefits of this type of parallel process are twofold. There is less disruption in the field, and there's a longer reaction time since historical data can be input from any time period and evaluated without the rush of trying to obtain results before the next parallel period has ended. In addition, those responsible for processing the live payroll can complete that work and then focus on the new system without having to process both in relative real time. The disadvantage to this type of parallel is that it's not a true test of the input processes or the human element. Employee proficiency in using the system will not have been tested. Often, adjustments and manipulations taking place in the old system are whitewashed, eliminating the opportunity to shake out issues before going live. In addition, the mock parallel requires more involvement of the project team and may require some programming to simulate or automate the flow of data.

Which method of parallel testing and proving you decide on depends on your confidence in the survey and system configuration processes because part of what you are proving is that everything needed has been

Guidelines for parallel surveys

1. Know what you want to find out about or test
2. Ask questions that require a quantifiable answers, i.e., answers that give you measurements.
3. Ask yes-or-no questions whenever possible, but only if you plan to do something as a result of what you learn.
4. Ask open-ended questions, but be prepared to have to read all the answers and somehow compile them.
5. Have the respondents identify themselves. It's important to know the source of the answers.
6. Offer an incentive to participants if possible in order to encourage feedback.
7. Publicize the results and tell participants how the information was used to improve the system. Let them know it mattered that they spent time completing the survey and participating in the parallel.
8. Send out the survey before the parallel so they will know what to expect. Prompt participants to complete the survey as soon as possible.
9. Evaluate the responses for:
     a. Cost implications
     b. Consistency with the overall vision and scope
     c. Problems that result from related systems or processes and are not limited to, or originating from, the current system under review.
     d. Short term versus long term issues and goals
10. Have an escalation plan to route problems uncovered in related systems to the appropriate business owners who can resolve those issues.
11. Consider having participants provide feedback again after they have used the system for a longer period of time. Determine if their responses changed over time and why.
12. Archive the data, and review it later for "Lessons Learned" for future projects.

designed into the system. It also depends on how much practice you think everyone needs with the new system before you depend on it for payroll and credible data capture. This is where the human element plays a large role in parallel testing. If survey respondents did not answer honestly or completely, or if configuration analysts did not accurately understand the needs and did not translate them into appropriate system settings as a result, there will be gaps in the processes and errors in the payroll outputs. Further, it's important to keep in mind when planning is done that the new system will be a workforce management technology tool in addition to a payroll processing system. This is something that's almost impossible to mimic without a parallel that involves users and managers in real-time. Management tool elements aren't so much about data as they are about data flow, timing, access, the parsing of data and actions in real time. However, the tool element can be proven gradually as users gain familiarity with the system and expectations grow.

Insuring Actionable Feedback

Another important element of the parallel process is feedback. There is feedback, and then there is "feedback." Don't think that simply taking complaint calls means you are getting the feedback you need. Hoping the phone doesn't ring during the parallel and thinking that means you got good feedback isn't "feedback," either. Parallel feedback is a measurement of how things are working. Notice I said "measurement" and not "opinion." The purpose of gathering feedback isn't to placate participants who weren't happy about having to participate in a parallel, or who did not feel involved in the implementation process. Feedback is a tool to insure the system is working effectively. Getting good information of this type requires planning.

I recall a TV show, or maybe it was a movie, in which a young lawyer was being scolded for asking the wrong question in court. The older, wiser attorney told him "never ask a question you don't know the answer to." For our purposes, we should modify that advice to "never ask a question that doesn't have a system-specific purpose." In other words, it's important to ask questions whose answers may result in a potential change to the system or processes. If you don't intend to change a particular aspect, you don't really need to ask about it. It may be interesting to know if users like the new system in general and whether they find it easy to use. But ask yourself, would such vague feedback prompt the implementation team to change anything?

Be specific in a way that can be measured. It may be useful to find out such things as, "Were there errors in calculating hours or computing the proper net pay?" Answers to this could identify users who had to manipulate the system to make it work, or who had to correct problems outside the tested system.

The answer to, "Were you able to make changes to the data that you normally edit?" could alert you to problems with the user's access profile. "Were you able to toggle between modules within 30 seconds or less?" can measure the expected wait time that results from the current system infrastructure of servers, band width, processing speed, and so forth.

Another might be: "Did you contact customer support for help? If so, please describe the issue, how many customer support representatives handled your call, and how long it took for customer support to resolve your issue." This question will reveal how effective training was for both users and support personnel. Common problems might prompt a revision to a section of training material. NOTE: If your organization has a sophisticated problem tracking system for customer IT support, query that database for feedback on how the system is working.

This may be a good time to give a little pep talk I often give customers and prospective clients. A time and attendance project will likely be the most *highly visible project* they will ever undertake. No other system touches every employee every day. Every supervisor will be involved. The system will involve a significant investment of the company's money. If something goes wrong with the system, everyone will know it. Employees are not patient about payroll errors and management will not be supportive if the objectives are not met or their personnel are significantly inconvenienced or distracted from business activities. All this is why it's important to invest the time and the proper resources to plan effectively and manage this project carefully. It's often said and probably true that for each hour spent in the planning phase, many hours are saved in implementation phase and in system rework.

Selling the Benefits of the New System

Without a doubt, the new system will bring changes that represent benefits to the company and "takeaways" to the employee. But a well-designed system will also deliver benefits to employees and changes that may represent costs to the company in terms of control and infrastructure. A good way to communicate the changes is to put them in terms of a balance sheet showing pros and cons to both company and employee. For example, improving the company's ability to control overtime expenses will reduce some hourly employees' earnings. On the other hand, the reduced cost due to less overtime will result from equalizing hours among the staff, thereby increasing the earnings of those who will now get more hours. It will also increase the quality of life for those who will have to work less overtime. In addition, a reduced overtime expense may translate to more retained earnings and potentially higher base pay rates.

Another example is the elimination of pay program stacking. This control mechanism benefits the company with lower labor costs per hour. While it will result in a reduction in pay for those who enjoyed or engineered a lucrative alignment of their payroll stars, it also demonstrates to employees that their employer is spending its hard-earned revenue wisely and getting smart about spending. Just ask a laid-off or downsized laborer if they'd prefer less pay to no pay. This type of line item on the balance sheets assumes employees understand the value of long-term strategic financial planning. If it doesn't impress the more shortsighted wage earner, an entry opposite this on the balance sheet might be an unrelated benefit such as employee self-service or flex scheduling. Remember the benefits of employee involvement and empowerment and relationships with bosses.

The point of such a balance sheet is to articulate to the workforce the impact the new system will have on them and their employer. Rest assured, nothing will go unnoticed, so it's best to get ahead of the conversation and put coming changes in the right perspective.

Maintaining Morale During the Changeover

People are naturally resistant to change, which is why obtaining buy-in from all levels of personnel will be important to the success of the new system. The new technology can result in significant changes in processes, responsibilities and controls, and it can result in much higher visibility of individual and group performance levels and activities. The high profile of the implementation of such a system demands a good communication plan. Include a clear connection to corporate goals and an indication of strong executive support for the system. The goals should be to create positive acceptance of the new system and its benefits and to clearly communicate the reasons behind its implementation along with the new policies and processes that are part of it. This is the key to obtaining a good response to the changes.

If it's true that employees will be adversely affected by the new system in any way, do not ignore or attempt to sidestep this. A reduction in net pay won't be overlooked by employees. If an individual doesn't happen to notice, coworkers will be certain to clue that person in. Plan to communicate to managers, supervisors and employees why these changes are necessary. There is a benefit to the change — share it or at least be honest about the implications.

In today's economy, employees are cognizant of the fact that it's a competitive marketplace. Every day brings news of layoffs and plant closings and unions and employee groups accepting pay cuts or reduced benefits. Unhealthy companies currently are struggling to become financially viable. If, for example, reducing overtime expenses is a financial objective to make the company more profitable — explain why that's a good thing to employees. The fact is that it's better to have a job that offers less overtime than to have no job at all. If an automated scheduling system will improve staffing and result in higher customer satisfaction — connect the dots between happier customers, more revenue and employee job security. Don't expect front line management to articulate these issues. This should come directly from the top and be reinforced by everyone on down the line.

If your employees don't know how competitive your industry is, what kinds of concessions others have accepted and where the future lies if changes aren't made then it's time to educate the workforce and to put the new technology into perspective.

Project Champions

As touched upon earlier, the implementation of a time and attendance system is a highly visible activity. Managers and employees at all levels will be talking about the changes. Those leading the project should be engaged in the conversation and working to direct sentiment in favor of the initiative and new ways of doing business. This is why the communications plan also should include a cadre of Project Champions who are fully versed in the business rationale for the changes. They need to be kept up to date at all times on the progress of system implementation and be the first to receive communications as they are distributed throughout the organization. A clear expectation should be that these individuals will represent the project in a positive light and work to minimize negative talk or grumbling among their team members. They are also a source of feedback to the project sponsors so that concerns from the workforce can be addressed effectively.

The communications plan should be bi-directional. Politicians have perfected the use of Project Champions, whom they call "front men," and arm them with talking points to carry the torch for the issue at hand. These are hand picked individuals, so keep in mind that titles or positions in the organizational hierarchy are not the only factors to consider. Those chosen need to be the best individuals to carry the message and must understand the importance of supporting the party line. They need to be credible and enthusiastic. Project Champions must be pro-active. They should not wait to hear negative rumblings, but rather should at each opportunity take whatever the issue might be to the staff. Project Champions state the vision of the new system in terms employees can understand by relating it to issues and concerns people have on their minds.

Obviously, Project Champions need to consider the implications of project decisions and changes and be able to anticipate how the workforce will react. Ideal Project Champions contribute by submitting their concerns and suggestions about the system. It's a job, and a job description with clear expectations should be created for these leaders. Knowing exactly what they will be expected to do and when and how they will do it will help them perform that job well.

Gauging Success and Attitudes

Finally, some mechanism should be in place for gauging the success of these project representatives. This might be done, for example, through spot checks of how the project is perceived in the field by speaking with individuals during various phases of the project implementation, who are completely uninvolved in the project. Secretaries and administrative assistants can be good barometers of employee reaction if they are in positions to hear what's going on.

A WMT system can help to boost morale and help keep employees from jumping ship, or it can cause a lot of grumbling and a negative atmosphere if it isn't sold correctly during the implementation phase. It's important to realize that both the upside and the downside are in the hands of those who design and install the system. I suggest goals be set to use the system to improve employee retention, if that's an issue. A strategy and specific actions also ought to be identified and implemented to keep everyone in the loop and things on a positive note while the new system goes into effect.

Keep in mind that change is tough for most people. What makes it more difficult is not knowing what to expect — what's on the other side. Plan for the communication plan to evolve as the system is rolled out and to incorporate positive feedback and success stories from those operational areas that are enjoying its benefits and rewards. If certain areas had difficulty, highlight how those difficulties have been overcome and how the team is planning on avoiding those for future groups that will come on board. Praise your project team and let the field know how hard they are working to make this a good system for the organization.

Part Four
Getting from Concept to Project:
Finding a Solution
Selling it to Decision Markers
Designing the System for Success

Chapter Eleven: The Need for a Business Case

Before we get started on this section, let me give anyone who has read this book from the beginning a heads up. Every now and then you are going to come upon something that may cause you to think, "Gosh, didn't I read something similar already?"

Well, yes, you probably did. And there's a reason. Some of those who purchase this book may simply flip through the first part and not begin reading in earnest until they reach this point. They may already be aware what Workforce Management Technology (WMT) can do and may be more interested in how their company or organization can get it.

This section is meant to:

1.   Help anyone serious about upgrading to a state of the art system develop a business case to present to top management.

2.   Guide you in evaluating your business relative to the unique aspects of this technology.

3.   Explain what it will take to insure that the system successfully delivers improvements to the organization and supports the business mission.

Now, let's get started.

Why a Business Case?

The business case seeks to answer the question, does a state of the art Workforce Management Technology (WMT) system make sense for your company? Will the payback be there? Will it meet the business needs and fit the culture of your company? After all, if you pay for a powerful system but have to implement in a way that doesn't employ all the technology purchased, or if you cannot support the system, money will have been poured down the drain.

Today's business environment places ongoing pressure on companies to improve efficiency, timeliness and quality and to reduce operating expenses. Simultaneously, an organization may be struggling to meet the demands of investors and customers, to abide by government regulations and to get the job done in an ever more challenging labor market. To address the challenges, executive and middle management must maintain, improve and grow the business using carefully crafted strategies that insure the organization not only survives but prospers.

Given this backdrop, new initiatives must make good business sense. At minimum, the cost of a project and the staff time commitment required must not jeopardize productivity and the volume of output needed to maintain status quo. Funds for special projects are limited in most organizations. Many proposed undertakings have merit, but not every one can be supported. Ideally, the investment should deliver improvements in operations and help in the effort to reduce expenses.

The Value of a Business Case

A well-written business case can make or break a project. When the facts and pertinent information are laid out in a compelling way, a company's executives will have a relatively easy time making an appropriate decision and justifying funding. Even so, proposals often are made without much documentation or rationale to support them. This can be a huge mistake. Managers are accountable for the decisions they make, particularly when a significant investment is involved. No wonder some proposals are rejected and others simply stall and eventually die on the vine.

Laying The Groundwork

Developing a successful business case is a process that requires those charged with it to wear many hats, including those of teacher, salesman, analyst, organizer, problem solver, champion and, with luck and hard work, hero. The best approach I've found is to tackle the job as though selling to another business — not to the familiar guys upstairs who ride the same elevator every day. Most successful salespeople do a good deal of homework before they even make a call. They know how important it is to thoroughly understand an organization and to identify where and how the product they have to sell might fit. Labor management technology can answer many issues concerning costs, staffing, productivity, risk and revenue. To maximize the likelihood of making a sale, the problems recognized as those causing the most acute pain in an organization, or the challenges representing the biggest opportunities, must be identified. This is step one.

Next is to articulate these problems relative to workforce management technology. Why? Because you want people nodding their heads. Perhaps the most crucial factor in gaining support for your business case is an audience that recognizes the problems you believe WMT can solve. When you make your case, it shouldn't be the first time the issues come to the attention of the audience. Imagine walking into the CFO's office and saying, "Mike, I've got a business case here that will solve our attendance problems" when Mike isn't aware of any significant attendance problems. You want your business case to stand out as the savior and solution in a cacophony of communications about the issue.

If an issue isn't already front and center, you might start out by having informal conversations about it and sharing with your manager what you know, along with possible solutions. Get him or her energized about the idea that your area may be able to deliver a solution. Your job is to familiarize and educate management about what they should know about the problem. If you do not have a routine meeting with higher ups, ask for opportunities to present introductory information up the ladder. Managers at the top must understand the problem and how not addressing it could prevent them from reaching important goals. If management does not accept that a problem exists, and if they don't understand the proposed solution, your proposal may languish forever in limbo or be rejected without comment.

Don't limit your conversations to upper management. A dialog with all those affected by the project should start at the beginning of the process. This will help build a sense of being in the loop on something important among potential supporters. Be sure to conduct these chats as two-way conversations — their perspective may give valuable information you hadn't considered. You certainly don't want to overlook anything, or to make inaccurate assumptions.

Where Does the Business Case Fit in the Project Investment Life Cycle?

```
Project Investment Life Cycle (PILC)

1. Idea Management
2. Project Request
3. Feasibility Study
4. Business Requirements
5. >> Business Case with ROI
6. Funding Approval
7. Project Charter
8. Activity Based Work Breakdown Structure Development
```

The exhibit above shows the flow of a project from the inception of an idea to the beginning of the implementation of the project. Some ideas will never evolve past the concept phase. Others will be retired when a project request is rejected. Some of the early phases may be somewhat informal and involve very few individuals until something formal is approved, such as a go-ahead to develop a business case.

You may find the complexity of this process and its formality strange. Most organizations are familiar with System Development Life Cycles (SDLC) for systems development. New regulatory guidelines and the need for accountability have caused organizations to formalize internal processes for the selection of projects, which now more than ever before need to be based on clearly defined corporate priorities and evaluated according to their appropriateness in this regard. This new process is known as the Project Investment Life Cycle (PILC) and is a methodology for the examination of issues to insure decision makers make well-grounded selections.

You might look at preparing a business case as you would putting together a resume for a job because, in a sense, a business case is your project's resume. The project is a candidate — a suitor vying for a role in the organization. Your project will be competing with other candidates for acceptance. Careful consideration needs to be given to how the project stacks up against other potential initiatives that those in upper management may be considering. Every project that comes along cannot be funded, and it would be foolhardy to spread people who will be doing the implementation too thinly.

**The Business Case includes
numerous informational areas:**

• Executive Summary	• Manpower Needs
• Purpose	• Costs and Timeframe
• Background	• Business Risks
• Project Officers	• Project Risks
• Business Requirements:	• Alternatives
- Strategic	• Economic Assessment:
- Operational	- Costs and Cashflows
• Justifications	- ROI (NPV/MIRR)
• Project Goals/Objectives	- Funding Source
• Scope of Project	• Recommendation

The Business Case includes numerous informational areas. These areas are summarized above. A great deal is on the list. It needs to be done correctly, with all areas covered. What's unique about WMT systems is that the current systems and processes in place may not be well understood or appreciated. Some of these subject areas may be more difficult to develop than you might expect.

The Process of Developing a Business Case

Once you get the nod to proceed with your suggestion, the place to start is by examining what the company is experiencing today. The first step is to conduct a Feasibility Survey. Such a survey consists of high-level discussion about problems, opportunities, directives and constraints related to a system, or lack of a system, in the organization. The survey helps an organization determine if there truly is a business need and if it is severe enough that a resolution is required. Having the results of the survey will also provide important information to be used in system planning and for development of specifications for the purchase of software and hardware to address the needs.

The important thing about a Feasibility Study is that it screens out issues and problems that are not the result of a system or process. It begins to focus on the real problems rather than the symptoms of problems. The Feasibility Study should provide the first indication that a solution truly addresses the problem from a high level.

The survey reviews issues related to performance, information management, economics, controls, efficiencies and services to the internal and external customers of that system. The study also identifies potential solutions and suggests approaches that may address the existing issues.

After Feasibility is Determined

Once a Feasibility Survey has been completed and proves there is a rationale for finding a better solution to a problem that exists, the next step is to do a detailed System Study. This analysis involves a detailed examination of the current system and processes. Conducting a System Study involves reviewing all of the materials, systems, processes and personnel involved in the current situation. Legacy systems and manual processes are identified, described and measured. Problems and opportunities are isolated through root-cause analyses, the process of which is discussed below. The key is to focus on "what is" rather than spending time and energy at this point on potential solutions. This helps assure that solutions developed later are not Band-Aids placed on symptoms.

The Right Questions to Ask

Some of the questions to ask and answer in your analysis are:

"What systems and processes are in place and how do they work today?"
"Who is involved?"
"What are the problems and short comings?"
"What is the cause?"

217

"Is anything else broken?"

"What else should it be doing?"

"What is the impact of this problem?"

"Where is the company headed? What are some of the larger issues at play internally?"

"What are the possible solutions?"

"Can the organization support the solution?"

This process is similar to what's used in Six Sigma root cause analysis. The question "Why?" is asked at least five times until the root cause of a problem is identified. You might think of it as peeling away the layers of an onion. For example, a capillary tube soldered to a bellow leaks:

- Why does it leak?
  The welding does not seal properly.
- Why doesn't it seal properly?
  There is a deposit of a material inside the capillary tube.
- Why is a deposit on the inside the capillary tube?
  Washing the tube did not clean it.
- Why did washing not clean it?
  The detergent used was not working effectively.
- Why did the detergent not work effectively?
  The detergent formula was not effective on this particular type of deposit.

This allows a solution that will truly solve the problem to be imposed — using a detergent that will work.

The Phases & Deliverables of Discovery & Analysis

The deliverables produced from the System Study may include a Summary Analysis of the current systems, a Recommendation for Approach explaining how the organization should plan to acquire a solution, and possibly a Survey or Questionnaire based on the findings to assist in the next phase of the development of the Business Case. The survey's outputs ocus on "what is" and are not a detailed list of new requirements. The survey's purpose is to focus the next steps needed to find the solution to the real problems.

Once the System Study is evaluated and the approach is confirmed, next comes a Requirements Analysis. The purpose of this step is to document all the features and functions that will be required of the new solution. These include:

1. Existing functionality that must be maintained
2. Features that will address the problems identified in the System Study
3. New capabilities that will help the organization meet its strategic goals
4. Attractive features that are not required and will not justify additional expense, but if offered as part of the package offer desirable capabilities

The Requirements Analysis has a functional focus. It is not the same as a Technical Specification used to design a system, detailing specific system components. At the functional level the company understands what is needed but is not specifying *how* it will be accomplished. The different vendors will provide the detail on how their product delivers the most viable solutions. The Requirements Analysis prioritizes the needs and assists in evaluating costs against these needs. It helps the company evaluate where they get the most bang for the buck.

The outcome of the Requirements Analysis is the development of the Request for Proposal (RFP), or Request for Quote (RFQ). Either one of these documents can be delivered to vendors who in turn submit their bids for consideration. The RFP/RFQ creates a framework that each vendor must use to present products and solutions. This will result in a consistent format of responses to the same set of requirements from different potential vendors, making it easier to compare "apples to apples." In the same way, you will drive the focus of the presentation. It gives prospective vendors the opportunity to highlight their most relevant features showing the customer which offers the best fit when measured against your needs. Organizations that don't control the proposal process and don't precede it with an independent evaluation of their own requirements can be easily distracted by the bells and whistles of vendor demonstrations and proposals. The result may be that the vendor proposals become the "requirements" and a customer's choice will be diverted by features that may or may not end up delivering a cost-effective impact on an organization's actual problems and needs.

The final phase is the Decision Analysis. This effort is intended to determine the best approach (e.g. purchase a new system or fix existing processes) and assess options (e.g. evaluate vendor proposals, study new processes, and so forth) to address identified problems. This is where the culmination of all of the research, internal discussions, vendor demonstrations and customer referrals — and the cost and return on investment

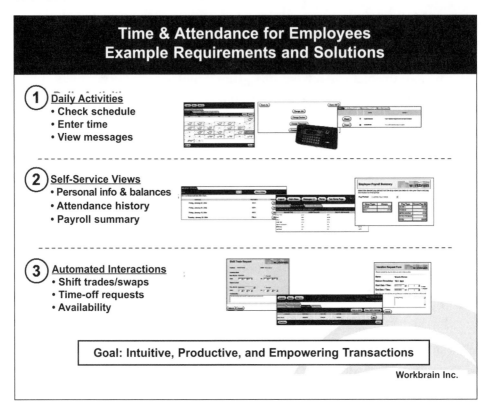

analyses — take the form of a recommendation, which is a request for approval to make a selection of a vendor and a product to move the company forward.

Developing a Document

The time is near to present the recommendations to the decision makers. The next step is to develop a document to support your proposal that contains all the information that management needs to approve the project. This will contain the detailed information gathered, analyzed and organized, showing an awareness of the benefits, impacts, risks, assumptions and financial costs. In doing so, it will demonstrate how the solution is in sync with the organization's mission.

The purpose of this document is to define what is being proposed to support and improve the business in a way that will make a compelling argument for approval of the proposal. This document, the Business Case, can be considered a contract with the organization that will provide direction and parameters for implementation of the system.

Why this Process Makes Sense

The process described above — beginning several sections back — may be somewhat foreign to you or it may not fit the approach that is commonly taken at your organization. It may seem very formal and involved. There are a number of steps to be taken, many documents to prepare, people to involve, and a good deal of critical thinking to be done. But don't let that deter you. If this is a new concept here are some reasons to consider introducing it to your organization:

1. An approach designed around thorough discovery and analysis insures real problems are identified and decisions are in line with corporate objectives.
2. The approach addresses concerns surrounding accountability and protects decision-makers from taking on inappropriate, risky projects.

3. The detail required will cover all the bases, allowing indecision due to a lack of information or the absence of proper assessment of alternatives to be avoided.

4. A document-driven approach provides a history of all the analysis and it binds participants to the decisions ensuring continuity and consensus.

5. A professional looking presentation will enhance credibility and show decision makers what they can expect when the project reaches execution.

6. By following this approach, you may introduce a methodology that will take hold in your organization and elevate the manner in which such projects are considered.

7. You are competing against other initiatives and demands for corporate resources and manpower, and you want to win. A thoughtful and thorough approach such as this has the potential to reflect well on you.

Business Case Development is a Team Effort

A good business case is generally the result of a team effort. At the outset of a study we like to get all the stakeholders and prospective team members together in a room and introduce them to the project. This might include IT, Payroll, Accounting, and Operations. What we don't want are conflicting agendas in the various corporate fiefdoms. It's important for everyone to be on the same page and in agreement about where we are headed and want to arrive. We will examine the reason or reasons a hard look is being taken at this new technology and raise the question, what does each area want to get out of the effort?

This meeting is an opportunity to bring everyone into consensus in order to avoid conflicts down the road. If things go as they should, we will come out of it with everyone in agreement about the issues and their approximate order of priority. It's also important to identify who is going to lead the project and what the overriding goal is.

We try to anticipate objections some might raise about a new system and to answer as many of these as possible before they become obstacles. What we're doing falls into the area of change management and managing perceptions. After all, things will be different once the new system goes in.

Since there will always be those who are resistant to change, it doesn't hurt to do a little proactive public relations. In fact, once you are further along and have a clear picture of what the new system will entail, we will develop a full blown communications plan and identify champions whose job it will be to communicate to others about the new system. More was said on this in a previous chapter.

For instance, people should know that the new system will bring consistency, that everyone will be treated the same and in a fair way. The new system will also introduce more efficient and accurate processes. People will have more information available to them and this will be available in real time. They won't have to wait to get answers because they will be able to access certain data themselves. They'll be able to make better decisions and work smarter.

Team Roles & Responsibilities

The group of individuals who will work on the Business Case should include the Project Sponsor, the eventual Business Owner of the new system, the Project Manager and the Product Manager. The Sponsor needs to be a high-level, primary stake holder who is most concerned with the eventual outcomes of the project and the systems to be implemented. The Sponsor may be someone in a position to expect the greatest benefit from the improvements. As such, he or she should provide direction and set priorities throughout the development of the proposal and ultimately the project. The Sponsor should also be expected to allocate the needed resources and insure the project receives ample support throughout the organization. The Sponsor may be less involved on a day-to-day basis but has to be available when needed to resolve conflicts and to insure the project succeeds.

The Business Owner is the individual who will lead the area that will eventually take ownership of the new system and be responsible for its care and feeding. For a WMT system, the Business Owner is often the

Payroll Manager or HRIS Director. The Business Owner is often responsible for the current system and processes and is integral in understanding how the change to the new system must occur.

The Project Manager owns the task of leading the project from inception to completion. Once the business case has been approved, the Project Manager will shepherd the project from the conceptual stage through design, testing and training to delivery. He or she will use the business case in the development of the charter, scope and schedule of the project, and will rely on its contents to provide the vision of what is to be accomplished.

Finally, the Product Manager should play a role in the development of the business case, taking the lead in addressing issues that pertain specifically to the vendor and system or systems to be purchased. This individual is most likely to be in tune with how the proposed solutions will fit within the existing infrastructure and be aware of prerequisites that must be in place before change can occur.

The leaders who form this core group need to control the development of the Business Case and, upon its approval, lead the project. They are the primary decision-makers but do not comprise the entire task force. They represent their respective areas and serve as conduits between the business units and the other team members for the concerns and issues that may surround the proposal. Having them develop the Business Case and be in charge of the project will help insure continuity, so that the original vision for the new system will be maintained. This will also involve the eventual owners, users and caretakers of the system early in the selection and design process, thus avoiding the potential of a disconnect between those who "buy" the system and those who must "live with" the system. You might think of it as buying a house. Would it make sense to have your brother and your sister-in-law select a house for you to live in?

Casting: Involve All the Right Players

The document impacts several functional areas of an organization, some at a fairly sophisticated level. The project initiator may hail from the Payroll or HR area but the gathering of information will likely involve operations, finance and information systems (IS) among others. If those on the Business Case development team neither know nor have access to the information needed from their area, they need to get the right people involved. This may mean bringing on an outside consultant who has the experience and technical skills to assemble the information and conduct the analysis. Mike King, who has written a book on this topic, explains that it's a common mistake for organizations to "dumb down" the information being presented. He believes it is the responsibility of executive managers and the proposal team to educate themselves about the complexities in order to insure the survival and prosperity of the organization.

An inclination to simplify the Business Case may stem from a fear the document itself will be too overwhelming, too intimidating to complete, too difficult to understand, or that delving deeply into the data and an analysis of it will take too much time. This may come from a concern that a great deal of detail will overcomplicate the project and makes mountains out of molehills. In some cases this may be true. What's important, however, is not to gloss over disturbing details or to brush past difficult questions. If you can't answer the tough ones now and don't invest the time to assess the impact of disturbing trends, do you really have what's needed to justify and undertake the project?

The purpose of the Business Case is to define the problem, recommend and justify a solution, and assess the potential impact of all the possible alternatives, including the option of doing nothing. The Business Case will answer, "How much?" "Who?" "When?" and "With what result?" for each scenario. A team representing a cross-section of business areas and expertise can insure the best answers to these questions.

Internal versus External Subject Matter Experts

It will probably make sense to involve an expert from outside the organization. Time is one of the benefits of this. Internal resource personnel already have full-time jobs. Adding the development of a Business Case to their plate not only will tax them, it's likely to slow things down or prevent important tasks from getting adequate attention. Moreover, internal resources may lack expertise in important areas. Getting up to speed will take even more time and effort. Outside consultants, on the other hand, can be fully dedicated to the project. Their time will be efficiently spent because they will not be distracted by day-to-day business issues. They bring experience, knowledge and training on the technology that can greatly accelerate the process. They will be in position to understand which issues are most critical, quickly see potential opportunities, and understand timetables and client expectations. And very important, they can compare what they know from prior projects to the information gathered in yours to readily spot omissions as well as gauge how reasonable the data appears. There's almost no doubt an external subject matter expert will make the process happen faster, with fewer hiccups, and the end result will likely be more thorough.

An important differentiator between internal and external subject matter experts lies in the area of expertise. An internal resource will likely be an expert when it comes to the business. He or she knows who to go to and how things work. He can maneuver effectively within the organization, garner cooperation and encourage collaboration and openness. It is quite likely, however, he will lack technical expertise on WMT technology. After all, it is still new and rapidly developing. If the company is in the investigative stage, it's likely he hasn't had his hands on it yet — unless he's a new hire from somewhere else that has a state of the art system. However, by the time the new system is installed that system may be a version or two behind.

A good external consultant can anticipate and project how business requirements can be satisfied by the technology. Based on experience, he or she should be able to uncover requirements or glitches that may create critical issues or significant obstacles. The term "best practices" is somewhat overused in today's business conversations. Nevertheless, we all know how valuable going straight to a best practice is, as opposed to stumbling through a rugged learning curve. Experienced consultants advise their partners on appropriate strategies and direct the course of the discovery process in developing the Business Case. Knowing the destination helps them lay out the best course to get there.

The management of some companies often assumes these projects will not require outside assistance. This may stem in part from a lack of understanding both of the technology and of the tremendous change that's about to occur. In the past, management may not have paid much attention to managing labor expenses or to what, for example, goes into getting payroll done. It just seems to happen week in and week out, fostering a misconception that a time and attendance project will fall into the same category. What it comes down to is that management doesn't know what they don't know. Not until an implementation has stalled or targets have been missed will they begin to see that the internal resources tasked with the conversion would have benefited from the experience and expertise of outside help.

There's something else. An internal, do-it-yourself approach breeds an informal attitude that may result in a decision not to go to the trouble of developing a formal Business Case and request for approval. One result of this we've seen has been that many initiators have had difficulty in getting projects off the ground. The project simply goes nowhere. The best advice is not to give in to the temptation to take the "easy way." Assemble a formal, well-represented proposal team and put forth the effort to develop a document.

Taking a Project to a Higher Level

An external consultant can provide the critical expertise and perspective necessary to build a Business Case that accurately connects the system to the high level benefits executive-level decision makers care about. Such a consultant's participation can increase the credibility of assertions made in a Business Case, particularly when the consultant has an extensive and impressive background with the technology.

One of the current trends in the IT market is for companies to treat every IT related project the same. More and more companies have a tendency to undertake these projects in house. In line with this is the trend to extend "in house" to include engaging resources only through Tier 1 or partner IT resource outfits. These organizations act as temp agencies and generally provide resources for networking, data center, specific pro-gramming needs, and off-hours (overnight and weekend) support as well as temporary technical support. Such technical resource needs are well suited to this business model, and IT sourcing firms have rosters of qual-ified personnel to fill these needs. But you might also say that such resources are a basic commodity. By definition an individual must have a specific skill set and be able to perform a closely defined set of tasks. Typically, such individuals are assigned to the same job over and over at different customer locations.

On the other hand, Workforce Management Technology subject matter experts are far from "commodity" resources. No two WMT projects will ever be the same because the needs of almost every business, as well the strategic goals of most organizations, are almost certain to be different. These resources must be functional experts and have a broad range of skills and industry experience.

Every day I see advertisements from IT headhunters looking for appli-cation-specific resources as though having "Product A" on one's resume automatically qualifies an individual for a job in Workforce Management Technology. But that is not the case. In today's business environment where embellishment is king and former employers will provide little more than name, job title and employment dates — for fear of the legal implications of a negative referral — employers who seek resources in this manner are going to get what they pay for, and probably less.

A very important role an external consultant plays is that of translator. As with any highly specialized area, a special language is spoken that must be understood, articulated clearly and translated for those who are not experts in the field but need to understand the ins and outs and impli-cations. A professional consultant can help the organization learn this new language and introduce participants and decision-makers to the new inventory of systems and tools. Because a successful Business Case will be the foundation for the next steps in the project, having such things accu-rately depicted insures there will be a match between the company's needs and the selected systems.

External consultants who operate as part of a firm that specializes in workforce management systems are even better additions to the team than independent (sole operator) consultants. Engaging resources who work with a group of WMT specialists will provide continuity to the project as it progresses. Looking at the need for outside resources as an end-to-end solution will translate into ensuring that the project history is well understood and the objectives that are identified at inception carry through to the roll-out. Changing teams or injecting unrelated "newbies" into the project midstream means more ramp up time, the potential for oversights and the possible redirection of crucial system plans. Engaging a team makes the resources more vested in the project outcomes, insures coverage during absences or vacations and provides an added component of collaboration. Consultants who know they are there for the life of the project and understand they will be handing off specialized tasks to the team members take care to keep the project team on course and to impart project knowledge because they are obligated to pass it along to their cohorts. Unlike what may be the case with internal project managers, they have few competing distractions and priorities. Their mission is to implement according to The Plan, and they are more mindful of issues, bottlenecks, and the customer's expectations. Given the pace of growth and change in WMT, it is virtually impossible to know it all. So a good consultant networks with other experts in the field and mentors his team. The job requires having or finding the answers and solving problems. If a good consultant doesn't know an answer, he will know someone who does. It makes sense to take advantage of this.

Speaking the Same Language is Critical

I have been involved in projects for which the external consultant wasn't called in until after the vendor and product had been selected. In more than one instance, the customer and vendor had not communicated effectively on needs and functionality. Apples and oranges had been discussed, misunderstood and misconstrued. But neither party recognized the disconnect until I started looking at the designs and the system which had been purchased.

Here's an example. One of my customers that handled the early phases of a WMT project in-house wanted labor level validation. This means the general ledger (GL) account hierarchy needed to be enforced within the time and attendance system. In plain English that means an employee working as a RN should not be able to punch in as working in the housekeeping department. RNs are in nursing — always, no exceptions. This requirement was in the Request for Proposal (RFP). The vendor sales team responded that their product would "validate labor levels." So, "we need labor level validation" was responded to with "we offer labor level validation," except this wasn't exactly true, at least not in the way the customer expected. The system would indeed "validate" the labor level entry. If "1234 — Housekeeping" wasn't a valid labor level entry, it would be disallowed. But the system did not check to verify that a job (RN) and a department (housekeeping) were not a match. That's what the customer had meant by "validate the labor level." The result was that a product was purchased that didn't meet the business need. Ouch! What was the cost of living with that going to be? In 1607 a man named Edward Topsell referred to the reason this happened as being penny wise and pound foolish. The company saved on consulting expenses in the early phases of the project but those "savings" were quickly consumed.

When this discrepancy was identified, the relationship with this vendor was off to a shaky start. In addition, the absence of this feature may have been a valuable leverage point in negotiations with the vendor. It's what you don't know that can hurt you. Experienced consultants can insure good communication with vendors on technical issues.

The message is, don't wait to bring in an expert consultant, and don't look for WMT experts through your partner IT outsourcing agent. They simply don't know what to look for or how to qualify candidates. Understanding the technology requires extensive training, hands-on experience and a background in the business areas where these systems are used. If the IT outsource recruiter doesn't know the technology, how can he know what to ask or what is really required? Building a Business Case for a sophisticated business tool such as Workforce Management Technology takes much more than understanding how to install a product. Leading a WMT project involves more than a technician setting up the system. Making a positive contribution to a Business Case, and leading a complex project to deliver innovative business processes, require skills and knowledge that can only come from having previously been a key player in similar projects.

Expand Your Vision and Find the Right Angle

When you think of building a Business Case as a process, part of this is to put yourself in the position of your audience. Obviously, you get it and know why a WMT system makes sense for your organization. But your reasons for pursuing the acquisition of this technology may not be the same reasons that will sell the managers who will ultimately make the decision. Executive managers are held accountable not only for individual departments, decisions and project choices but for the overall success and profitability of the organization. They are hearing not only from you about problems, fixes, and budgets, they are also receiving competing requests for funding and resources from throughout the organization. They are responsible for choosing projects that support the mission and objectives that have been laid out for the future.

Erin Govednik of Cox Communications in Atlanta participated in a panel discussion, "Workforce Management System Implementation Best Practices," in the fall of 2006. She said she'd been involved in the preparation and presentation of proposals to invest in a new WMT system for several years without success. The first unsuccessful Business Cases focused primarily on the need for the system from an IT, Finance and HRIS perspective and did not cover all the potential benefits. Later, a Business Case was developed that explained the overall impact the system could be expected to have on the organization. This time, the proposal was accepted. Executive management bought into the wider benefits. The moral is that a Business Case that focuses on benefits too far down in an organization may not be able to beat out other funding requests. A winning Business Case will present benefits that high level decision makers can easily understand and relate to.

Executive Level Concerns

Nowadays, executive management is also probably worried about complying with Sarbanes-Oxley regulations and an increased level of scrutiny from corporate boards and investors. Top executives know they can be held accountable for their decisions. A Business Case should be designed to address these concerns and to provide detailed information. A well written case will demonstrate how the initiative will transform the organization and contribute to meeting strategic, operational and financial objectives.

It also may help to understand that managers in the position of making decisions about strategic, companywide initiatives make this kind of decision differently than they do those affecting operations. Operational issues are generally decided based on prior decisions, trends and known factors to do with maintenance, growth and regulation. Rather than starting with a blank page, such tactical decisions often may be more of a selection from a limited set of alternatives. Conversely, a Business Case must compel leadership to forge into new territory. Without a strong and thorough case having been made, the path of least resistance may be to make no decision at all, which is the same as deciding against the project.

A Good Business Case is Both a Map and a Contract

So how is a strong case made? On any journey, it's important to know where you are before starting out. This is why a good Business Case will begin with an examination of where the organization is today — a place it presumably does not want to be. It will then provide a map to a destination that is clearly more desirable.

The map will show the way, of course, but it might also be viewed as an agreement or contract. It will outline the project and the new system for all parties and serve as a written consensus among those who support or approve the project and those who will carry it out. It can be considered a formal, auditable document focusing on ramifications of and recommending solutions to specific problems or needs.

The term "auditable" represents a new concept for many. We say it is auditable because once it is approved, the document becomes a contractual agreement that can and most likely will be reviewed and tracked to insure that the called-for resources were made available and the corresponding results were delivered.

The Business Case defines scope and expectations and assures future accountability. Top managers almost always must answer to boards of directors, investors, and regulators. Such a document provides a certain amount of cover to whoever approves it, thus increasing the likelihood he or she will sign off on the request. For stakeholders. it insures continuity because it binds current and future project leaders and participants to expectations that have been set down on paper and agreed on. In large organizations in particular turnover is likely to happen. The approved Business Case prevents new team members from attempting to redirect the project in midstream.

What are some other reasons proposals fail to achieve their goal? Why are they unable to gain the support needed to move forward? It probably won't surprise anyone to read that internal politics may play a role. Players with their own personal motivations may repress or spin information and attempt to influence decisions in the direction they want things to go. Regulatory issues can also thwart an otherwise sound effort. It's important to anticipate these potential obstacles and address them early on. Often they can be mitigated during the effort made to create awareness of the "problem" the proposal is designed to solve. A good salesman knows that it makes sense to raise potential objections before someone else does and to shoot them down early.

Be Thorough — Don't Be Set Aside

A number of other factors can sidetrack a proposal. For example, if not enough information is given, decision-makers may be left with unanswered questions and set the proposal aside. They may also have concerns about failed or underperforming projects in the past that were not delivered as promised. Those issues might have been overcome, but they may still need to be addressed. Indeed, as many issues as possible should be anticipated and dealt with when building a case.

Going through the process you will either demonstrate the merit of an undertaking and debunk its naysayers or demonstrate for yourself and others that — although the project may appear sound on the surface — the timing, required funding and resources or the likelihood of a desired outcome makes it inadvisable to undertake under present conditions. Although as an initiator you may feel you've failed, the process of building a Business Case will actually have saved the organization the time and trouble of pursuing what would likely have turned out to be an ill-timed investment.

Chapter Twelve: What to Look for and Consider

Through all of the phases of getting from concept to project it's vitally important to spend time and energy up front thinking through the process and systems the company now has in place, whether they should be replaced, and, if so, what should replace them. In doing so you also need to consider how a new system will best be implemented. It's been my experience that a great deal of time, energy and heartache can be saved during the implementation stage and into production if a thorough job analyzing and planning has been done. Workforce management technology is unique. It's a conglomeration of functional and technical information and concerns. It involves old, familiar data and new possibilities for value-added data. It depends on inputs from people, external databases and internal calculators and gauges. It is constricted by policy, contract, regulation, expectations, people and infrastructure. It will make changes necessary in other systems and processes in order to deliver its powerful improvements to the operations side of the business. It is expensive but can deliver significant return on investment if deployed appropriately.

Focus on Benefits, and Consider the Alternatives

Envisioning what can be and communicating it effectively to decision makers is the key to obtaining approval and getting it done. The content of the Business Case should not be too technical in nature. It should describe technical system needs, but it is best to keep the discussion focused on what the proposal will do for the business, rather than how it will work technically. People respond positively to benefits, so focus on benefits.

For example, management will want to know how the system will allow them to implement strategies and tactics and how it will facilitate decision making. The system will do so because it will assemble and present information in a way that allows meaningful comparisons to be made that point to logical conclusions, decisions and actions. It will help in other ways as well. Just how this will be accomplished will be covered in the next chapter.

Executive management will expect those involved in preparing the Business Case to be proactive and to investigate the details. As many questions as possible need to be anticipated and answered. Every viewpoint and perspective should be examined. In addition to information being well organized and logically presented, the Business Case should also demonstrate knowledge, capabilities and management skills that will lessen the risk of failure and strengthen the likelihood the project will be a success. In other words, who will do the work and what are their qualifications?

It's also important the case be honestly presented, regardless of whether every fact supports the author's personal objectives. Putting forth information that does not entirely support the proposal builds credibility. Most executives simply aren't going to believe a case that has no downsides. Of course, the positives must outweigh the negatives, or the project cannot be justified.

Looking at alternative directions is also important. Often, one of the biggest roadblocks to project approvals is the question, "Is there something else out there that may work better?" If you've identified all of the possible alternatives and show that what you are recommending is the best approach, the question will not be asked.

There is also a great deal the audience won't know and will not expect to be included. But it's your job to make certain it is included. A collaboration of internal and external subject matter experts ought to insure this.

Let's turn now to some common things to be on the lookout for in your survey and analysis.

Look Out for Hidden Practices

WMT systems are likely to impact the policies and processes now used to pay people. Workers at every level care a great deal about what they are paid. A number of factors, including the complexity, lack of standardization and amount of individual discretion found in many existing pay systems often aren't fully appreciated. Policies to do with payment for certain work activities may not be documented. What is down in writing may not be what's actually done in practice.

How can this be? Much of what goes on may not be visible beyond an employee and his supervisor. It's simply buried in payroll totals. Don't be surprised to find supervisors are putting a significant amount of creativity to work in the name of "getting the job done" when it comes to paying certain employees.

These hidden practices are often well entrenched, and when this is the case, they become ingrained in the psyche of managers and employees. As such, understandings are formed and held concerning what constitutes fair compensation for the jobs in question. In some cases a practice that's been in place for a while can actually become an entitlement for employees. After a time, the company may be obligated to continue the practice in spite of its inconsistency with company policy or even union contracts. Uncovering these situations and properly handling their conversion will be an important part of the project. The Business Case may not identify all of these outliers but it should point out that a new system is not simply a "plug and play" installation or a zero impact upgrade. If a new system cannot accommodate all of today's needs — including maintaining employee morale or getting the work done — it might not be practical to implement, given a particular business climate.

Transitioning to Electronic Approvals

Approval processes also need to be reviewed as part of the analysis. WMT systems almost always automate something that has been manual, ad hoc or off the radar. These items didn't reach certain levels of management or the Payroll area until someone gave them the go ahead — someone other than the employee himself. What needs to be approved, when and by whom? Are the appropriate levels of management approving reported activity that will ultimately end up in someone being paid? Appropriate oversight is a must.

Transitioning paper approval processes to system processes can be challenging. Paper travels a physical path and becomes inaccessible to parties once it is passed on. A stack of time sheets can be sorted, subdivided, copied and stapled to other documents. It can contain information that is unrelated to time collection. It allows for ad hoc entries, what I call the "text messages" of yesteryear, such as workers' handwritten notes in the margins. It can be modified by the owners; columns can be used for other purposes such as adding data or information. All sorts of alterations may be used in the approval process. Ways need to be provided for this when the process becomes electronic.

Streamlining Approvals

WMT can eliminate steps. A new system can make it virtually impossible for invalid data to be entered into the system, and this will eliminate the need for some forms of verification and approval. For example, when a company moves from paper timecards to data entry by telephone, automated number identification (ANI) can be used to determine the location of the telephone an employee is using. No further validation is needed that he or she was on site because the system can be set to prevent an employee from punching in or out if he or she calls in from a phone other than the one designated.

The same system can also eliminate the need for an employee who moves around from one location to another to give this information when he or she calls in. The system will automatically know and record it, thus streamlining the process.

There are countless ways to automate the approval and qualification processes. If it can be reported and it needs to be approved, that's important to know.

Types of Data and Where it Resides

The next thing to look at is the types of labor activity. In connection with this, it's important to evaluate all of an organization's pay practices. This involves poring over HR and Payroll policy manuals and documents. Sample timecards need to be studied. The general ledger account and a paycheck register should be examined to determine and understand what defines the activity that's being reported. And it doesn't stop there. All sorts of inquires need to be made into what employees do and how it's reported.

238

Activities as they relate to billing and customers need to be considered as well as the types of regulations and industry standards an employer is subject to. The demographics of employees and how the physical layout of the facility plays into operations should be taken into account. Who does what, where and when and who needs to know all need to be mapped and organized into groupings, lines of business and hierarchal structure.

It's important to know what sort of information technology infrastructure already exists at a company, as this will determine the software options. Is it SQL , Window-based or on a mainframe such as IBM?

In our discussions with clients about enhancement possibilities, we try to determine what sort of activity-based information might be helpful. For example, would the client like to track piece-rate or specific client activity? Is there value in tracking projects for work orders? What about activity tied to premium or bonus pay? This starts a dialog, and through these discussions we are able to communicate what the various products out there have to offer. This will often generate ideas about the possibilities, and we use the resulting feedback to determine what's important and what isn't. This is critical information to have when the time comes to make a selection between vendors. A good consultant will make sure few gaps exist between what his or her client wants and needs on the business end and what a particular vendor has to offer.

In the next chapter we will cover how a mission-based system is developed. In our discussions, we try to make it clear such a system will deliver payroll data, but it can also focus on the activity, projects, demographics, clients — anything that management wants to track. Once we determine what kind of data will be valuable, we assess whether it can actually be captured. The activity has to be measurable, have a defined beginning and end and as such be consistent in how it is characterized.

Is it a unique activity?

Is it something that's repeated across the organization?

Does it make sense to ask people to segment their time? Is there a specific start time and stop time for the activity? Or is the activity interspersed with others? Concurrent activities can be tracked, but not all the software available does this.

Does someone wear several hats? Does the activity need to be charged to more than one business unit?

Data: Who, What, Where and When?

WHO: Time and effort needs to be spent determining where data will come from and when. It can come from employees themselves. It can come from a separate scheduling system or another piece of technology such as work orders when entered in an ERP system. It might come from homegrown in-house systems. It could come from templates or from projected historical data.

WHAT: If the data is to come from employees, it's important to know whether having them provide this information will impede their work. In other words, if they have to stop what they are doing and punch in every hour, the question must be raised, is that really a productive use of their time? Will what's gained be outweighed by the loss in productivity? Is there a way to soften the impact and still get the data in time?

WHERE: Workers can report certain types of activity when they check out at the end of a shift. This saves having to make a number of calls or trips to a data collection device during the day as they move from one activity to another. In other situations, time is more critical and employees are required to report activity throughout the day. Workbrain has customers who use bar code readers to track quantities throughout the shift from workers in production environments located right in their work area.

WHEN: Let's face it, we all live by the clock. We schedule our lives on the hour. Labor activity reporting can be like this, too. Everyone will be coming to work at the top or bottom of the hour. The collection of data is condensed into wedges of time, like pizza slices, near the twelve and the six on the clock face. Something to consider is whether stepped up pressure will clog or bring down the system because a large number of workers will be inputting data at the same time. Let's say there are 2,500 employees in a company and they will each make four punches on average during the day. That adds up to a lot of traffic condensed into a short period of time. For a detailed discussion of the implications, see the

"Scalability" section of Chapter Ten. Suffice it to say here that those designing the infrastructure for telephony-based WMT data collection must be diligent in sizing the system to handle the call volume correctly. Erlang B calculations are used by call centers to calculate the hardware required to handle various amounts of anticipated call volume on a phone system. It's important to understand what the expected call volume will be and apply these mathematic systems to an organization's metrics in order to design an adequate system. It's important to consult with some-one who has worked specifically with WMT technology and can share expected call patterns and durations, hang time, busy signals, line man-agement, and so forth.

Other data collection devices — timeclocks and computers — have their own volume and location issues as well. The logistics, capacity and speed of these systems, based on user traffic, also need to be carefully evaluated when purchasing and laying out a new system.

Labor Level Architecture

Labor levels are loosely associated with general ledger accounts. They are used to assign labor activity and costs to cost centers — the business units that employ the labor and are responsible for the expense. In a pay-roll register, labor costs are charged to departments, divisions, regions and so forth. Time and attendance systems allow the same structure to be built, but this can be broadened or broken down in different ways in order to capture more meaningful data. For example, management may want to assemble information that relates to a physical location that has nothing to do with the general ledger. An example might be the different wings or floors of a medical or retail complex, or a production line in an assembly plant which represents different teams or disciplines or lines of business. The different ways to break out data need to be based on how employees are being expensed and managed. Defining these groups and locations is important because it drives such things as security and access, who will see what data, and how it will be sorted and rolled up into summaries.

Some WMT systems have a parallel hierarchy setup commonly known as organizational mapping. These structures within the system allow a user two different hierarchies for two distinct purposes. The labor level structure generally handles the expense function. The organizational map charts where people are assigned, physically. These mappings may not line up with the general ledger. They represent how teams are structured. Org maps allow for work to be assigned in the system in the same way this occurs in the real world. Scheduling may not be built around general ledger accounts. Org maps also facilitate creating schedule templates that show job slots that need to be filled, or populated, by the assignment of a worker to a position or task.

Organizational maps are often very informal and undocumented. They can vary in structure with one area having multiple levels and another area very few. As such, they can be disjointed and fluid — changing to accommodate business needs — and this may make them difficult to capture. The recent introduction of org maps into the technology has significantly advanced the ability to accommodate existing business practices. The ability to configure around the interplay of labor levels and org maps has allowed expense processes to "play well" with scheduling processes for the first time. This allows companies with even the most complex scheduling processes to feed the time and attendance system with the background logic needed to compare and report on worker activity, bringing dry payroll data to life and giving it value. [Bob just punched in an hour early at the wrong location and Kathy was required to log into her secondary job when she transferred to a different department.] Inert schedules can now supply important real-time information. [Nobody showed up to work the front desk, and there aren't enough workers on the line to maintain production levels.] A state of the art system links what managers need to know with what is being reported — now!

Defining Pay Codes

Pay codes, earnings codes or wage types are the buckets that time goes into in order to calculate pay, report activity or create flags. These need to be identified, standardized and defined for the new system. This includes productive and non productive time, benefit time (PTO, vacation, sick, leave, jury duty, and so forth) and even expenses (e.g., mileage) or units (e.g., piece rate info).

Companies can redefine pay codes to track certain types of activity. The possibilities are endless with WMT systems. Even if limits exist in related Payroll and HR systems, this doesn't keep the WMT system from parsing time into very detailed subcategories and then rolling the numbers into more generic buckets for export to outside systems. The WMT system can provide much greater detail and summary information by using more pay codes to categorize activity and time.

Well-defined pay codes are crucial in helping managers of an organization better understand what makes up their labor expense. Program stacking or pyramiding is easily revealed, showing where a single shift of work activity begins to earn multiple rates of pay or pay premium. If a business operates in states or under contracts that call for multiple types of overtimes (weekly, daily, consecutive day, and so forth) how can that added expense be managed if it cannot be determined when the overtime is occurring? Can it be done by better managing daily shift length or total hours per day? How about by managing weekly total hours worked? I have yet to meet a customer who broke down overtime pay by type in a manual system. This being the case, there was no obvious attempt to understand and control this cost.

WMT configuration opens up an entirely new world of labor expense control possibilities. If a manager can't see the origins of payable activity, how can he manage it? How can anyone measure whether money is being well spent?

The System Should Be a Platform

A WMT system should be a platform for integration. Sharing information across systems and databases will reduce the duplication of effort. Instead of the HR Department keying in new hires, setting up social security numbers and age — then department personnel doing the same thing for the payroll system — it can all be done in one place and fed into the other systems. WMT systems can use the data the company already collects and maintains for employees, accounting, billing and operations and bring it all together to provide meaning to the labor activity data.

For purposes of cost accounting and project or job management, a system can be integrated with an existing ERP system. It can also be integrated with a CRM (Customer Relationship Management) system, so that employees might be tracked according to the customers with whom they interface. For example, suppose "issues" exist with several customers, or sales from certain customers have been trending down. It might be interesting to see if these customers are evenly divided among the sales force and customer service personnel, or if the same employees pop up frequently as being those who are interfacing with customers in decline.

What's great about integrating workforce technology into an environment that already has ERP, CRM and SCM (Supply Chain Management) systems is that these existing systems may have fully matured while stopping short of intervening in the process of labor deployment. They have great data but it has never been applied to human capital management. Now the next logical step can be taken.

All Related Systems Must Be in Sync

WMT systems draw on information in related systems such as HR, Payroll, Finance and Operations and so must be in synch with the other repositories of business data such as employee information (e.g. name, job title, hire date, employment status, work location, supervisor, and so forth). The Business Case should take into account these other systems in a way that dovetails with their current state. For example, if the HR system is about to be replaced, this pending undertaking is likely to require the time and attention of many of the same project resources. Having two systems that will closely interact in a state of redesign probably would not be smart. Granted, there is a bit of a "chicken versus egg" issue when deciding which system should be updated first. Each will depend on inputs and outputs from the other and be required to house information so both can handle their respective processes. And each will "own" certain areas of compensation processing (i.e. calculating, assigning appropriate rates of pay, allocating, and so forth). If your organization recognizes that an upgrade to HR or Time and Attendance is imminent, my recommendation is to evaluate where these processes will reside. Which system will do the work? The risk of not understanding the needs and placing them in the wrong system can be very costly. You can lose functionality and reporting capabilities, and require complex interfaces and program customization to accommodate the decisions and purchases.

Standardization

For a system to perform up to its potential, policies and practices should be standardized across the organization. This may be difficult to accept since many of these inconsistencies are well entrenched and have their justifications. But standardization will make administering the systems much easier and it will make the outputs consistent and meaningful across the organization. Maintaining nonstandard systems will be much more costly both in the initial implementation phase and on an ongoing basis.

If business reasons exist that prevent complete standardization, the organization needs to assess how complex the variety of differences will be and whether the WMT system being proposed can handle the complexity.

The introduction of a global WMT system into the organization presents an opportunity to corral departments that may be fudging a bit on employee practices. When the system becomes global, the company has a strong argument for ensuring employees are being treated equally and fairly, and this requires having standard policies and implementing them consistently in an evenhanded way. For example, what constitutes an exempt versus a non exempt employee needs to be consistent in all locations. It's also important that job titles reflect similar skill levels, training and responsibilities. Otherwise, comparisons between areas and locations made from rolled up reports showing jobs, departments and divisions won't be worth as much.

Another area where standardization can be an issue has to do with holidays. Many localities have their own local holidays. One way to deal with this is to go to floating holidays. Let's say a company has seven days off for holidays during the year. Are these seven holidays the same everywhere?

I had one customer who insisted during the initial discovery phase that the company had six standard holidays across what was a very large organization. This was supported in the holiday policy documentation at the corporate office, but in reality it turned out to be very different. There were more than 40 holidays observed across the organization that were based on contracts, local labor market expectations and business practices predating the acquisition of some by the parent company. It's just a good thing the system was able to handle them.

Some companies prefer to standardize the definition of shifts, also called zones. Others want the flexibility of having a variety. One of my customers has 150 different shifts or zones, which can make things very complicated. Does the second shift start at 4 p.m. and go to midnight, or does it start at 2 p.m. and go to 10 o'clock? What if the employee clocks in a few minutes early? Is that time part of the scheduled zone or the prior zone?

Rounding is another system setting that is better when handled consistently across the organization. Should an 8:07 punch be rounded to 8:00, to 8:10 or not at all? Variation does allow the company to schedule and compensate people the way management wants, but it can make interpreting the data and passing it to other systems difficult.

Standardization of components has many benefits including ease of training, common expectations across the organization, consistent pay practices based on these standard settings and less background maintenance required to manage a very complex system.

The WMT System Time Warp

Dumb technology, such as paper timecards, is very patient and forgiving. Paper timecards don't demand setup before they can be used. You can write all over the paper and it won't care if the "name" field hasn't been filled in. You can even wait until the very last minute of the pay period to pencil in all the data for the previous two weeks. A timecard filled out at the last minute of the pay period works just as well as one that was prepared with all the right information from the very first day.

Unfortunately, computer systems are often less patient and forgiving. Mr. Nuhire won't be able to punch into the system if his information isn't in the computer yet. Much has to happen behind the scenes to get the system ready to recognize Mr. Nuhire and accept his inputs.

It's easy to dictate what the new guidelines are for submitting paperwork and inputting data into the new system in time for employees to use the system appropriately. It's not easy to insure it happens that way in the real world.

In the real world, employees show up for their first day of work and no one has yet told HR they have been hired. What is the employee to do that first day? Use an old paper timecard? Perhaps, but then a crutch has been introduced. I've worked with some customers to set up a quick "mini hire," allowing last minute arrivals to be set up with the bare essentials so that they can use the WMT system from the start.

It can happen with changes to an employee's job, too. A promotion, a wage increase, a transfer to a new facility. All of these changes have to be communicated to the WMT system, ideally *before* they occur.

What's important in the planning and design stages is to know what to ask when doing discovery. How flexible is the HR system to a "mini hire" setup process? How receptive will the HR area be to such a divergence from their practice of holding Payroll hostage until all the required paperwork is received? Is someone willing to follow up or is the system capable of making certain the mini-hire converts to a full hire? How quickly can the HR system finalize inputs and export them to the WMT system? What are the options if a mini-hire isn't feasible? What's the best way to accommodate these issues inside the WMT system and processes? What can be done to alleviate the time warp between WMT and HR systems?

Achieving Integration

Often, integration is accomplished through data warehousing. More and more, leaders of companies are realizing the value of the data they have in the different systems under one roof, and that it makes sense for those who can put it to good use to have access to it. A data warehouse can house the information and make it available to anyone who is authorized. So instead of Payroll running a report in the time and attendance system and a budget report out of the finance system and then trying to reconcile the two, operators who use the various systems can go to the data warehouse, access and gather the information they need, combine the data and run the report from there. This not only gives these various users access to information from throughout the company, the processing burden is taken off each individual system, thus freeing up computer power. WMT systems can be allowed to focus on managing today's operations and collecting data, and not be burdened with excessive reporting. Migration to data warehouse systems of processes that drain business systems of resources and performance maintains the ability of these systems to accomplish their primary missions.

One Vendor and Its Suite of Solutions versus "Best of Breed"

A popular school of thought exists about the selection of software applications. It's not uncommon to hear people in organizations say their preference is to purchase the "best of breed" in every application. This means they want to buy the equivalent of the Consumer's Digest's #1 rated application on the market. They don't want to settle for second best. I suppose the rationale is that if the product is rated highly it must be the best solution available. Perhaps it's easier to justify large expenditures when there is a perception that "we're buying the best product out there." Is there an aura surrounding these "best in breed" products that gives a subliminal message that the organization is certain to be satisfied and benefit from the choice? Whatever it is, I'd like to challenge the concept that "best in breed" is necessarily the best approach.

There are advantages and disadvantages to the single vendor suite. Risks are involved but there also can be rewards. The point I'd like to make is simply to consider the advantages of aligning everything with a single vendor and weigh them against the advantages of product-specific requirements. Sometimes what people in organizations *think* they are get-

CASE STUDY
Vendor: API Software, Inc.
Customer: A community hospital in northern Ohio

In 1998 this customer began a search for a Time & Attendance system. A team of five key personnel representing IS, Payroll, HR and Operations selected API Software's Payrollmation product. Not long afterward, the organization decided to add access control and staff scheduling functionality to their automated solutions. Again, the organization chose API's products – ActiveStaffer and SecurAll. In the next phase, several years later, hospital management wanted to upgrade its HR and Payroll systems and to integrate employee cafeteria purchases in a single system. This time, the team committed fully to the existing vendor and purchased API's solutions for these systems as well. Overall, they went from having more than two systems and many manual processes that were poorly integrated back in 1988, to one suite of applications from a single vendor today. What kind of advantages did they experience? What was the down side?

PRO's
- 1 vendor owns any problem, no finger pointing
- Communication & Administration – single point of contact for system support, commonality for maintenance, vendor has responsibility for keeping systems in sync through upgrades, etc.
- Integration – the systems work well together, one platform supports all systems, no translations between systems required
- Easier implementation and training effort – one "look & feel", common GUI tools
- No loss of functionality from any application because a related system cannot support a feature
- Reduced interface costs and maintenance
- Badges worked on multiple devices (timeclocks, door locks, swipe for meal, etc.)
- Highly vested vendor – stronger position for customer in negotiations, may offer cost efficiencies

CON's
- Risk – customer is greatly impacted (multiple systems affected) if: vendor goes out of business, customer service is poor or the relationship deteriorates; customer must be certain vendor is financially strong and viable for the life of the products
- Bugs or problems with the software could be systemic and not limited to one application
- Limited by one vendor's ability to keep pace with technology improvements
- Costs – customer is subject to one vendor's pricing cycle and position
- Other vendors may offer greater functionality in one or more of the applications – customer may miss out on features so that they can take advantage of single vendor suite benefits.

ting doesn't always become reality because systems don't always integrate well, are expensive to maintain communication between or fail to deliver the expected results because a piece of the process for delivering the desired outcome was housed in a sister application that wasn't purchased because it wasn't "best of breed." Suite may be more "sweet" than you think.

Portal Technology

Time and attendance systems work well with portal technology. As mentioned above, a number of systems may exist in an organization. Portal technology allows users to sign on in one place and maneuver between these systems. Not only are people spared the inconvenience of having to go through multiple sign-ons, the technology makes it possible to share files and data among many users. It also directs users to workspaces the company wants them to use. If managers should be monitoring the deployment of labor to insure it is in tune with production, they need to be in that workspace in order to get the information.

Managers and workers in the not so distant future will be using wireless technology devices to free them from the need to be at the computer. But in the meantime, periodic "attendance" in the WMT workspace can be facilitated through portal systems that make it a one stop shop.

Another advantage of using portal technology is that everyone will have the same, up to date version of company knowledge and decisions. This is important because data is constantly being compiled and updated in a real-time system. Company documents and policies are routinely edited and revised. In this way, a portal system avoids the potential confusion that can come about because an individual may be working with a record or document that no longer coincides with the one someone else may be using.

A portal system can be thought of as a library that's kept constantly up to date. Every cardholder is able to check out any document, any schematic, any procedure or protocol, any report or legal finding he or she might want, and they can all do it at the same time. It delivers tremendous efficiency, control and improved communication to the organization. One of our customers worked with Quilogy, a Microsoft partner, to engage portal technology in concert with their workforce management system training program. They learned how to use applications they already owned to deliver the program across the organization and control content from a central location. That's a space companies will enjoy operating in.

Access and Security Issues

Workers are like kids . They want to do and see what everybody else can. But employers are like parents. They know that's not always a good idea.

In the most sophisticated WMT systems there are many available levels of security access. In Kronos' systems, for example, more than 240 control points drive what a user is allowed or denied access to in its Function Access Profiles. Control points are used to enable or disable what specific users can view and what they can change. There are a few primary access categories — who, what and in some cases when. One person might have access to all the employees in a department. His manager needs access to employees in five departments but not his own record. Some users will be privy to hourly rates, time worked to date, PTO and so forth. Others might need to be restricted from confidential information such as rates. Some will have the authority to make changes or to add comments. Others will not.

WMT systems provide different modules users need access to, such as timecards, schedules, employee records, running reports, maintaining the system settings, creating ad hoc queries, sending e-mails, and so forth. If a company had one flavor of user, then all this complexity won't be an issue. If a company has many different locations or lines of business or levels of hierarchy, the details of how access is set up can be critical. If access can't be controlled appropriately, features may have to be "turned off" for the entire company because access setup isn't robust enough to accommodate the limits. Again, mission-based configuration is an approach that requires taking a careful look at the users and what they need to see and do. Controlling data access is critical. Not enough functionality will diminish the chance of reaping all the benefits from the system. Too much functionality may be risky for the organization and allow some to go beyond the boundaries of a user's true needs.

Security also comes into play beyond the application itself. Regulatory requirements, news events and the recent upsurge in the need to protect people in the workplace from terrorism and violence, as well as to secure corporate secrets, are making workplace security an ever bigger management concern. Companies such as Identatronics are at the forefront of providing integrated solutions that address these issues. Paper guest books are being replaced by visitor access control systems that provide instant access to information about who is on premises, where and who they visit, and so forth. Visitors can swipe a driver's license or other identification and be issued a temporary badge. The system can simultaneously send an e-mail to the person expecting the visitor letting them know their guest has arrived. Badges can even be set to expire automatically preventing visitors from extending a stay without permission.

Sarbanes-Oxley regulations require public companies to keep records concerning who visits around the time financial reports are made public. External auditors can be given limited access to temporary offices or conference rooms, thus limiting the access they can have to sensitive areas.

Some employers use access control technology to provide a secure work environment and prevent unwanted visitors from entering large facilities. One of Identatronics' customers — a steel processing plant with less than fifty employees — took on the system to improve inventory control. Hiring security guards for their many exit doors simply wasn't financially viable. Indentatronics provides a full line of security products including CCTVs, badge makers and other devices that work hand-in-hand with the firm's time and attendance applications. Customers find that when they begin to manage time and labor, these processes line up naturally to provide solutions to other concerns about who goes where and when. It's great when one vendor can answer all of those needs.

Hosted Solutions — Application Service Providers (ASP)

This list of considerations wouldn't be complete without mentioning the options for ownership of these products. It's true the majority of companies seek to purchase these products outright and administer the applications in-house. However, that isn't the best option for all companies, particularly companies that are small to mid-sized in terms of the number of employees and the size of the IT and HR/Payroll areas. There are providers in the market who offer some of the same products in the form of a hosted solution. ADP is perhaps the largest company in the U.S. that offers hosted workforce management applications, but there are others in the industry that also do. Some are fairly small operations. For example, my friend Gary Huntoon, who owns Advanced Payroll Systems in Louisville, KY, focuses on attracting companies who want a more personal relationship with their payroll services provider. Their customers can't afford in-house data base administrators, system specialists and product trainers, but they do want to work with and get to know one or two dedicated individuals.

Application Service Providers (ASPs) — from the very large like ADP to smaller outfits like Advanced Payroll Systems — offer a cost efficient alternative to owning and administering these applications. Outsourcing time and attendance allows the organization to enjoy the benefits of the technology with fewer of the responsibilities. If funding, resources and expertise are concerns, it may make sense to consider a provider that will host the software for you. In addition, if the organization is already outsourcing Payroll or HR services it may make sense to have the provider host time and attendance as well.

Going with a hosted solution could also be a first step in a phased approach to automating these processes. If the technology proves worthy and the capabilities are on board, then phase two could be to bring the application in-house after a trial period. This ASP model may be worth considering.

Chapter Thirteen: Creating a Mission-Based WMT System

Once we fully understand the current system, including its strengths, weaknesses and shortcomings, we begin to see ways new technology can be put to use. For this reason, the next stage of our work involves returning to the Business Case and the vision for the technology as a business tool and creating an inventory of enhancements to be pursued that are designed to save time and money and help management run the business more effectively. The core of this is usually time and attendance, but the scope of the possible enhancements may include functions such as scheduling, employee self-service, absence management, the budgeting process, business intelligence, access control and human capital management (HCM). WMT is increasingly expanding into HCM, integrating the recruitment, retention, training and development processes. Labor management is being viewed as an ongoing path and is closely linked to compensation and deployment practices.

You might think of a Business Case as a story. That's right, a story about the company and where it is today, what its problems are, what has been done to address those problems, what works, and what doesn't work. And like most stories that strike positive notes with their audiences, it's one with a happy ending. It paints a picture of the business environment both as it is today and as it is projected to be in the future, how the company will benefit, and what a better place it will be once the solution has been successfully embraced and installed.

The company may be looking for ways to control and reduce labor-related expenses and to deploy the labor force more effectively. It may recognize a need to reduce the level of effort required to manage and track labor and attendance. Or it may be looking for ways to improve its ability to attract, select and retain the right employees in an increasingly tight labor market. Issues may also exist to do with integrating training, travel, gatekeeper controls or even the need for billing through a centralized system. The Business Case will explain how a WMT system will resolve one or more of these issues. This should be done in such a way that the audience will understand how the solution will benefit the organization.

Determine System Requirements

Once the problems and issues have been determined, it's time to figure out how to deal with them. We call this a "Requirements Analysis." What this means is that all the functions that the new system needs to offer have to be identified. This requires isolating a solution for each problem or issue and identifying the functionality the new system needs in order to meet this and thereby move the organization forward toward accomplishing tactical and strategic goals. In addition to existing problems and issues, new requirements must be addressed. Further, those existing functions that do not need to change but have to be maintained should also be included.

This represents the first opportunity to rank the importance of the various requirements. This ranking will be instrumental in developing estimates of costs as well as time requirements for project scheduling. It will help determine what must be included versus what may only be nice to have. It will contain the deliverables to be used later in the Request for Proposal r Request for Quote. And, when the time comes to select a vendor, the analysis and the ranking will help the team stay focused on real needs rather than be swayed by the bells and whistles that sales people like to show off.

You may actually be surprised by the outcome of building a Business Case. The process can be time consuming and costly. But you have to ask — What if the wrong decision is made? What would that cost? How much difficulty could that cause?

And think about this: What if the company doesn't actually need a new system? It may be possible to fix a problem by simply tweaking what is already in place, thereby saving a great deal of money.

A Blind Doctor

Let me digress for a moment to quickly illustrate how important it is to do a little research. Imagine a doctor who is examining a child, but this doctor is blind. He places his hand on the child's forehead. It feels very warm. Is the child sick? It's easy to conclude that the child has a fever. But what if the doctor asked a few questions, did some simple tests? How did the child feel? What has he been doing? The child's hot skin could be a symptom of a sunburn as well. Is the solution a fever reducer or a sunburn remedy like aloe vera? If you don't dig into the cause, you might be trying to fix the wrong problem.

A Case History — the Importance of Root Cause

A manufacturer in the West called on me to help with a problem. As is true with many companies, this large manufacturer has maintenance workers in its plants who spend time fixing and maintaining equipment. Several large buildings were scattered around this particular location, each one handling a different phase of the processing of raw materials into consumer products. Each building had its own maintenance workers.

Different buildings would from time to time have emergency issues arise that led to maintenance men from one building being called upon to help in another building that wasn't their home base. The problem was that the time worked would often be charged to their home departments rather than to the business unit they had helped out. Each building represented a profit center, and sometimes a lot of overtime would be incurred. As you can imagine, this caused a good deal of consternation among the managers of the various business units who had budget responsibilities.

Every morning these maintenance men would come in and pick up a stack of work orders, each representing something they needed to work on. A group of managers who was up in arms wanted the maintenance men to clock every time they moved to a different work order, so this would be recorded. The vendor had shown them a system module they could purchase that would allow them to track this activity. On the surface, this seemed to make sense. My mandate was to determine if the additional module would in fact make this work and be the best solution.

From a systems analyst's perspective, it didn't take much time to answer the initial question because verifying that the system could track this activity was not a problem from a technical standpoint. So if things were as simple as they appeared, the module could provide a workable solution. The important question was whether it made practical sense to do so. You see, it may not always be reasonable or feasible to have people punch in and out between tasks. These were big buildings and a lot of distance would have to be covered between where work was being done and where a clock could be punched.

Let's say, for example, a work order called for a repair to a blower on the roof. The nearest clock, however, was located by the entrance to the building. It could easily take 15 minutes to climb down from the roof in order to punch the clock.

Did it make sense for the worker to finish the job on the roof and spend 15 minutes walking down to the clock before moving on to the next work order? If the job after that happened to be all the way on the other side of the plant, the worker could easily lose half an hour in the process.

Someone asked, "What about using a PDA or some other type of hand-held device?"

PDAs aren't cheap and maintenance men have to crawl into some pretty tight spots to work on equipment. A PDA would have to be strapped to a repairman's belt. Chances are a man might go through a lot of expensive equipment just in the course of doing his job. So, although the "system" could handle the data, the operations couldn't support getting the data into the system.

During my investigation, another issue was uncovered that had to do with the nature of repair work. Sometimes a part would have to be ordered, or the machine would have to cool down, before the next step in its repair could take place. In these instances, the repairman might work on another job while waiting. Would the system allow someone to be working on two projects at one time? Did periods of waiting or multi-tasking need to be tracked in real time during the work day?

As the investigation developed, it became apparent that the way to resolve the issue was to determine the root cause of the reporting problem, including the real needs, and how they could be met.

The company had an ERP system that was supposed to be capturing and tracking maintenance workers' time and activity. They were required to write down on a work order how much time they spent on each particular job. A supervisor's assistant was supposed to key this information into the ERP system. But this step was apparently being missed with regularity.

So this company actually had a system and a process in place to solve the problem. It just wasn't being used — at least not consistently. A few people simply were not doing their jobs, and the information wasn't being collected correctly. The managers knew the data wasn't credible and were looking for a way to get good data. These processes and systems didn't have the logistical issues and expenses that the WMT system solution presented.

The bottom line was it made the most sense to have the supervisors' assistants use their current system and improve the reliability of that process, and this was the decision made. It seemed clear that had the company purchased the additional module, it could not have been supported in the "real world" environment. Addressing the problem's root cause was the best way to get the desired results.

Building a Business Case doesn't always mean writing a prescription for a purchase. The person who owns the task should consider him or herself a doctor diagnosing a patient to come up with the best possible treatment plan.

Exploring Functionality

In the Requirements Analysis stage, we explore the potential functionality of a new system and the scope and the vision of the project. Typically, we use a whiteboard and introduce the business pyramid hierarchy, which will be discussed shortly, showing how driving individual decisions and tasks with specific policies and procedures can ultimately lead to the accomplishment of goals. In addition to department goals, we will explore the company's overall goals, which might include everything from cost cutting, to improving productivity and sales growth or increasing employee retention, customer satisfaction or sales. We talk about any policies and programs which are being contemplated or put in place to support these.

We may identify the specific tasks that might lead to the accomplishment of certain goals and see how these tasks might be linked to labor data.

Mission-Based Configuration

There are real life companies that are driving their business success through WMT. The owner of 30 of the most profitable Subway stores uses the latest technology to bolster his sales. He knows that adequate staffing, for example, particularly at peak times, is an important key to success. No one wants to wait in line for a sandwich on their all-too-short lunch hour. What can WMT do? New, relatively inexpensive devices are now available that will alert managers when someone doesn't show up for work. This enables a manager who is not physically at a store location to address the issue. In the meantime, no one on the front line, delivering food to customers, will be distracted because he or she has to deal with staffing an unplanned absence.

How Tasks Lead to Achievement of Goals

Suppose upper management has a number of specific goals it wants the company to achieve. One overarching goal, for example, might be to increase profitability. This needs to be placed at the peak of a pyramid. One objective established to reach that goal might be to insure full staffing on all shifts. This is put on the second level of the pyramid and is assigned

to mid level directors. One strategy for improved staffing coverage might be to be notified immediately of absences. This is placed at the third level and is assigned to managers.

The directors set specific policies and targets for staffing goals. These policies are supported by procedures that relate to how managers expect to accomplish the objective. For example, a target might be a 20% reduction in understaffing, and the policy for reaching that goal would address absenteeism. Under the policies are the processes to support them. This forms the base of the Business/System Mission Hierarchy. This is where front line supervisors begin to use the system in support of the overall goal of greater profitability. For example, the system could be set up to track attendance and periodically reward employees with a financial incentive. In addition, supervisors could be immediately notified when someone fails to show up for their assigned shift. Supervisors are instructed to manage the schedule and replace them with those with fewer hours worked. The system could be set up to automatically select and rank the best candidates for shift duty — those who meet objectives, for example, of avoiding overtime payments, having the strongest skill match and keeping labor expenses at a minimum. Any supervisor who failed to take action or made a selection that was not on the list would be accountable for his divergence from the processes because his actions would be auditable in the system.

This is just one, very basic example. What has been accomplished is that day-to-day activities that result in the unwanted outcomes (absences and understaffing) are channeled through a system that

- encourages and tracks desired behavior,
- alerts employees to action,
- guides them to the next step,
- analyzes the options and
- provides timely solutions aligned with the overall objective.

Further, these actions are entirely visible to managers, are measured against the targets, and are visible to the manager's director and to the director's boss, the CEO.

Data Flow Analysis

How are the tasks identified that support objectives and ultimately corporate goals? The first step is to clearly define the goals, who can help reach them or keep them from being reached, the responsibilities of these individuals and the processes they currently follow. This will allow a planner to drill down to the actions that can drive the desired results. This process will require collaboration between those who understand the business and those who can envision how the technology can become a way to help manage activities or processes. Data flow diagramming is a methodology that can map these relationships.

How should such an analysis proceed? One way is a "punch to paycheck analysis." This is a study, including a flowchart, of how the company collects labor data and of every step between that and the points at which the company disburses and the employee receives compensation. Other charts can be overlaid on this punch to paycheck diagram in order to integrate the management of other processes, goals and employee activities. These charts lay out the current interplay of employees, managers, and the tools of labor activity planning and reporting. You see, to accomplish objectives, things may need to change.

These diagrams illustrate the current flow of workers, materials, equipment and information. They can be modified to show the change from current condition to the recommended condition. Decomposing the charts may be required in order to show more detailed levels of complexity or ownership and personnel, which helps identify the players, such as the departments, personnel, outside vendors and systems that are involved in the process. Decomposing also shows the bottlenecks, such as where things routinely get delayed or piled up, and the redundancies, such as where data gets collected, sorted, reviewed or processed again and again. It identifies the gaps in communication, such as who is and isn't in the loop. The timing is included, such as deadlines, sequencing of inputs, processes and outputs, as are the proper audits/approvals, i.e., who is and who should be keeping tabs on various steps in the process. All the good, the bad and the ugly aspects of labor activity and compensation are there. This analysis provides an opportunity to focus on the individual components and determine where each may be underperforming.

Another requirement is to develop specific objectives or targets for the various work areas and employee groups and the action plans that will lead to reaching the targets. Actions, or the results of decisions made based on input provided by the new system, should be measurable. The faster such a measurement can be made, the better, because this leads to visibility.

Such targets might be "time to complete," attendance percentages, hours worked, the amount paid out in premium pay, sales volume, production quantities, time to process (rate of work flow), throughput, quality levels — such as in the case of Nucor Steel — and even improved employee turnover. These tools create a blueprint for improvement, a script for managers and employees to follow. That's how tasks are identified and goals are reached. But there's more too.

Making Sure the Data Is Actionable

In today's work environment, it's possible to have too much information. There can be so much it becomes impossible for any one person to digest it all, much less do anything about it. This is compounded by the fact that some managers believe the solution to every problem is to generate a report about it. That's all well and good, but the report will not be of much use if no one knows what he's supposed to do about it. That's why it's imperative to make sure whatever information the system is set up to provide is actionable. It needs to be an idiot light that says, "Hey, there's a problem here. This flag tells you there's a problem and here's your next step."

Take for example, the missed lunch punch we discussed earlier in this book. The supervisor needs to find out whether or not the person took lunch or worked through it. Once he does, he needs to make the necessary inputs, such as enter a comment, approval, or the missing punch into the system.

The way to insure data is actionable is first to take a hard look at what management would like to control. Is it how much is being spent on an

System Mission Hierarchy

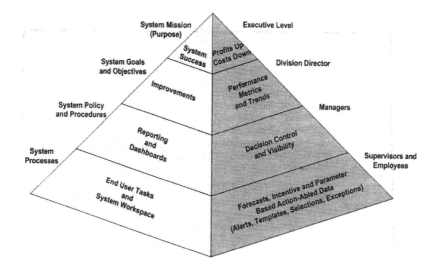

On the right side of the pyramid are the company and its hierarchy of business objectives. On the left is the system. Its processes and features are paired with the business mission. From the executive level on down to supervisors and employees, and from the end user task and system workspace on up to system success, all team members and all aspects of the system have roles to play in accomplishing the mission. Each end user task and each instance of manager oversight will have a positive impact on the mission.

A successful system will involve every level of the hierarchy. High level benefits are derived from actions at every level. There should be no gaps in the process of working towards the goals. The business case will illuminate these connections.

Based on this, for any new technology, the primary goal of the business case is to demonstrate how it will support the business and how the technology will help insure the success of the overall corporate mission. When this is achieved, executive management will "get it,"and the business case will make good sense to them.

activity? Is it a failure to adequately schedule? Does it have to do with lost revenue or high employee turnover? Is it making sure overtime is offered to the person next in line under union contract provisions?

If, for example, the problem is too much overtime, a report about what happened last week won't do much good. What's needed is an alert that notifies managers that these people are headed into overtime unless certain interventions are taken.

The next question is "who needs to have the data?" If it's department supervisors or scheduling coordinators, they need to get the alert via a mechanism they have easy access to, and they need to get it in a way that enables them to respond with the appropriate action. Sometimes this is where real changes in processes are necessary. The outputs of the technology cannot impede the recipient's primary job.

It's critical to understand what the most important activity is a supervisor performs. Understanding what is required to make a good business decision when alerts are generated is also important. In a manual system, perhaps only the manager had enough information to make a judgment about the course of action. With the new technology, the information, validation and judgment can be designed into the system making the reaction more automate. Maybe the best use of the manager's time isto be present on the shop floor, where he can help solve problems and open up bottlenecks. Responding to an open position on the production line is rudimentary and the alert and action can be handled lower down the chain of command, shifting the responsibility for the process to another role — freeing the manager to manage the work rather than spending his time on administrative tasks.

Finally, can an action itself be automated? Can a system be created that is intelligent enough to handle certain administrative tasks? Imagine how beneficial this would be. Not only would less time be wasted, the possibility someone might drop the ball would be eliminated. It would mean mission accomplished a hundred percent of the time.

Cost Considerations

Before bringing this book to a close, let's talk about money. Your analysis should take the costs of the new system into account. These costs can go far beyond just the software, hardware, and implementation effort. There are recurring overhead expenses related to owning any technology. With WMT systems a recurring licensing fee may be included, and it's important to consider how this cost and others will grow as the company grows.

An effective ongoing training program should be planned, for this will be needed both during the initial rollout and over the life of the system as new users come on board. Additional personnel costs may also be involved because it will take people to administer the system. There will be database administrators, network administrators and system analysts who monitor the system and swing into action if the database, network, clocks or phone lines go down. A functional expert who understands the business needs and translates them into system features will be required. This support may come from highly trained in-house personnel or an outside consultant who partners with your company to provide ongoing system support. These experts will be able to tweak the system, administer changes, add new functions, add profiles for new business units, and so forth. The system will continually evolve just as the company does.

The budget should also include funds for attendance at user conventions and for ongoing training for personnel as new functionality is added and the product matures. Contingency plans should include reserves for handling employee turnover in highly specialized positions. A departure of key personnel may mean that temporary staff must be engaged — often consultants or vendor resources — to cover critical areas of system support. These specialized resources can be expensive and often must travel to the customer location, which can add to the cost.

It makes sense to plan as well for the possibility that existing systems may have to be upgraded. Underlying programs and utilities may not be the latest versions or capable of handing the new software's outputs. System speed, monitor size, printers, report programs, network infrastructure and operating systems — any one of these and more may be out of date. The cost to replace these components of the company's infrastructure may be significant. Nevertheless, with upgraded business tools the additional costs are likely to be justified.

Although the number of technical sections of the Business Case may be limited, these areas should not be omitted even if they may be unfamiliar. It is better to educate yourself and others, if necessary, than to appear as though some ideas and concepts associated with your proposal are over your head. This may be an area where you will need to call in an expert, but remember, if you want others to support your initiative, the investment will be worth it. An expert should be able to tackle the technical details quickly and teach others what they know.

Sometimes a project team will try to reduce the cost estimate, the time required for implementation, or the overall effort the project appears to require. Team members may argue that by keeping down the cost, or by describing the time and effort as modest, winning approval is more likely. Perhaps. But unfortunately, this may mean that additional funds will be needed later, or that more time will be required and the business will be disrupted longer than expected. As a successful business executive once said, "It's a lot better to underpromise and overdeliver." The point is to err on the conservative side so that the project will be properly funded and the schedule will be workable. You will be glad of this later. After all, you can only go to the well so many times. Make certain that if you do have to go hat in hand, it won't look like incompetence was the cause or that there was an intentional effort to mislead.

Risk Analysis

What we've touched on are not only the known costs but the potential risks that may be involved with the new technology. There can also be unexpected expenditures or costs that are difficult to estimate accurately. A cost estimate will be based on many assumptions. There are tools we use to identify the assumptions, the likelihood of bad things happening and the impact on the project in terms of dollars, time and quality. Don't

ignore this. Embrace the assumptions as the foundation of your estimate and be prepared for unexpected events to occur. It makes sense to take a conservative approach and to figure monetary contingencies into the financial picture of the Business Case.

The Role of Cost Estimates

The cost sections of the Business Case are where details are perhaps most important. Cost estimates are an integral part of the contract the Case represents so you can bank on them being referred to in the future. While executive management may only review the summary, others will need the details in order to direct, structure and drive the project. Keep in mind that no one likes surprises. And, as always with projects and contracts, "if it is not documented, it does not exist."

My husband and I have a number of friends who work for the Department of Defense. Those who have visited a lot of military bases tend to agree that the Air Force has nicer facilities than, say, the Army. The inside joke is that the Air Force builds the infrastructure first — housing and airplane hangars are erected, as are office buildings, officers clubs, gyms, and hospitals. Then, when the money runs out, they say, "Hey, we've *got* to have a runway." Of course, you can hardly have an Air Force base without a runway, so more money is allocated to make the base complete. Unfortunately, most businesses don't work that way. Make sure the cost of your "runway" is included.

Return on Investment

Our discussion of things to consider wouldn't be complete without mentioning return on investment. Everyone wants to know how we put this together. I wish there was one, easy answer. Unfortunately, an ROI analysis is unique to each project and customer. There is no template, no simple spreadsheet and it's not a black box of proprietary calculation tools. ROI analysis is very hands-on and specific to the needs, opportunities and constraints of each organization.

To prepare an ROI analysis the specific ways the WMT system will impact the organization must be understood. There can include personnel, processes, system, and information. Each area impacted must be measured in its present condition and a value put on the present state. Then an estimate of the future condition and the rate of change, whether gradual or instantaneous, must be taken into account. Activity Based Costing (ABC) is a method for obtaining this information. An industrial engineer isn't required, but an understanding of how to track activities and flow is.

The ROI analysis will require input from experts in several areas. Because it involves technology, the IS department will need to assess the impact on current systems and infrastructure. The new hardware and software will have to be maintained and administered, and estimates of personnel, time and cost should be included. No doubt HR and Payroll will be impacted. Job responsibilities will shift, and personnel changes may result. Operations also needs to be included because the system touches every person every day, and responsibilities and processes will evolve as workers engage the new technology. The impact on management at various levels should also be assessed because of the new and improved information and the system's impact on productivity and output.

If the organization is really working outside the box and aligning the system to help reach goals such as increased sales or customer satisfaction then input from marketing and public relations may be required to gauge the impact.

Finally, finance should be involved in ROI when numbers are crunched and cash flow, opportunity cost, time value of money, hurdle rates and financing are integrated into the overall ROI analysis. Each organization has its own format and guidelines for these financial indicators and the ROI analysis should fit these.

It's surprising to me that some companies have said they don't need an ROI analysis — they know they need the technology, and demonstrating ROI either isn't a requirement or perhaps even an expectation. Here we again encounter the pervasive idea that it's just a payroll system or it's just another piece of overhead — an unavoidable expense with little impact on the organization. I hope by now you will agree that a WMT system will have an impact and should produce a noticeable and perhaps significant ROI. The question is really how much and from what aspect of the implementation the return will come. Everyone needs to know what to expect and where to focus attention. ROI analysis figures aren't just hopeful numbers representing optimistic predictions about what the technology will deliver. They should be a target the system aims to hit and the ultimate definition of success.

Price Negotiations

Sometimes customers want me to help in the negotiation process with vendors on price. I can say with confidence that I've been able to tell when a customer is getting a really good deal. It is more difficult to determine if they should be getting a better deal. In my own business, price is a factor of many variables. Every business has to make a profit and those that gouge their customers won't be around long. Sometimes a business is hungry and will take anything that comes along, and sometimes the plate is full, and only a lucrative price will entice the business to take on the extra work. This technology can seem expensive. Consulting support can seem expensive too. The underlying value — the benefit each brings to the company — is what's important. If they take a business to a better place — to greater profits, to more effective delivery of product or service, to improved employee and customer satisfaction — the money will have been well spent.

My philosophy is that a good consultant should be a mentor. Experts who come in and pretend they have a black box only they can understand rub me the wrong way. Consultants are being paid to share what they know. If it's rocket science, let the customer know, but do so with a level of respect and suggest a way for the customer to become a rocket scientist if he so desires. Customers should always receive excellent service and this includes a willingness to impart information so that the customer feels better off having worked with a consultant — beyond just receiving the deliverables promised. A good consultant elevates his customer, leaving him wiser after the project is completed and with the knowledge and documentation that will be needed to continue independently. When this is the case, consulting dollars will have been wisely spent.

In Conclusion

Up to now, most Workforce Management Technology has taken the form of simple automation and reporting. Supplying a sufficient volume of labor and adequate payroll reporting was pretty much all that has been expected. You might say the old paradigm was concerned with how many, when and where. The primary measurements of these processes are typically budget and trending with a few high-level relative indicators. The value of such systems is limited, however, because they are reactive rather than proactive. The lag time required to get information all but eliminated the impact they could have on daily operations.

But WMT has developed into and can now be employed as a proactive business tool. The new WMT — what this book has been about — will allow companies to expect volume — whether production, census, traffic or any demand factor — as well as quality and cost to be factored into workforce decisions. There can be no doubt this will transform workforce management from part art form, part relationship-driven decision-making into an applied science — infusing the business intelligence of an ERP system into the process, thus pushing a business or organization to perform at peak efficiency.

This sophisticated new technology provides a forecasting tool. It can help determine what is needed, identify the best solutions, and quantify financial and operational impacts. The tool kit it provides will enable supervisors to quantify the attributes of all available resources, the demand for them, and deploy and invest accordingly.

In addition, WMT enforces accountability because decisions and performance are visible to management in real time and can be measured impartially in terms of dollars and cents. Let's face it. The big variable in workforce management is behavior. Perhaps more than anything else in recent years — as the the work ethic of some has declined — managers have been searching for how to instill and enforce accountability. WMT is the way. More than any tool developed to date, WMT can offer the ability to influence and even to control behavior. Using it, the organization can channel decisions by supervisors and spur performance by employees. Individuals can be made accountable for productivity, quality, and costs through a system that alerts them to operational needs, defines options, and controls actions. Companies can use this technology to plan the most productive use of capital assets, to meet customer satisfaction goals, to maximize sales and to reduce labor costs to a minimum. And this means higher productivity and greater profits.

As our time together comes to a close, I don't think it is too much to say WMT is the future — the future of workforce management.

And you know what? Having read this book, you might say you hold the future in your hands.

Especially for Payroll Managers

Why Payroll's Time Has Come

A renaissance is underway in labor management. Leaders from varied backgrounds who possess diverse problem solving skills and different market issues are coming together in this revolution, causing it to grow and flourish as the first Renaissance did 500 years ago. Then, too, people from varied backgrounds converged — artists, tradesmen, bankers, and scientists — and together, brought forth a new age.

You can be a leader of this movement, participate in the discussion, and contribute to the evolution of labor time and activity management. As you've read this book, you doubtless were able to relate to many of the stories and situations that businesses find themselves in when managing staff and labor expenses. What I wanted to reveal are problems and the opportunities that exist and to show how to get the most out of the newest technology. I also attempted to show how to insure that the right software is selected from the many programs available and to give you the necessary questions to ask in order to insure a successful implementation. My goal was to energize you with real-world examples of companies taking labor data far beyond what's needed to calculate paychecks. And, like the Renaissance men and women of centuries ago who came together, I attempted to connect you with leaders from different industries — heathcare, retail, manufacturing, education — in order to open up new perspectives on your business and to expose you to new ideas that can help you meet goals and separate your company from the pack.

The Evolution of Payroll and HR

Let's explore the evolution of the Payroll Department. The origins of payroll and accounting, bookkeeping, and paper and coin currencies can be traced to the beginning of ancient civilizations and have evolved slowly over a long period of time. Although the practice probably dates back many thousands of years, the earliest disbursement records still intact are stone tables dating to the Athenian state for the period 418 B.C. to 415 B.C. Of course, Rome and other empires had to pay their armies, which were scattered all over the known world. The word "salary" comes from the Latin word salarium, which literally means "salt money." Apparently it started out as money paid to Roman soldiers for their allowance of salt. According to some historians, Roman emperors had their likenesses put on coins to remind the troops who they were working for. And why not? The source of the jingle in your pocket can make a difference when the time comes to make a decision that involves a question of loyalty.

Payroll Today

Today, the Payroll Department is much like Accounts Payable. A business activity occurs — employees work — and costs are incurred. People need to be paid and taxes need to be disbursed. The Payroll Department is also comparable in some ways to the Human Resources area. Both departments administer employee-related services and benefit programs such as insurance and retirement programs, employment incentives, banking services including direct deposit, savings plans, et cetera. And they manage regulatory requirements. For Payroll this might include processing attachments such as garnishment payments and ensuring compliance to wage and hour regulations. But despite these similarities and practically an equivalent level of importance in the organization for much of the last couple of centuries, the two — HR and Payroll — today are positioned quite differently in most organizations.

It is not uncommon for Payroll and Accounts Payable to exist at an almost equal level in the organization reporting up through the Finance division. Depending on the size and complexity of the organization, these departments have at least one or more layers of management between a department head and senior management. Human Resources, however, has ascended to a much higher level in many organizations.

Why have Payroll and Human Resources evolved so differently?

A logical explanation exists. Government and industry rules and regulations, reporting requirements and benefit programs have exploded over the last few decades. Our political leaders and government bureaucrats at the federal, state and local levels have been busy satisfying the demands of their constituents and of special interest groups. Businesses, institutions, non-profits, schools — all forms of organization — have become subject to regulations such as those in the Equal Employment Opportunity Commission (EEOC), the Family Medical Leave Act (FMLA), anti-discrimination, sexual harassment regulations, the Federal Labor Standards Act (FLSA), Occupational Safety & Hazards Act (OSHA), retirement plan regulations and on and on. Someone in each organization needed to become an expert on these rules and the demands they make on the company in order to keep the Feds and lawyers from the door. In addition, the workforce became more highly educated and increasingly transient, and the pool of labor was no longer limited to local resources. As a result, employees demanded more competitive wages and attractive benefit packages. They could easily shop around for the best opportunity and often left unexpectedly for greener employment pastures. This resulted in a corresponding increase in the effort to manage and supply labor to the organization. All the government information and market data that was generated had to be organized and available, resulting in operational pressures that mandated the use of more technology. Regulators required reports and verification. Disgruntled employees threatened the organization with litigation and potential financial liabilities. Compliance, risk mitigation and holding down benefit costs also became big concerns. The cost of heathcare, for example, has been escalating at a dizzying rate.

As the HR Department became increasingly vital and visible, its profile was raised above Payroll and Accounts Payable. Along with this, it became apparent the director of Human Resources needed to be accessible to top management and so the position was integrated with executive leadership — so much so that now the HR leader sports a C-level title at many organizations.

Payroll managers, on the other hand, typically remain down in the organization in relative obscurity — in the Finance department or perhaps even reporting up through Human Resources to the HR director. The truth is, Payroll is not seen as an owner of an important part of the business and is not credited with managing much more than payroll disbursement.

In my view, this is not as it should be. Today's Payroll Department can be as vital and potentially as influential as many other areas of operations. Changing the way organizations view their Payroll Department and the people who manage labor costs and utilization is my personal mission. I truly believe Payroll and the people who manage labor costs and utilization will become important in almost every organization in surprising ways as the future unfolds.

I'd like to see the Payroll Manager's job elevated in terms of respect. That has been one intent of this book — to provide evidence that Payroll is the owner and conduit of valuable labor management data and can become empowered by using the latest technology to bring significant benefits to the organization. I haven't just written about payroll theory, nor have I speculated about what might happen. Rather, I have related case studies that come from real companies and explained the successes they have achieved so that you would be able to see how the technology can be applied to your situation.

Why Payroll Deserves More Attention

Payroll Departments handle huge sums of money. In many organizations, labor costs are the single largest expense. Despite the complexities, frequent changes and tight deadlines that Payroll Departments operate under, the work they do is almost always highly accurate and timely. At the same time, Payroll may be the least "managed" cost. It is treated more like a fixed cost and a flat biweekly obligation than a controllable disbursement of the company's valuable funds.

How often will an employee overlook an error on his paycheck? Never, unless the error is in his or her favor. Think about it. The IRS doesn't accept estimates, inaccurate wage calculations or late deposits of tax withholding. Everyone who depends on the Payroll Department expects perfection. This puts on the pressure, but the good news is that this perception can be a big plus. When it comes to numbers, Payroll has credibility out of the gate. Payroll is assumed to be staffed with administrators who are sticklers for precision and timeliness. Who, then, would be better to put in charge of labor data technology?

The right processes, controls and procedures can make a big difference to a company's bottom line. In addition, the value of the data that Payroll can provide is tremendous because the efficiencies and cost savings can be enormous if the data is used correctly.

As previously mentioned, nowadays Payroll tends to be viewed the way Accounts Payable is viewed. Accounts Payable doesn't drive sales. It doesn't increase revenues or make the business end of the organization operate any better. Accounts Payable pays vendors. Payroll pays employees. But this perception is about to change. I'm not an expert in Accounts Payable, and there are certainly professionals in this area who perform important functions. But assuming they are not actively involved in front-end procurement — the buying decisions, contract negotiations with vendors, and in supply chain management — their job is to expedite the processing of payable invoices. Accounts Payable may have influence over the terms of payment. The people in Accounts Payable may determine the legitimacy of charges and the allocation of expenses to the General Ledger. There may be value to improving the data collection process for this area as well — but that's for another book. The big difference between Payroll and Accounts Payable is that AP has little opportunity to proactively impact the costs incurred by the organization because AP is the central and final repository of costs incurred by other areas. The regulatory requirements and competitive demands driving these purchases are already being managed by the areas incurring the costs. Industry is already aware of lean manufacturing, just-in-time (JIT) supply chain management, competitive material bidding, and so forth.

Payroll, on the other hand, is in charge of what has been up until now an unmanaged expense. But the opportunity exists to change this — for Payroll to actually provide a tool to manage this expense.

The all too common and pervasive attitude toward wages has been that they represent a fixed expense relative to the number or type of employees. An employee is hired at a fixed rate — either an annual salary amount or an hourly amount. The hourly employee may be eligible for some additional wages via overtime, shift premiums and an occasional bonus, but these are also seen as static and are usually "budgeted" with an expectation of only small variations. In addition, the payroll expense is a continuing obligation eliminated only in extreme situations.

Wouldn't vendors love to be assured their services would be needed 40 hours a week indefinitely?

Payroll has remained unmanaged from within the organization, perhaps because outside entities took the first steps to dictate how labor expenses would be paid. States and localities have imposed numerous industry standards and practices on employers. The resulting rules and responsibilities for compliance on the organization and the Payroll Department have been substantial. Each state has a unique set of guidelines dictating the terms of employment and impacting such things as rest breaks, overtime, minimum wage, how minors are treated, the types of activity different classifications of employees can perform, total hours, and so forth. Add to this the complexities of union contracts which must be applied to the payment, scheduling and treatment of employees. No wonder we have been lulled into thinking *someone else* is managing labor costs. By way of proxy, Payroll has thus become the administrator for these outside management guidelines.

When regulators imposed rules on labor practices and payments, they did so from the perspective of the worker, the state and the public. Few, if any, of the wage and hour guidelines or union contract mandates were designed to use labor resources more efficiently or to improve operations. Certainly, no one outside the organization can be credited with collecting any data, designing compensation programs or constructing work scenarios that are designed to make the company more profitable. Allowing the process of administering third-party regulations — which Payroll does quite nicely — to substitute for conscious management of labor expenses and utilization by the company seems absolutely absurd to me. So why have we been allowing it to be this way for so long?

Payroll data is the natural convergence of labor cost and business activity. It's where the mechanism for getting an organization's product to the market — employee performance — meets the cost of that undertaking in the form of production labor costs. When rules were imposed from the outside, payroll administration was logically identified as the most efficient place to monitor and administer them. To comply with these controls, which are more accurately described as constraints and penalties, takes time and effort. They are written in the way laws that tell us what penalty will occur if we exceed the speed limit are written. The result is, emphasis is typically placed on making sure whatever is triggered by exceeding a limit is complied with, rather than putting mechanisms in place to be sure the limits are not exceeded in the first place. This is a lot like someone driving a car with the attitude that "I'll slow down when I get a speeding ticket." At this point, it's too late. A penalty has been incurred, and points have been posted on that person's driving record. That's why most of us don't go much over the speed limit. It's safer, it's more fuel efficient, and we will avoid the extra cost of the speeding ticket — or better yet, a costly or deadly accident. It doesn't make sense to slow down only if and when we get pulled over by the man in blue.

Wouldn't it likewise be better if we operated our businesses the way we drive our cars? But we keep paying the proverbial "ticket" every pay period, over and over again. As though our business only operates at one speed — reckless!

Why Payroll Should Manage Labor Costs

Let's step back and consider why Payroll is the best place to begin to manage these constraints. Let's face it, employee activity determines everything. Machines don't run on their own. Customers don't buy a product with robots standing by. Patients don't get well just by lying in a hospital bed. Widgets don't travel to stores on their own two legs. The point is, your organization uses people to make it happen, and it costs money every time they show up at work. Every strategic initiative the organization undertakes requires employees to get it done. Because Payroll is the point where activity and costs merge, it's the right place for integrating all the information and decisions related to labor activity and expense. The truth is, it has held this position for a very long time, but without the ability to take advantage of it — until now. Recent developments in workforce management technology now make it feasible. This is why the time has come to reevaluate the payroll function and workforce management. I'll say it again. In the last five years, developments in technology have transformed labor data into a valuable tool for controlling a major expense while at the same time influencing performance in a positive way.

The time has come to stop managing labor using shorthand, manual typewriters, and adding machines with a crank. It's time to collect and analyze labor data, then wisely put it to use. It might even be time for Payroll managers to get a little more assertive regarding their role in the organization, and for C level executives to reassess how they can — no, how they *should* — leverage this knowledge to their companies' advantage.

Lisa Disselkamp
December, 2006

Especially for Owners and C-Level Executives

The Role of WMT in Mergers and Acquisitions

Having good labor cost and productivity data can be valuable in positioning a company for sale.

How so?

A lot of time and effort is spent tending to the assets of the company, but what about tending to the company as an asset? Business leaders, including those in small, privately owned companies — not to mention corporate executives of large, publicly held institutions — benefit when they look at their companies as they would a commodity on the market for sale. These "owners" are responsible for the health and appearance of the company. When a company is available for purchase, outsiders are going to examine it closely from an operational and financial perspective.

For smaller, privately held companies, owners are eventually going to be concerned with succession planning or with positioning their company for sale at retirement. Why should workforce management technology be part of the business brokerage process?

You've heard it said, no doubt, that the three most important things to consider when buying a house are location, location, location. When buying a business, it's not so simple. Prospective buyers of a business will look at profitability and cash flow. As has been said, the only way to obtain a return is through profitable operations, and the only way to pay bills is through positive cash flow.

WMT can provide data that will help a prospective purchaser understand the business and what its true costs are, as well as its sources of profitability and true profit potential. The numbers can be scrutinized from every angle. They can be reviewed by business line, profit center, individual product, or whatever the case may be, which should give a prospective purchaser a high degree of comfort about what he will actually be getting. If the buyer has a question, such as how much is spent to staff this or that unit, or the cost of maintenance or rework, it should be relatively easy to answer.

Another concern from a buyer's perspective has to do with the distinctive competencies of the company's management. Labor data merged with business data can draw the connection between managers and profit centers and reveal the productivity of groups and individuals. This can give prospective buyers an opportunity to identify key personnel as well as workers who may be more expendable. This will help buyers understand who is essential in maintaining continuity following the acquisition or merger.

1. *Management.* Management's ability is usually the key asset sought after in an acquisition.

2. *Cash flow.* Cash flow or potential cash flow of the acquired assets is critical. Profitable operations are essential to obtain a return, and positive cash flow is the only way bills get paid. The time period for positive cash flow is unique to the acquirer.

3. *Opportunity/Strategy/Capital.* Is there a meaningful opportunity, and are there effective strategies and appropriate capital assets, to reach desired objectives? Key aspects of a strategy might include customers, products, services, footprint, competition, business model, and so forth.

Finally, WMT will make the transition to a new owner go more smoothly since a methodology for controlling labor deployment and labor costs will be in place. New management will not have to learn through trial and error while getting up to speed. The system can automatically schedule people, enforce policies and union rules, and manage such things as projects and billable activity. WMT technology can also act as an effective change agent for companies that must administer major transitions when merging two companies together. Managing labor deployment, activity and costs within these systems gives leadership the ability to direct those efforts across the organization consistently and continually without physically micro-managing every supervisor and worker on the shop floor. If the parent organization has a better way of doing business, those guidelines can be set up within the system and applied to every manager's workspace. His actions will be automatically aligned with the new order of business and instantly observable.

Finally, employee-centric business tools combine data and decisions in the hands of the drivers of change in the organization. Production or Operations, HR, and financial system initiatives alone are not enough to maintain the economic viability of many organizations. Because the time to value is short, the savings from WMT systems are immediate, and funds become available for other transformations. Using the technology to save time and money frees up company resources for other projects.

A good realtor tells his client to pay attention to curb appeal. A good business broker should consider how WMT dresses up a business and gives potential buyers a positive picture of the "property."

END NOTES:

1. Nucleus Research, Inc. Research Report D69 2003.

2. Exceptions exist by industry and worker category — check with KY Wage & Hour.

3. Mercer Human Resources Consulting and CFO Research Services, 2003.

Topical Index

About the Author

Lisa Disselkamp is President of Athena Enterprises, a management consulting firm specializing in time and attendance and labor data technology systems design and implementation. Her clients range in size from a few hundred employees to more than 50,000. A frequent speaker at industry conferences, she has addressed groups such as the American Payroll Association, the Institute of Management Accountants, The Society of Human Resource Managers, the Society of CPAs, and the Service Corps of Retired Executives. She is the founder of the Louisville Technical Market Analysis Group and a member of Vista - Society of Industry Leaders. She was a National American Business Women's Scholar and graduated with honors from Earlham College with a degree in Japanese and International Management. You can contact the author at WorkingTheClock@athena-enterprises.net.